2194

READINGS ON

WALT
WHITMAN

OTHER TITLES IN THE GREENHAVEN PRESS LITERARY COMPANION SERIES:

AMERICAN AUTHORS

Maya Angelou
Stephen Crane
Emily Dickinson
William Faulkner
F. Scott Fitzgerald
Robert Frost
Nathaniel Hawthorne
Ernest Hemingway
Herman Melville
Arthur Miller
Eugene O'Neill
Edgar Allan Poe
John Steinbeck
Mark Twain
Thornton Wilder

AMERICAN LITERATURE

The Adventures of
 Huckleberry Finn
The Adventures of Tom
 Sawyer
The Call of the Wild
The Catcher in the Rye
The Crucible
Death of a Salesman
The Glass Menagerie
The Grapes of Wrath
The Great Gatsby
Of Mice and Men
The Old Man and the Sea
The Pearl
The Scarlet Letter
A Separate Peace

BRITISH AUTHORS

Jane Austen
Joseph Conrad
Charles Dickens

BRITISH LITERATURE

Animal Farm
Beowulf
Brave New World
The Canterbury Tales
Great Expectations
Hamlet
Heart of Darkness
Julius Caesar
Lord of the Flies
Macbeth
Pride and Prejudice
Romeo and Juliet
Shakespeare: The Comedies
Shakespeare: The Histories
Shakespeare: The Sonnets
Shakespeare: The Tragedies
A Tale of Two Cities
Wuthering Heights

WORLD AUTHORS

Fyodor Dostoyevsky
Homer
Sophocles

WORLD LITERATURE

All Quiet on the Western
 Front
Antigone
The Diary of a Young Girl
A Doll's House

THE GREENHAVEN PRESS
Literary Companion
TO AMERICAN AUTHORS

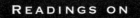
READINGS ON

WALT WHITMAN

Gary Wiener, *Book Editor*

David L. Bender, *Publisher*
Bruno Leone, *Executive Editor*
Bonnie Szumski, *Series Editor*

Greenhaven Press, Inc., San Diego, CA

Every effort has been made to trace the owners of copyrighted material. The articles in this volume may have been edited for content, length, and/or reading level. The titles have been changed to enhance the editorial purpose. Those interested in locating the original source will find the complete citation on the first page of each article.

Library of Congress Cataloging-in-Publication Data

Readings on Walt Whitman / Gary Wiener, book editor.
          p.   cm. — (The Greenhaven Press literary companion to American authors)
     Includes bibliographical references and index.
     ISBN 0-7377-0077-7 (alk. paper). —
ISBN 0-7377-0076-9 (pbk. : alk. paper)
     1. Whitman, Walt, 1819–1892—Criticism and interpretation. I. Wiener, Gary. II. Series.
PS3238.R38   1999
811'.3—dc21   98-44753
                                                             CIP

Cover photo: Archive Photos

Copyright ©1999 by Greenhaven Press, Inc.
PO Box 289009
San Diego, CA 92198-9009
Printed in the U.S.A.

"I sound my barbaric yawp
over the roofs of the world. **"**

—*Walt Whitman*

CONTENTS

Chapter 2: Themes

Chapter 3: Analyses of Individual Poems

Chapter 4: Influence: Other Poets Evaluate Whitman

FOREWORD

*"'Tis the good reader that
makes the good book."*

Ralph Waldo Emerson

The story's bare facts are simple: The captain, an old and scarred seafarer, walks with a peg leg made of whale ivory. He relentlessly drives his crew to hunt the world's oceans for the great white whale that crippled him. After a long search, the ship encounters the whale and a fierce battle ensues. Finally the captain drives his harpoon into the whale, but the harpoon line catches the captain about the neck and drags him to his death.

A simple story, a straightforward plot—yet, since the 1851 publication of Herman Melville's *Moby-Dick*, readers and critics have found many meanings in the struggle between Captain Ahab and the whale. To some, the novel is a cautionary tale that depicts how Ahab's obsession with revenge leads to his insanity and death. Others believe that the whale represents the unknowable secrets of the universe and that Ahab is a tragic hero who dares to challenge fate by attempting to discover this knowledge. Perhaps Melville intended Ahab as a criticism of Americans' tendency to become involved in well-intentioned but irrational causes. Or did Melville model Ahab after himself, letting his fictional character express his anger at what he perceived as a cruel and distant god?

Although literary critics disagree over the meaning of *Moby-Dick*, readers do not need to choose one particular interpretation in order to gain an understanding of Melville's novel. Instead, by examining various analyses, they can gain numerous insights into the issues that lie under the surface of the basic plot. Studying the writings of literary critics can also aid readers in making their own assessments of *Moby-Dick* and other literary works and in developing analytical thinking skills.

The Greenhaven Literary Companion Series was created with these goals in mind. Designed for young adults, this unique anthology series provides an engaging and comprehensive introduction to literary analysis and criticism. The essays included in the Literary Companion Series are chosen for their accessibility to a young adult audience and are expertly edited in consideration of both the reading and comprehension levels of this audience. In addition, each essay is introduced by a concise summation that presents the contributing writer's main themes and insights. Every anthology in the Literary Companion Series contains a varied selection of critical essays that cover a wide time span and express diverse views. Wherever possible, primary sources are represented through excerpts from authors' notebooks, letters, and journals and through contemporary criticism.

Each title in the Literary Companion Series pays careful consideration to the historical context of the particular author or literary work. In-depth biographies and detailed chronologies reveal important aspects of authors' lives and emphasize the historical events and social milieu that influenced their writings. To facilitate further research, every anthology includes primary and secondary source bibliographies of articles and/or books selected for their suitability for young adults. These engaging features make the Greenhaven Literary Companion series ideal for introducing students to literary analysis in the classroom or as a library resource for young adults researching the world's great authors and literature.

Exceptional in its focus on young adults, the Greenhaven Literary Companion Series strives to present literary criticism in a compelling and accessible format. Every title in the series is intended to spark readers' interest in leading American and world authors, to help them broaden their understanding of literature, and to encourage them to formulate their own analyses of the literary works that they read. It is the editors' hope that young adult readers will find these anthologies to be true companions in their study of literature.

INTRODUCTION

In the mid-to-late 1800s, any list of America's great poets would have included such names as Henry Wadsworth Longfellow, James Russell Lowell, and John Greenleaf Whittier. Walt Whitman would not have appeared. Like many innovators, radicals, and freethinkers, Whitman was not recognized by his contemporaries as a major voice. Even his own family was not impressed by Whitman's magnum opus, *Leaves of Grass.* His brother George summed up their opinion: "Mother thought as I did—did not know what to make of it." The great poet of democracy, the man who celebrated America in all of its glory, would find during his lifetime a more appreciative audience in Europe than in his own country. In 1876 a British article scolded America for not appreciating Whitman, calling him a "Golden Eagle . . . pursued by a crowd of prosperous rooks and crows."

For generations most high-school students would have known Whitman only for his singsong, banal piece on the death of President Lincoln, "O Captain! My Captain!" Whitman certainly understood the irony that his best-known piece was among his weakest: "I'm almost sorry I ever wrote the poem," he said. But as the twentieth century progressed, many poets and critics read and were influenced by Whitman's more substantial work and spread the word. As Longfellow, Lowell, and Whittier have come to be accorded only minor status, Whitman has emerged as the premiere American poet of his era. Whitman's influence has been so wide-ranging and important that it would not be much of an exaggeration to say that all modern American poetry derives from him, as Hemingway said that all modern American literature is similarly indebted to Mark Twain's *Huckleberry Finn.*

America's belated acceptance of Whitman could have been expected. From the beginning he purposely set out to be different. His work rarely used the conventional poetic techniques of meter and rhyme, and to some it resembled prose more than poetry. He considered subjects that other poets would not touch, and his acceptance of sexuality in particular scandalized readers who might have otherwise been receptive to his writing. An 1889 volume entitled *Our Authors* remarks that Whitman's poetry "contains passages of a very objectionable character, so much so, that no defense that is valid can be set up." Whitman wrote of the average American worker, not the exotic heroes who served as protagonists for most literary works. He always looked to the future instead of the past, even going so far in poems such as "Crossing Brooklyn Ferry" as to address an audience of one hundred years hence. He did not cultivate the contemporary image of a poet and used the informal name of Walt Whitman instead of the elaborate polysyllabic monikers of his peers. He posed for pictures in workman's clothes instead of the ornate costumes that the public believed all poets wore.

Whitman wrote, "I hear America singing," and finally, America has heard Whitman, too. "Song of Myself," "Crossing Brooklyn Ferry," "Out of the Cradle Endlessly Rocking," "When Lilacs Last in the Dooryard Bloom'd" and "Passage to India" are now counted among the great American poems. "O Captain! My Captain!" has faded into a historical footnote along with Longfellow, Lowell, and Whittier.

In his poetry, Whitman often addressed the reader directly, inviting us to join him on his poetic journey. He ended "Song of Myself" with the words "I stop somewhere waiting for you." Elsewhere he wrote, "To have great poets, there must be great audiences, too." *Readings on Walt Whitman* will enable the reader to understand better the unconventional brilliance of this important American poet and perhaps to join the great audience that has come to appreciate Walt Whitman.

WALT WHITMAN: A BIOGRAPHY

Legend has it that Walt Whitman published *Leaves of Grass* on July 4, 1855. Whether or not this is true, the date is certainly apropos, for with the publication of this small volume, the father of modern American poetry announced himself to the world:

> Walt Whitman am I, a Kosmos, of mighty Manhattan the son,
> Turbulent, fleshy and sensual, eating, drinking and breeding;
> No sentimentalist—no stander above men and women, or apart from them;
> No more modest than immodest.

Before this declaration, there had been no poetry, American or otherwise, quite like it. Afterward, poetry would never be the same.

Whitman was born on May 31, 1819. He was thirty-six years of age when he published the first edition of *Leaves of Grass*. He died on March 26, 1892, at the age of seventy-two. Thus *Leaves of Grass* was published at the very middle of his life, and in so many ways divides his life in two. Before, he was a teacher, printer, journalist, carpenter, and more. After, no matter what else he did, he was a poet. He spent the rest of his life revising, editing, updating, adding to, and reissuing his masterwork. There were nine major editions in all, the last, or deathbed edition, appearing in 1892. Ultimately the small volume of 1855 would stretch to over four hundred pages of poetry.

In many ways, Whitman's life coincides with the rise of writing in America. Only a year after his birth, in 1820, Sydney Smith of Britain's *Edinburgh Review* could disparage American literature as a whole with the words, "In the four quarters of the globe, who reads an American book?" By 1892 America had produced James Fenimore Cooper, Edgar Allan Poe, Herman Melville, Emily Dickinson, Mark Twain, Ralph Waldo Emerson, Henry David Thoreau, and more. Walt Whitman's America would become a major force on the world literary scene.

Whitman was born in Long Island, New York, the fish-shaped island that juts out over one hundred miles into the Atlantic Ocean. Two of the island's counties, Brooklyn and Queens, form part of New York City. The other two counties are, from west to east, Nassau and Suffolk, the last of which contains West Hills, or Huntington, as it is now known. Today Whitman is as much identified with Long Island as John Steinbeck is with the Salinas Valley in California or Emily Dickinson is with Amherst, Massachusetts. Whitman loved Long Island dearly as the place of his childhood, and he often referred to it in his poetry by the Native American name of "Paumanok."

THE POET'S PARENTS

Walter Whitman Jr. was the second son of Walter and Louisa Whitman. His father's ancestor John Whitman had come to America with the English Puritans in 1640 and settled in Massachusetts. The first Whitmans moved to Long Island in 1664. His mother's family, the Van Velsors, was descended from early Dutch settlers. For generations, both sides of the family earned their living by farming. The women kept house, cared for the children, made clothing, and cooked meals. The men worked the fields and tended herds of livestock.

The house that Walt was born in had been built by his father, "a first rate carpenter." Mr. Whitman had learned carpentry as a youth and served an apprenticeship in New York. He was not an easy man to live with, being "strong, self-sufficient, manly, mean, anger'd, unjust," if we can take Whitman's lines about the father in the poem "There Was a Child" as autobiographical, as critics often suggest. But this harsh, moody man, given to excessive indulgence in alcohol, could also be quite thoughtful. He read widely and brought books into the home. Something of his patriotism is evinced in the names of three of his sons, George Washington, Thomas Jefferson, and Andrew Jackson Whitman. He raised his children as radical Democrats, aligned with the farmer, the laborer, the small businessman, and the people, and taught them to oppose the banks and the establishment as the enemy. He was a friend of Elias Hicks, the Quaker preacher, and took Walt to hear the liberal thinker's sermon on at least one occasion. He taught his children to think for themselves.

Nevertheless, until Walter Sr.'s death in 1855, the younger Whitman harbored resentment toward his father and believed that most of the inspiration for his life and writing came from his mother, as he wrote in an early poem: "Starting from fish-shape Paumanok where I was born,/Well-begotten and rais'd by a perfect mother." Louisa Whitman was a large, strong woman of ruddy complexion; Whitman inherited these physical characteristics as well as her manner of walking and her voice. She was not a reader like her husband but had a gift for storytelling: "She excelled in narrative," Whitman later wrote, "could tell stories, impersonate; she was very eloquent in the utterance of noble moral axioms—was very original in her manner, her style."

EARLY YEARS

Having leased the land on which he built the West Hills home, Walter Whitman Sr., who could obtain little work in his chosen field, soon found that farming would not pay the bills. In spring 1823, the family moved to Brooklyn, New York, where Whitman's father had heard that carpenters were needed. By this time there were three Whitman children—Jesse, the eldest, followed by Walt and Mary—and Louisa Whitman was again pregnant. There would be eight younger Whitmans in all. Their father, whose plan was to buy houses, fix them up, and sell at a profit, was never very successful. During the early period of Walt's life, the family moved to a new house almost every year. Walt attended District School Number One and was hardly an outstanding student. He did not appreciate the strictness of an institution where students were routinely given corporal punishment for even minor offenses. Even years later, as a journalist, he would campaign in print for an end to such barbaric treatment of children.

Additionally, as would be the case all of his life, Walt preferred idleness to nose-to-the-grindstone labor. A supreme irony in the life of Whitman is that the writer who produced thousands and thousands of pages of writings, including journalism, letters, poems, nonfiction, short stories, and even a novel, was often content merely staring into space or up at the sky. When Whitman writes in the opening of "Song of Myself,"

I loafe and invite my Soul;
I lean and loafe at my ease observing a spear of summer grass

the repetition of *loafe* is wholly intentional. Numerous friends, relatives, bosses and acquaintances would remark on Whitman's idleness, often with disdain. Biographer Philip Callow writes,

It was natural and it was also part of the game with him to appear lazy. It fooled others. . . . If one moved slowly, determined not to be hurried, arriving in one's own time even if it meant coming in last, was that stupidity or stubbornness? Whitman's innate resistance to the will of others was part of his sly, undeclared disobedience, a refusal to go along with the world. If his mother said worriedly, "What will people think?" her strange son with his contradictory moods, his changeable, restless nature, would answer quietly, "Never mind what they think."

As his brother George observed, from an early age Walt refused "to do anything except at his own notion." But clearly it was this penchant for idleness that allowed him to be the keen observer and poet that he was. In 1840 Whitman wrote, "Of all human beings, none equals your genuine, inbred, unvarying loafer. What was Adam, I should like to know, but a loafer?"

Whitman's formal education ended when he was only eleven years old, and he began working as an errand boy in a Brooklyn law firm. Then, as now, New York City attracted the rich and famous, and Whitman's trips around Manhattan island enabled him to come in contact with such people. On several occasions he delivered messages to Aaron Burr, the former vice-president who gained notoriety for killing Alexander Hamilton in a duel. Another time he chanced to see John Jacob Astor, the richest man in the world, and the memory of Astor, "bearded, swathed in rich furs, with a great ermine cap on his head," fixed itself in Whitman's mind for years to come.

Whitman's employers, James and Edward Clark, treated him kindly and encouraged him to read. Edward Clark gave him a library subscription, which Whitman later acknowledged to be "the signal event of my life up to that time." He particularly enjoyed romantic tales, including the *Arabian Nights,* and the novels of Sir Walter Scott, author of *Ivanhoe,* and James Fenimore Cooper, who wrote *The Last of the Mohicans.* He also read some of Walter Scott's poetry, and would later comment that it marked the first time that poetry had meant something to him.

Whitman next worked as an office boy in a doctor's office, but this job did not last long. When he was twelve, Whitman worked as an apprentice for the newspaper the *Long Island Patriot.* There he met William Hartshorne, a newspaperman who had grown up in Philadelphia during the American Revolution. While working, Hartshorne would regale his apprentices with personal anecdotes about such notables as George Washington, Thomas Jefferson, and Ben Franklin. Whitman would later immortalize this friendly, cheerful man in "Song of Myself":

> The jour printer with gray head and gaunt jaws works at his case,
> He turns his quid of tobacco while his eyes blur with the man-uscript

Amazing as it seems, Whitman actually published a few small articles in the *Patriot* during this time, though they did not bear the writer's name.

At thirteen, Whitman left the *Patriot* and took a job with a rival Brooklyn paper, the *Star*. During the early 1800s the newspaper business boomed in the United States. In 1830, there were thirty-six daily papers in the country. Twenty years later, there would be over 250. Newspapermen frequently moved around, and Whitman would switch papers with abandon during this time.

In 1833, Whitman's father moved the family back to Long Island just after his wife gave birth to their eighth child, Thomas Jefferson Whitman, or "Jeff," who would become Walt's favorite sibling. At fourteen, Whitman was already closer to adulthood than childhood, and he stayed behind in Brooklyn, signaling the end of dependence on his parents. Upon finishing his apprenticeship, he went to work as a printer.

NEWSPAPERMAN AND TEACHER

At fifteen, chubby cheeked, and as large as a grown man, Whitman continued his work at the *Star*, and, discovering in himself a passion for writing, he placed articles in Brooklyn's *New York Mirror*. (As with his previous articles for the *Star*, these too were printed without bylines, and scholars have been unable to trace them.) Whitman discovered another new love, the theater. He attended numerous melodramas (plays that blatantly cast good characters against evil ones) that were popular at the time, including *The Last Days of Pompeii* and *The Murder at the Roadside Inn*. He also saw plays by Shakespeare and was especially taken by the performance of the famed actor Junius Brutus Booth in *Richard III*.

In August 1835 a conflagration, or huge fire, broke out in New York's publishing district. The area was destroyed, and thousands of newspaper workers found themselves suddenly unemployed. While many left for jobs elsewhere, Whitman

doggedly hung on until May 1836 when he was forced to re-
nounce his much-loved independence and return to Long Island to join his family. Still, there was no way Walt would
submit to working on the family farm. He and his father apparently engaged in some fierce arguments over the son's refusal to do farm chores, but Walt remained his usual stubborn self. He secured a job as a teacher in Norwich, not far
from where his maternal grandfather lived. With little formal
education, seventeen-year-old Walt took charge of a one-
room schoolhouse, teaching a mixed classroom of children,
some of them nearly his own age. He often found residence
with the families of his students. Many, including his
younger brother George, who was one of Walt's pupils, remembered him as quite a good schoolmaster. Others complained of his halfhearted attitude toward his work, that he
tended to focus more energy contemplating and writing. As a
result, between 1836 and 1841 he held at least eight different
teaching appointments. As in publishing, it was fairly easy to
obtain work in teaching at the time, and schoolmasters, like
printers, tended to switch jobs frequently.

It was during his stint as a schoolteacher that Walt began
to write short stories. Many of these stories he published in
the 1840s centered around a son being treated badly by his
father, causing scholars to wonder about their autobiographical nature. In between teaching jobs, he often moved back in
with his family, and his running feud with his farmer father
resumed. In one of his stories, "Wild Frank's Return," a boy
runs off rather than submit to his father. But he returns,
homesick, and not wanting to go inside the house, falls
asleep under a tree. There is a thunderstorm, and Frank's
horse, attached to his arm by its bridle, bolts in terror, killing
the sleeping Frank. The horrified father and mother later find
the dead boy's body.

At home, Whitman assumed almost a parental role, seemingly as a way to displace his rival, the elder Walter Whitman.
To George Whitman, it seemed "as if he had us in his
charge. . . . Now and then his guardianship seemed excessive."
Walt gained much pleasure in spending time with his siblings.
By now there were eight children all together, and Walt was a
companion and playmate to the others as well as a surrogate
parent. "Though a bachelor," he wrote in one sketch, "I have
several boys and girls that I consider my own."

In 1838 Whitman bought a used press, rented space above
a stable, and went into business for himself by founding a

weekly newspaper, the *Long Islander.* The first issue appeared soon after Walt's nineteenth birthday. Here he published local interest stories plus weather and harvest reports and an occasional news story. In keeping with the role he had assumed while living at home, he was fond of writing columns giving parental advice. He bought a white horse, Nina, and rode through the Long Island countryside delivering his paper. But his business went flat, and he was forced to give up the paper in the summer of 1839.

Whitman took more teaching and newspaper jobs, but employers were as unimpressed by his lazy work habits as they were impressed by his thinking and writing skills. He continued to write short stories and produced some rather uninspired, traditional poems. According to critic Gay Wilson Allen, these poems, "which Whitman contributed during the 1840s to popular magazines were so conventional, sentimental, and trite that it seems almost a miracle that Walt Whitman could have written the 1855 poems" of *Leaves of Grass.* Whitman also produced a novel, entitled *Franklin Evans,* during this time. But he was never proud of this temperance (antidrinking) novel, which tells the melodramatic story of a young man from Long Island whose life is destroyed by alcoholism. Whitman would come to be embarrassed by it. He would even joke that he wrote the novel in a few short days, aided by a bottle of liquor or two. But *Franklin Evans* did accomplish one goal. As a potboiler, or a novel written for the chief purpose of making money, *Franklin Evans* sold more copies during his lifetime than any of his other productions, including *Leaves of Grass.*

During the 1840s Whitman first acquired and then lost printing and editing jobs at one New York newspaper after another. By September 1845 he had been employed by ten different papers, including the *Aurora, Evening Tattler, Sun, Democratic Statesman,* and *New York Democrat.* Sometimes his politics caused friction between the owners and himself. Other times his laid-back attitude alienated his bosses. On occasion he left a paper for a better offer elsewhere.

In 1845 Walter Whitman Sr. decided to give carpentry another try and moved his family back to Brooklyn from Long Island. Walt, now twenty-six and out of a job, crossed the river from Manhattan to live with them. Walt was glad to be with his family once again, and he became particularly close to his younger brother Jeff, now a schoolboy. Both loved the outdoors. They were fond of long walks on the Long Island beaches together. Walt soon found work with the *Long Island Evening Star,* one of the papers on which he had formerly served an apprenticeship. But in February 1846, the editor of the more prestigious *Brooklyn Daily Eagle* died suddenly and Whitman was soon after offered the position. Though he annoyed his bosses at the *Star* by doing so, Whitman jumped at the chance to work for the *Eagle,* a partisan Democratic paper whose politics coincided with his own. Whitman would later describe his time at the paper as "one of the pleasantest sits of my life." The owner of the paper gave him freedom in its production, the pay was good, and the work not too strenuous. He was able to write numerous editorials on any and all subjects that interested him. He held this job for two years, until political differences with the owner led to his dismissal. Rumor had it that the brawny Whitman had kicked a visiting politician down the office stairs.

Unemployment did not faze Whitman. Not long after being fired, he ran into a man who was starting a newspaper in New Orleans. On February 11, 1848, with his fourteen-year-old brother Jeff in tow, Walt left New York to work on the *New Orleans Crescent.* Like so many others, this position turned out to be short-lived. Jeff was homesick during the entire stay, and Whitman the journalist found himself muzzled due to his untrustworthy Northern opinions. New Orleans was a center of the slave trade, and Whitman was never comfortable with having this unsavory business thrust in his face. The Mexican War had recently ended, and Whitman, like many other so-called Free-Soilers, was fearful that any new territories gained from this victory would become slave states. But he had to keep these opinions to himself in the pro-slavery South.

Nevertheless he was often amazed at the "populous" city of New Orleans, which, as he later wrote, imprinted his brain "with its shows, architecture, customs, traditions." Material from his trip South would surface in one of the more famous poems from *Leaves of Grass:*

> I saw in Louisiana a live-oak growing,
> All alone stood it and the moss hung down from the branches,
> Without any companion it grew there uttering joyous leaves of
>   dark green
> And its look, rude, unbending, lusty, made me think of myself.

Whitman's relationship with the *Crescent*'s owners deteriorated rapidly, and by June of the same year, after only four months, he and Jeff were already back in New York. He worked on several other newspapers in the late 1840s, including one short-lived Free-Soil paper he founded himself, but as his father's health began to decline, Walt became more involved in the family real estate business. He moved back in with his family and essentially took control of the household and the business, calling himself a carpenter but actually seeing to the paperwork and finances while his carpenter brothers, George and Andrew, performed the physical labor. Along with the buying and selling of houses, Walt continued to contribute articles to local papers, ran his own printing press and stationery store, and attended Free Soil Party meetings.

AMERICAN BARD

In March 1842, the renowned writer and philosopher Ralph Waldo Emerson, of Concord, Massachusetts, had come to New York to deliver a series of lectures on "The Times." In the lecture on poetry Emerson declared that, while America had not yet produced a great poet, "The genius of poetry is here." To doubt that America's poet would soon appear, Emerson insisted, "is to doubt of day and night." Whitman had attended the speech as editor of the *Aurora.* His newspaper review declared Emerson's lecture to be "one of the richest and most beautiful compositions, both for its matter and style, we have heard anywhere, at any time."

Emerson's lecture that evening was a forerunner to his famous essay "The Poet." Part of the essay reads, in Emerson biographer Robert D. Richardson's words, "like a cue for the entrance of Walt Whitman." As Emerson wrote:

> Our log-rolling, our stumps and their politics, our fisheries, our Negroes and Indians . . . the northern trade, the southern planting, the western clearing, Oregon and Texas, are yet unsung. Yet America is a poem in our eyes; its ample geography dazzles the imagination, and it will not wait long for meters.

It was a message that Whitman took to heart, even while Emerson asserted that he had not yet "found that excellent combination of gifts in my countrymen which I seek."

There was no straight progression from the Emerson speech to *Leaves of Grass,* despite Whitman's claim that he had been "simmering" and that Emerson had brought him to a boil. The Whitman of the 1840s, who produced, in critic Lewis Turco's opinion, execrable poems, was certainly not yet the man Emerson sought. According to biographer Justin Kaplan, between 1846 and 1850, Whitman produced "scarcely a line" of poetry. What happened to turn the poetaster, or inferior poet, of the 1840s into the brilliant bard of the 1855 *Leaves of Grass* is the subject of much speculation. Biographer Paul Zweig believes that Whitman even tried to obscure any record of these years "in order to keep intact the mystery of his poetic origins." But a passage from Emerson's "The Poet" may offer a clue to Whitman's mindset:

> Doubt not, O poet, but persist. Say "It is in me, and shall out." Stand there, balked and dumb, stuttering and stammering, hissed and hooted, stand and strive, until at last rage draw out of thee that dream-power which every night shows thee is thine own; a power transcending all limit and privacy, and by virtue of which a man is the conductor of the whole river of electricity.

And persevere Whitman did. Feeling that he did not have the education necessary to be the great poet he dreamed of becoming, he set out to educate himself. According to Zweig, "Whitman began to clip out of magazines articles that interested him on a variety of subjects: literature, of course; but also history, geography, geology, even law." Other interests that absorbed him included Italian opera, Egyptian mythology, and phrenology, the nineteenth-century pseudoscience that attempted to explain human psychology by studying the bumps on a person's head. For years before Whitman released *Leaves of Grass,* he carried a series of notebooks, in which he at first kept business records but later filled with notes for a new brand of poetry. "Make it plain," he told himself. "Lumber the writing with nothing—let it go as lightly as a bird flies in the air—or a fish swims in the sea." He would stand alone, independent of the great literary minds that had preceded him: "Make no quotations and no reference to any other writer," he insisted. Seeking to avoid the artificial style and language of much European poetry and its American imitators, he set out to write in "A perfectly transparent, plate-glassy style, artless, with no ornaments." By the mid-1850s, the "long foreground" that Ralph Waldo Emerson would later suggest led up to the extraordinary volume *Leaves of Grass* was complete.

LEAVES OF GRASS

Whitman self-published *Leaves of Grass* in July 1855, having even set some of the type himself in the Brooklyn, New York, print shop of James and Thomas Rome. The first edition of his masterwork was an anonymous ninety-five-page volume containing a preface and twelve untitled poems. Discerning readers had two clues as to its authorship. The first was the title page picture of a robust-looking, bearded man, his collar open and his hat tipped to one side, with one hand in his pocket and the other on his hip—in short, a man who looked more like a carpenter than a poet, the standard image of which had been set in the early 1800s by dashing English poets such as Lord Byron, who were often photographed decked out in formal attire that included such accoutrements as capes and canes. The second clue appeared on page twenty-nine in the long poem "Song of Myself" where the poet announced himself to the world as "Walt Whitman, a Kosmos, of Manhattan the son."

Despite Whitman's self-promotion—he even wrote anonymous articles praising the volume and placed them in several newspapers—*Leaves of Grass* was no commercial success. The very audience Whitman wanted to reach, the average American worker, had little interest in poetry, especially poetry that was daring enough to openly discuss the human body. Nineteenth-century American society was dominated by Victorian social values, and many writers and thinkers who might have responded to *Leaves of Grass* intellectually were scandalized by the poet's frankness. And so, as Paul Zweig observes, *Leaves of Grass* was largely ignored by an "American public that, four years before, had refused to read [Herman Melville's epic novel] *Moby Dick* and, only a year before, had found nothing worth remarking in [Henry David Thoreau's] *Walden*." Such a reception could have been predicted. One New York paper, the *Criterion*, had called *Leaves of Grass* "a mass of stupid filth." As Whitman's own spiritual mentor, Ralph Waldo Emerson, had observed in his essay, "Self Reliance," "To be great is to be misunderstood."

Emerson became Whitman's greatest early ally. Upon receiving a copy of *Leaves of Grass* from the poet himself, Emerson wrote Whitman one of the more famous letters in American literary history, welcoming the new poet to the forefront of American writers and praising "the most extraordinary piece of wit & wisdom that America has yet contributed." Whitman used the letter shamelessly to promote himself, knowing that the very mention of Ralph Waldo Emerson's name could open many doors in the world of nineteenth-century American letters.

Despite the first edition's poor sales, Whitman wasted little time in bringing out a second edition (1856) that was noteworthy for its inclusion of the whole of Emerson's letter and thirty-two new poems, including the masterpiece "Crossing Brooklyn Ferry." Again sales were poor, though Henry David Thoreau made a notable visit to Whitman after receiving a copy of the second edition. "There was nothing else to do but go back to journalism," as one biographer writes, so beginning in 1857, Whitman served another stint as a newspaper editor, this time with the Brooklyn *Daily Times.* His father had died in 1855, less than a week after the publication of *Leaves of Grass,* and Whitman desperately needed money.

In 1860 he received a letter from a Boston publisher, Thayer and Eldridge, who offered to publish *Leaves of Grass.* When Whitman journeyed to Boston to sign his first contract (he had self-published the first two editions), he also met with Ralph Waldo Emerson, who tried to persuade him to soften some of the more sexual poems in his volume. Whitman listened thoughtfully but ultimately decided against expurgating (or censoring) *Leaves of Grass.* "The dirtiest book in all the world is the expurgated book," he would say. One other result of Whitman's trip to Boston was that he met William O'Connor, a strident abolitionist whose antislavery novel *Harrington* was also being published by Thayer and Eldridge. O'Connor would soon become one of Whitman's most enthusiastic supporters.

Thayer and Eldridge were optimistic that the third edition of *Leaves of Grass* would be a big success, but before the year was out they had gone out of business, having earned only $250 for Whitman. Meanwhile, the United States was entering a crisis. In November 1860, Abraham Lincoln was elected president. Whitman was a strong supporter of the new president, having even written a political pamphlet in 1856 calling for "some heroic, shrewd, fully-informed, healthy-bodied middle aged, beard-faced American . . . to walk into the Presidency." But the South, worried that Lincoln would abolish slavery, threatened secession. On April 13, 1861, Southern forces fired on Fort Sumter in South Carolina. The Civil War had begun.

THE CIVIL WAR YEARS

Walt's brother George was among the first to enlist when President Lincoln called for volunteers. Many in the North thought the war would be short-lived. But when the Union forces were thoroughly defeated at the first battle at Bull Run in northern Virginia, any end to the war seemed a long way off. In December 1862, George Whitman's name appeared in the *New York Herald* (mistakenly reported as G.W. Whitmore) as one of the wounded at the battle of Fredericksburg. Whitman immediately left Brooklyn in search of his brother. In Philip Callow's words,

> His search for George was the first stage in a journey which would change the direction of his life irrevocably. In the slaughter ahead and its aftermath he would see with his own eyes the transitions and manglings that lie under so many of his poems, the rotting compost out of which his leaves spring so cleanly.

Whitman was relieved to discover that George had received only a superficial wound. Even so, he was shocked at the carnage of war and, after leaving George, went to Washington, D.C., where he spent much of the remainder of the war nursing the wounded and soothing the dying. Often he would bring small gifts such as candy, writing paper, and even ice cream to the patients. He became a close friend to many of the soldiers.

His former publisher Charles Eldridge was now working in Washington, and Eldridge helped Whitman obtain a job with the military in the army paymaster's office. Each day after work, he would visit one of the numerous area hospitals, cleaning and bandaging wounds and helping with operations, notably amputations. In his journal, excerpts of which would later be published as *Specimen Days,* Whitman set down some of the more grisly images of war. On the outside of a mansion used as a hospital, he noticed,

> a heap of amputated feet, legs, arms, hands, &c., a full load for a one-horse cart. Several dead bodies lie near, each cover'd with its brown woolen blanket. In the door-yard, towards the river, are fresh graves, mostly of officers, their names on pieces of barrel-staves or broken boards, stuck in the dirt.

Whitman also composed many poems about the war. These he collected into *Drum-Taps,* which would be included in a subsequent edition of *Leaves of Grass.* Among these poems were "Give Me the Splendid Silent Sun," "Vigil Strange I Kept on the Field One Night," and "The Wound Dresser," the last with its vivid lines:

> The crush'd head I dress, (poor crazed hand tear not the bandage away,)
> The neck of the cavalry-man with the bullet through and through I examine,
> Hard the breathing rattles, quite glazed already the eye . . .

Despite such graphic imagery, Whitman believed that "The real war will never get into the books." The war took its toll on the robust poet, and in June 1864 he returned to Brooklyn ill with the cumulative effects of his proximity to the horrific conflict. But six months later, Whitman was back in Washington, working as a clerk in the Office of Indian Affairs. He resumed his visits to soldiers and worked on the *Drum-Taps* poems. In April he took a leave from his job to visit his mother in Brooklyn and to arrange for publication of his Civil War poems. While he was there, the Civil War finally ended with the surrender of General Robert E. Lee at Appomattox Court House in Virginia. A few days later, Abraham Lincoln was murdered by John Wilkes Booth, the son of the famous actor Junius Brutus Booth, whose performance Whitman had enjoyed so much in *Richard III* many years before. Whitman was devastated. He returned to Washington and subsequently wrote his most well-known poem, "O Captain! My Captain!" about the death of Lincoln, a poem that would be recited by schoolchildren for generations to come. A harsh, but not unjustified, assessment of "O Captain!" comes from biographers Adrien Stoutenburg and Laura Nelson Baker, who in 1968 wrote:

> Strapped into regular, sing-song rhyme, ["O Captain! My Captain!"] is one of the weakest poems he ever wrote. Yet this actually maudlin poem has been the most quoted, memorized, and admired by thousands of undiscriminating readers over the years. Popular anthologies and many school teachers have forced it on the public and on children to such an extent that even today Whitman is best known for this piece of melodramatic doggerel.

Another Whitman effort on the subject of Lincoln's death, "When Lilacs Last in the Dooryard Bloom'd," is by every scholar's account the far superior poem, and one of his greatest, if not one of the greatest in all of American literature, but ironically it is far less well known.

THE GOOD GRAY POET

In May 1865, Whitman was promoted to the next level of his clerk's job at the Office of Indian Affairs. A month later, the new secretary of the interior, James Harlan, came across a copy of *Leaves of Grass* in Whitman's desk. Finding the material scandalous, Harlan fired Whitman. No amount of persuasion by Whitman's friends, particularly William O'Connor, could convince the conservative Harlan to reinstate Whitman, but the poet soon found a new clerk's position in the attorney general's office. O'Connor, still enraged that a man he considered the greatest poet America had yet produced could receive such shabby treatment, set about to defend Whitman against his legion of critics. In January 1866, O'Connor published the biography *The Good Gray Poet,* and the title has stuck with Whitman to this day. O'Connor presented a portrait of Whitman as half-genius, half-saint. He may have exaggerated in this appraisal, but the book served to put Whitman's name at the center of numerous literary conversations in America.

Whitman was also beginning to gain recognition overseas. William Michael Rossetti, brother of the renowned English poet Dante Gabriel Rossetti and a distinguished man of letters in his own right, put out an edition of Whitman's poems in England. This publication set off a chain reaction that soon gave Whitman a far more significant reputation in Europe than he would ever gain during his lifetime in the United States. Among the literary giants who now took an interest in Whitman's writings were the poet Algernon Charles Swinburne of England and the exiled Russian novelist Ivan Turgenev. A highly respected English intellectual and widow named Anne Gilchrist read a copy of Whitman's poems and fell in love with the poet from afar. She would write him a series of letters proposing matrimony and even come to America expressly to see the poet, who admired her but had little interest in marriage.

In 1865 Whitman had met a streetcar conductor, Peter Doyle, with whom he began what is believed to be the longest and most intense friendship of his life. Whitman had always admired young working-class men in his poetry and in his private life, and he and Doyle, who was many years the poet's junior, filled the role of close friends, comrades, and even father and son, for the next decade.

Whitman was also writing a new selection of poems. With the completion of the transcontinental railroad and the opening of the Suez Canal in 1869, events that rendered the United States and the world dramatically smaller, Whitman's dream of a united brotherhood of man suddenly seemed less far off. In celebration of technology's ability to bring people closer, Whitman wrote "Passage to India," his last great poem. He was fifty years old now and his health was failing. He suffered from dizzy spells and sweats. His hair was completely white. Despite "Passage to India," he knew that his poetic powers were also in decline. Though he would live another twenty-three years, toward the end of that poem, the poet who had always been aware of the inevitable cycle of life and death prepared himself poetically for his own end:

Swiftly I shrivel at the thought of God,
At Nature and its wonders, Time and Space and Death,
But that, turning, call to thee O soul, thou actual Me,
And lo, thou gently masterest the orbs,
Thou matest Time, smilest content at Death,
And fillest, swellest full of the vastnesses of Space.

His family, too, was growing older. In March 1870 his elder brother Jesse died. Jesse had always been mentally unstable and Whitman himself had five years earlier brought his brother to the insane asylum where he had spent his last days. George had married and moved to Camden, New Jersey, where he worked as an inspector in a pipe factory. The elderly Mrs. Whitman, who would die in 1873, was too frail to care for herself and left Brooklyn to live with George in Camden. Despite his own declining health, Whitman kept at work, in the early 1870s producing the fifth edition of *Leaves of Grass* and a prose work, *Democratic Vistas,* that both celebrated and criticized his contemporary America.

In January 1873, Whitman, still living in Washington, D.C., and working for the attorney general, woke up on the morning of the twenty-third unable to move. His entire left side was paralyzed, the result of a stroke. The once physically robust Whitman, the man who had proclaimed in "Song of Myself," "I . . . in perfect health begin,/Hoping to cease not till death," had hit rock bottom.

THE POET IN DECLINE

Whitman recovered from his stroke, but his rehabilitation was a long process. He had to struggle merely to walk. He took a leave from his government job and went to live with his brother George and his wife, Louisa, in Camden. He hoped to return to Washington, but in July 1874 the government informed him that he was being replaced. In February 1875 he suffered another stroke. Despite these setbacks Whitman produced a two-volume edition of *Leaves of Grass* in 1876 to celebrate the centennial, or one hundredth birthday, of the United States. Once Whitman was well enough to get out of the house again, he befriended an eighteen-year-old errand boy by the name of Harry Stafford. Whitman met Stafford's parents as well and took a liking to the family. The Staffords owned a farm about twelve miles from Camden, and soon Whitman was staying with them for weeks at a time, recuperating from his illness. He spent hour upon hour walking in the woods along a stream called Timber Creek that was near the Stafford property. Such outings helped to rejuvenate the rapidly aging poet and reawaken his love of nature.

By 1879 Whitman was well enough to embark on a long trip west. The poet who celebrated America and its manifest destiny had never actually been farther than Louisiana. Whitman traveled to Denver, then to the Rocky Mountains. He also stopped in St. Louis to visit his brother Jeff, and in 1880 journeyed to Canada to visit one of his greatest admirers, Dr. Richard Bucke, a future Whitman biographer who directed an insane asylum in Ontario.

A year later he traveled to Boston, once again to meet with a publisher about *Leaves of Grass*. James R. Osgood was the first commercial publisher to release Whitman's poetry since Thayer and Eldridge. The new version of *Leaves of Grass,* published with all of the sexual poems that had previously caused so much trouble, soon caught the attention of the district attorney of Boston. *Leaves of Grass* had been judged obscene. Unless the publisher agreed to expurgate the book, its distribution would have to cease. Whitman was not opposed to making a few alterations, but when the district attorney delivered a long list of changes, Whitman balked. Osgood recalled the books, and the Boston edition of *Leaves of Grass* was dead. Fortunately a Philadelphia press agreed to publish the book. Having been banned in Boston, *Leaves of Grass* obtained a new notoriety that led to better sales.

Whitman continued to live with his brother until 1884. Walt had always been an enigma to his practical younger brother, the pipe factory inspector, and living together again did not enable George to understand the poet any more clearly. George resented Walt's refusal to take a job that would pay for the family expenses and found his brother to be a stubborn and idle man. As biographer Justin Kaplan writes, George found it hard to reconcile Walt's apparent laziness "with the fact that year after year eminent, even dazzling, visitors from abroad journeyed to Camden, a place of few attractions, to call on the author." One of these visitors was the world-famous playwright Oscar Wilde, who "drank elderberry wine and hot toddies in George's house and then wrote a note to 'My Dear Dear Walt' to say, 'There is no one in this great wide world of America whom I love and honor so much.'"

In the spring of 1884 Whitman bought his own house on Mickle Street in Camden. But because his works had never sold particularly well, he had little money left. Gifts began to pour in from friends, admirers, and well-wishers. In 1885 a group of admirers pooled their money to buy Whitman a horse and buggy. He became a regular sight in Camden, driving through the streets alone or with a friend. In 1888, Whitman collected his new poems and published them as a volume entitled *November Boughs,* which he believed might be his last book. He began the volume with a long preface in which he reminisced about his writing career. "From a worldly and business point of view 'Leaves of Grass' had been worse than a failure," he wrote. Nevertheless he remained fiercely proud of his production. He first received a copy of *November Boughs* on his sixty-ninth birthday, which gave him two reasons to celebrate. But only a few days later, Whitman suffered a series of strokes that would incapacitate him. He no longer drove around Camden in his horse and buggy and relied on a wheelchair to negotiate his Mickle Street home. With his death still four years away, he spent much time designing a large tomb that would hold eight people. He composed an eighth edition of *Leaves of Grass* in 1888 but continued to revise and edit his life's work until just before his death. He lived long enough to complete one further project, the "deathbed," or final authorized, edition of *Leaves of Grass,* which was published in 1892. In January of that year, he wrote,

> Walt Whitman wishes respectfully to notify the public that the book *Leaves of Grass,* which he has been working on at great intervals and partially issued for the past thirty-five or forty years, is now completed, so to call it, and he would like this new 1892 edition to absolutely supersede all previous ones. Faulty as it is, he decides it as by far his special and entire self-chosen poetic utterance.

With this declaration Whitman saved future scholars a lot of guesswork of the kind that occurs with the works of Shakespeare and other great writers. There would be no doubt as to which version of *Leaves of Grass* Whitman wanted future readers to use.

BIDDING FAREWELL TO HIS CREATIVE POWERS

In the last poem in that last edition of *Leaves of Grass,* Whitman bids farewell to his creative powers that served him so well. The poem, "Good-bye My Fancy," reads in part,

> Good-bye my Fancy!
> Farewell dear mate, dear love!
> I'm going away, I know not where,

Or to what fortune, or whether I may ever see you again,
So Good-bye my Fancy.

Walt Whitman died on the evening of March 26, 1892, at his Mickle Street home. He is buried in Camden's Harleigh Cemetery, along with members of his family, in the tomb he designed himself.

CHAPTER 1

The Man and the Poet

READINGS ON
WALT WHITMAN

The Evolution of *Leaves of Grass*

Justin Kaplan

Throughout his career, Walt Whitman produced a single volume of poetry: *Leaves of Grass*. From its first publication in 1855 to the "deathbed" edition of 1892, Whitman continually edited, expanded, and revised the book. Here Whitman biographer Justin Kaplan traces the evolution of *Leaves of Grass* through its many incarnations. Kaplan includes the whole of Ralph Waldo Emerson's famous letter welcoming Whitman to the forefront of the literary ranks in America. Whitman shamelessly used the letter, and other slightly devious methods, to promote *Leaves of Grass* during his lifetime. Among Justin Kaplan's books are *Walt Whitman: A Life* and *Mr. Clemens and Mark Twain*, which won the Pulitzer Prize for biography in 1967.

In January 1892, a few months before his death at the age of seventy-two, a world-famous resident of Camden, New Jersey, prepared this announcement for the press:

> Walt Whitman wishes respectfully to notify the public that the book *Leaves of Grass*, which he has been working on at great intervals and partially issued for the past thirty-five or forty years, is now completed, so to call it, and he would like this new 1892 edition to absolutely supersede all previous ones. Faulty as it is, he decides it is by far his special and entire self-chosen poetic utterance.

The 1892 *Leaves of Grass*, for sentimental and promotional reasons dubbed the "Deathbed Edition" by Whitman's literary executors and his Philadelphia publisher, was a bulky volume of 438 pages and almost as many poems. Some were love lyrics, candid and explicit celebrations of sexuality, visionary musings, glimpses of nightmare and ecstasy, poems of loneliness, loss, and mourning, among them

Whitman's supreme elegy for Abraham Lincoln, "When Lilacs Last in the Dooryard Bloom'd." Others—"Song of Myself," "Crossing Brooklyn Ferry," and "Out of the Cradle Endlessly Rocking," for example—were personal testaments that also epitomized American vision and experience in the nineteenth century.

A LIFE'S WORK

The "ensemble," as Whitman liked to call the organized totality of his work, was willful and far too inclusive, showing him at his worst as well as his incomparable best; it is best read selectively, at least the first time. But "faulty" as it was, the final *Leaves of Grass* was so much the fulfillment of his entire life—its shaping "desire and conviction"—that he thought of it as a person, his sole comfort and heart's companion.

> Camerado, this is no book,
> Who touches this touches a man,
> (Is it night? are we here together alone?)
> It is I you hold and who holds you,
> I spring from the pages into your arms . . .

"Here I sit gossiping in the early candle-light of old age," Whitman wrote in a prose epilogue, "I and my book—casting backward glances over our travel'd road. . . . My Book and I—what a period we have presumed to span!" An exact contemporary of Queen Victoria and Herman Melville, he was born in a Long Island farmhouse in 1819, during the first administration of President James Monroe. He came from long-established native stock, landowners, farmers, builders and horse-breeders, who had slid into economic, social, and even genetic decline: of the eight Whitman children who survived infancy, one was the poet who proclaimed his perfect health and perfect blood, three were normal, but four were insane, psychotic, alcoholic, or feebleminded. At one time or another in his early life he was a printer, schoolteacher, newspaper editor, writer of popular fiction (including a novel about the evils of drink, *Franklin Evans; or The Inebriate*), storekeeper, and building contractor. In his early thirties, responding to complex inner and outer imperatives, Whitman awoke to a sense of purpose. Emulating [the Greek poet] Homer, Shakespeare, and [English novelist] Sir Walter Scott, masters all, he declared, "I will be also a master after my own kind, making the poems of emotions, as they pass or stay, the poems of freedom, and the exposé of personality—singing in high tones democracy and the New World of it through These States." A fragment of early verse suggests the profound personal transformation that was part of the foreground of *Leaves of Grass:*

> I cannot be awake, for nothing looks to me as it did before,
> Or else I am awake for the first time, and all before has been
> a mean sleep.

Together, Whitman and his book saw a young nation, irrepressibly vital and bitterly divided against itself, approach and then survive the terrible bloodletting of the Civil War. The United States, once a dubious political experiment ridiculed by critics abroad, overflowed its continental limits and became an industrialized world power. "I know very well that my 'Leaves' could not possibly have emerged or been fashion'd or completed, from any other era than the-latter half of the Nineteenth Century, nor any other land than democratic America, and from the absolute triumph of the National Union Arms." He had set out to write the poetry

WHITMAN REVIEWS HIMSELF

Whitman was a master of self-promotion. In the following anonymous review he celebrates himself.

To give judgment on real poems, one needs an account of the poet himself. Very devilish to some, and very divine to some, will appear the poet of these new poems, the *Leaves of Grass*; an attempt, as they are, of a naïve, masculine, affectionate, contemplative, sensual, imperious person, to cast into literature not only his own grit and arrogance, but his own flesh and form, undraped, regardless of models, regardless of modesty or law, and ignorant or silently scornful, as at first appears, of all except his own presence and experience, and all outside the fiercely loved land of his birth and the birth of his parents, and their parents for several generations before him. Politeness this man has none, and regulation he has none. A rude child of the people!—No imitation—No foreigner—but a growth and idiom of America. No discontented—a careless slouch, enjoying to-day. No dilettante democrat—a man who is art-and-part with the commonalty, and with immediate life—loves the streets—loves the docks—loves the free rasping talk of men—likes to be called by his given name, and nobody at all need Mr. him—can laugh with laughers—likes the ungenteel ways of laborers . . . does not make a stand on being a gentleman, nor on learning or manners—eats cheap fare, likes the strong flavored of America in the American language. To sing the song of himself, his nation, and his unloosened century, he had rejected conventional literary themes, stock ornamentation, romance, rhyme, formalism—anything that reflected alien times, alien traditions and social orders. Through Whitman and a handful of other midcentury writers, American literature came of age.

When Whitman published *Leaves of Grass* for the first time, in 1855, he was willing to risk everything on a daring proposition, "The proof of a poet is that his country absorbs him as affectionately as he has absorbed it." But in the evening of his life he conceded a measure of defeat. "I have not gain'd the acceptance of my time." His most fervent readers as a group were not the American workingmen, artisans, and farmers—the democratic leaven—to whom *Leaves of Grass* had been addressed. Instead they were British writers and intellectuals of the highest degree of cultivation: Oscar Wilde; [poet] Algernon Charles Swinburne; Robert Louis Stevenson [author of *Treasure Island*]; [poet] Gerard Manley

coffee of the coffee-stands in the market, at sunrise—likes a supper of oysters fresh from the oyster-smack—likes to make one at the crowded table among sailors and work-people—would leave a select soiree of elegant people any time to go with tumultuous men, roughs, receive their caresses and welcome, listen to their noise, oaths, smut, fluency, laughter, repartee—and can preserve his presence perfectly among these, and the like of these. The effects he produces in his poems are no effects of artists or the arts, but effects of the original eye or arm, or the actual atmosphere, or tree, or bird. You may feel the unconscious teaching of a fine brute, but will never feel the artificial teaching of a fine writer or speaker.

Other poets celebrate great events, personages, romances, wars, loves, passions, the victories and power of their country, or some real or imagined incident—and polish their work, and come to conclusions, and satisfy the reader. This poet celebrates natural propensities in himself; and that is the way he celebrates all. He comes to no conclusions, and does not satisfy the reader. He certainly leaves him what the serpent left the woman and the man, the taste of the Paradisaic tree of the knowledge of good and evil, never to be erased again. . . .

Milton Hindus, ed. *Walt Whitman: The Critical Heritage.* New York: Barnes & Noble, 1971. pp. 45–48.

Hopkins; Professor Edward Dowden of Trinity College, Dublin; Alfred Lord Tennyson, the Poet Laureate. So far as its own country was concerned *Leaves of Grass* in 1892 was still only "a candidate for the future" and would have to subsist "on its own blood." Looking ahead as well as backward over traveled roads, Whitman compared his modern epic to a tree with many growth rings, an elder daughter, a cathedral, a great city like his million-footed Manhattan. None of these comparisons is entirely adequate, but to the extent that the final and "authorized" *Leaves of Grass* is like a city, the six earlier editions are its substrates [foundation], each with its own spirit of place and time.

THE FIRST EDITION: A PECULIAR BOOK

The 1855 *Leaves of Grass* was a peculiar book in both makeup and content. Designed, produced, and published by the author himself, who also set some of the type for it in a Brooklyn printing office, *Leaves of Grass* came into an indifferent world as an album of ninety-five pages. The words "Leaves of Grass" were stamped on the cloth covers in tendriled letters that appeared to be taking root. Inside, the reader's eye was drawn to an engraved portrait of a bearded man in a hat and open-necked shirt, one hand on his hip and the other in his trouser pocket. In keeping with his assertive informality, the author's name appeared neither on the portrait nor on the facing title page. The text began with ten pages of eccentrically punctuated prose set in double columns, a preface that defined the modern poet as a prophet, hero, priest, and supreme arbiter who "judges not as the judge judges but as the sun falling round a helpless thing." Another bold statement—

I celebrate myself,
And what I assume you shall assume,
For every atom belonging to me as good belongs to you.

—introduced eighty-three pages of poetry, at first glance simply clusters of prose sentences printed like Bible verses.

Do you take it I would astonish?
Does the daylight astonish? or the early redstart twittering
    through the woods?
Do I astonish more than they?

The twelve poems of 1855 were untitled except for the insistent head caption for each, "Leaves of Grass." Readers who ignored the copyright page had to wait until they reached page twenty-nine to learn the identity of the bearded loafer of the frontispiece and the anonymous poet:

> Walt Whitman, an American, one of the roughs, a kosmos,
> Disorderly, fleshy and sensual . . . eating drinking and
>   breeding,
> No sentimentalist . . . no stander above men and women or
>   apart from them . . . no more modest than immodest.

RALPH WALDO EMERSON'S ROLE

Leaves of Grass was to grow and change over the next four decades, but it arrived in 1855 not as a "promising" book but as something stylistically and substantively achieved, at once the fulfillment of American literary romanticism, as articulated by Ralph Waldo Emerson, and the beginning of American literary modernism. Two of the longer poems, "Song of Myself" and "The Sleepers"—the one relatively sunlit, conscious in argument, and public in voice, the other nocturnal, secret, surreal—are the matrix of all of Whitman's work. Emerson himself recognized right away that *Leaves of Grass* was a decisive event in his nation's literature. It had answered his call for the emergence of a native genius who possessed "nerve and dagger" and a "tyrannous" command of "our incomparable materials." After some puzzlement over the unknown author's identity and whereabouts he sent Whitman a letter that remains unmatched for the generosity, shrewdness, and force of its understanding.

Concord, Massachusetts, *21 July, 1855.*

DEAR SIR—I am not blind to the worth of the wonderful gift of "LEAVES OF GRASS." I find it the most extraordinary piece of wit and wisdom that America has yet contributed. I am very happy in reading it, as great power makes us happy. It meets the demand I am always making of what seemed the sterile and stingy nature, as if too much handiwork, or too much lymph in the temperament, were making our western wits fat and mean.

I give you joy of your free and brave thought. I have great joy in it. I find incomparable things said incomparably well, as they must be. I find the courage of treatment which so delights us, and which large perception only can inspire.

I greet you at the beginning of a great career, which yet must have had a long foreground somewhere, for such a start. I rubbed my eyes a little, to see if this sunbeam were no illusion; but the solid sense of the book is a sober certainty. It has the best merits, namely, of fortifying and encouraging.

I did not know until I last night saw the book advertised in a newspaper that I could trust the name as real and available for a post-office. I wish to see my benefactor, and have felt much like striking my tasks and visiting New York to pay you my respects.

                                                                R. W. Emerson.

Without asking Emerson's permission Whitman released this private letter to the New York *Tribune*, arranged to have it printed elsewhere, and distributed it to editors and critics in the form of a broadside. "That was very wrong, very wrong indeed," Emerson complained about these exploitations; friends said they had never seen the Concord sage so angry. But having discerned Whitman's "free & brave thought," "courage," and sense of mission, Emerson should not have been too surprised to find in him also a disregard for conventional proprieties along with the ruthlessness of saints and tyrants. Throughout his career Whitman seized on such opportunities, generated controversy and publicity, arranged favorable accounts of his work, and even reviewed it himself anonymously and pseudonymously. "I have merely looked myself over and repeated candidly what I saw," he once said. "If you did it for the sake of aggrandizing yourself that would be another thing; but doing it simply for the purpose of getting your own weight and measure is as right done for you by yourself as done for you by another." As for the audience for these exercises: "The public is a thick-skinned beast, and you have to keep whacking away on its hide to let it know you're there." Whitman's incessant clamorings for attention have a certain purity—they were always and ultimately in the service of his sacred book, *Leaves of Grass*, not personal advancement.

Emerson's famous letter became part of the texture of Whitman's plans during 1855 and 1856 as he prepared the second edition of *Leaves of Grass*. In his notebook he sketched out "Crossing Brooklyn Ferry," the most significant of the twenty new poems he was to add to his original twelve:

> Poem of passage / the scenes on the river / as I cross the / Fulton ferry / Others will see the flow / of the river, also, / Others will see on both / sides the city of / New York and the city / of Brooklyn / a hundred years hence others / will see them . . . The continual and hurried crowd of / men and women crossing / The reflection of the sky / in the water—the blinding / dazzle in a track from / the most declined sun, / The lighters— the sailors / in their picturesque costumes / the nimbus of light / around the shadow of my / head in the sunset

Further on, along with trial passages for another major new poem of 1856, "Song of the Broad-Axe," is an entry of a different sort. Enclosed within a large bracket, it occupies a page to itself:

> "I greet you at the
> beginning of a great
> career"
>   R.W. Emerson

This Ali Baba formula appeared stamped in gold on the spine of Whitman's new book, at the end of which he once again printed the entire letter along with his own letter of response. He hailed Emerson as the prophet of "Individuality—that new moral American continent without which, I see, the physical continent remained incomplete." "Dear Friend and Master," he wrote, ". . . the work of my life is making poems."

LATER EDITIONS

By 1860 Whitman had eliminated all of this prose matter, which he considered superfluous, and had completely re-structured his book, so that for the first time it had organic unity as a sort of whole-duty-of-man or generic autobiogra-phy—a "New Bible," as he thought of it. Among the 146 new poems in the third *Leaves of Grass* were: "Starting from Pau-manok," an announcement of program and themes; the pro-foundly self-questioning "As I Ebb'd with the Ocean of Life"; "Out of the Cradle Endlessly Rocking," which Swinburne called "the most lovely and wonderful thing I have read for years and years . . . such beautiful skill and subtle power"; and "Calamus," a major cycle of lyrics, tender and per-turbed, on the theme of comradeship or "manly love." For the first time, too, *Leaves of Grass,* "in a far more complete and favorable form than before," was being "really *pub-lished*," Whitman said, not by him, but by an enthusiastic new firm, Thayer and Eldridge of Boston, who were certain they could sell his book to "the mass public" and do its au-thor some good, "pecuniarily." "I am very, very much satis-fied and relieved," Whitman told his brother Jeff, "that the thing, in the permanent form it now is, looks as well and reads as well (to my own notion) as I anticipated—because a good deal, after all, was an experiment—and now I am sat-isfied." But at the end of 1860 Whitman's affairs took a steep downward turn. Thayer and Eldridge went bankrupt and turned over their stock (including the plates of Whitman's new book) to a rival publisher they considered "illiterate" and a "bitter and relentless enemy."

On his forty-second birthday, in May 1861, a month and a half after the fall of Fort Sumter [the battle which began the Civil War], Whitman drafted a prose introduction for yet another edition of *Leaves of Grass*. "So far so well, but the most and the best of the Poem I perceive remains unwritten, and is the work of my life yet to be done. . . . The paths to the house are made—but where is the house itself?" The fourth edition that he brought out six years later included, as an "annex," *Drum-Taps*, sequences of poems in response to the Civil War, his service as a volunteer nurse ("wound-dresser") in the Washington military hospitals, and the death of Abraham Lincoln; much as he regretted having written it, "O Captain! My Captain!" written within a month or two of "When Lilacs Last in the Dooryard Bloom'd," became his only poem to make the anthologies while he lived. But the core of his postwar book—*Leaves of Grass* proper, as distinguished from its annexes—was the 1860 edition so extensively reworked that it seemed almost to be published for the first time. All but 34 of the 456 pages show some sort of revision, ranging from punctuation and single-word corrections to wholesale deletions and additions. A conscious and deliberate craftsman, Whitman reshaped, tightened, and clarified individual poems, rearranged them in order and by group, rejected forty. His revisions, he said, give "a glimpse into the workshop," and the work went on, for even this new edition was transitional in design and massed effect—unfinished and perhaps, like a city, unfinishable. In 1871 he brought out a fifth *Leaves of Grass*, which included "Passage to India," and in 1881 a sixth, in which the poems (exclusive of annexes) were arranged in definitive order. The authorized edition of 1892 was the seventh but, had he lived beyond its publication, it might have not been the last.

PROBLEMS AND CENSORSHIP

"From a worldly and business point of view," Whitman said, looking back over four decades of vicissitude, *Leaves of Grass* had proved to be "worse than a failure." He had seen it take its place in world literature, but in his own country it remained to a certain extent an outlaw book that had subjected him to "frequent bruises," ostracism, and public humiliation. "I don't know if you have ever realized what it means to be a horror in the sight of the people about you," Whitman said of his standing in literary America. One early reviewer had dismissed *Leaves of Grass* as "a mass of stupid filth." Another asked, "Who is this arrogant young man who proclaims himself the Poet of the time, and who roots like a pig among a rotten garbage of licentious thoughts?" In 1865 he was fired from his clerkship in the Interior Department because the secretary found *Leaves of Grass* to be outrageous, offensive, and in violation of "the rules of decorum and propriety prescribed by a Christian Civilization." For Whitman, and for the small band of partisans who had begun to surround him, his well-publicized dismissal crystallized a ten-year pattern of injustices; the prophet mocked and dishonored in his own country became "The Good Gray Poet," sage, martyr, and redeemer.

During the 1870s he orchestrated an international controversy the main issue of which was his alleged neglect and persecution. And in 1881, just when it seemed that L*eaves of Grass* was once again to have a Boston edition, the district attorney there put Whitman's publishers under notice. He warned them that in his opinion the book fell "within the provisions of the Public Statutes respecting obscene literature" and recommended that they withdraw and suppress it. The publishers proposed a list of deletions, including extensive passages and three poems in their entirety: "A Woman Waits for Me," "The Dalliance of the Eagles," and "To a Common Prostitute." Whitman refused to make any concessions and soon after managed to find a home for his book in Philadelphia. "As to this last & in some sense most marked buffeting in the fortunes of *Leaves of Grass*," he reflected at the time, "I tickle myself with the thought how it may be said years hence that at any rate *no book on earth ever had such a history.*"

The Philosophy Behind the Poetry

Joel L. Swerdlow

Joel L. Swerdlow, a self-proclaimed "C" student in English who rarely picked up a book of poetry, here attempts to discover why the average person can understand Walt Whitman's poetry. Swerdlow follows in Whitman's footsteps, starting with the poet's birthplace, in order to understand the poet's philosophy. Swerdlow talks to various Whitman experts along the way (including the teacher who was the model for the movie *Dead Poets Society*) and even to a clown, and comes to understand why Whitman is indeed America's poet. Joel L. Swerdlow has authored and edited books including *Beyond Debate: A Paper on Televised Presidential Elections* and *To Heal a Nation: The Vietnam Veterans Memorial.*

"Stranger," Walt Whitman says in *Leaves of Grass*, "if you passing meet me and desire to speak to me, why should you not speak to me? / And why should I not speak to you?"

I never listened. Despite a passion for books, I read Whitman and other poets only under duress. I received a C in college English and never took another literature course after my freshman year. *Leaves* still sits on my bookshelf. This passage—which I underlined during a homework assignment—shines like a beacon, a voice I heard long ago but did not answer.

Whitman did for poetry what [Spanish novelist] Miguel de Cervantes did for the novel, [German playwright] Bertolt Brecht did for theater, and Pablo Picasso did for painting: He redefined the rules. In terms of style and subject matter most 20th-century poets in the United States—and many throughout the world—are his grandchildren. Poems from *Leaves of Grass*, furthermore, are required reading in America's

Reprinted from "America's Poet: Walt Whitman," by Joel L. Swerdlow, National Geographic, vol. 186, no. 6, December 1994, by permission of Joel L. Swerdlow and the National Geographic Society.

schools and have been translated into dozens of languages.

These translations line bookshelves in the old farmhouse in which Whitman was born. I have come to West Hills, Long Island, looking for clues. Who was Whitman? What have I been missing?

Schoolchildren's pennies helped buy this house in 1951, saving it from bulldozers. The house has Dutch doors and ax-cut beams—all from the hands of Walter Whitman, Sr., a carpenter and sometime farmer. By the time Walt was born in 1819, the Whitmans had lived on Long Island for nearly 200 years. Patriotism pervaded their household. One of Walt's five brothers was named George Washington Whitman, another Thomas Jefferson Whitman, and another Andrew Jackson Whitman.

VISITING WHITMAN'S BIRTHPLACE

The house is now on a four-lane highway, diagonally across from the Walt Whitman Mall. Inside the mall five teenagers are eating pizza. "Do you know about Walt Whitman?" I ask. Four have heard that Whitman is a "cool" poet, but one responds, "I thought he was the guy who owns the mall."

When I settle into my motel room, it is time to confront poetry once again. In the 30 years since freshman English, I have attempted to read poems only once. In 1984 someone I loved had a fatal illness. His girlfriend found solace in poetry and recommended a particular collection. I glanced at a page, liked it, and for a week walked around with the poems in my hip pocket. Their physical presence provided comfort, but I never read more than a few lines.

Now I select a Whitman poem entitled "Out of the Cradle Endlessly Rocking," which literature professors consider one of Walt's best. "Out of the mocking-bird's throat, the musical shuttle, / Out of the Ninth-month midnight, / Over the sterile sands and the fields beyond, where the child. . . ."

My eyes drift over the next few pages, looking for something to happen. By "the lilac-scent was in the air" I feel sleepy, and at "Low hangs the moon, it rose late" I reach for the remote control.

I feel guilty, but I enjoy a good movie on television.

FOLLOWING WHITMAN TO BROOKLYN

Although the Whitman family moved to Brooklyn just a few days before Walt's fourth birthday, he retained his love for the Long Island countryside—"Sea-beauty! stretch'd and basking!" As a young man he often went swimming, clamming, and fishing. He walked the deserted beaches at Coney Island, where he says he recited Shakespeare and Homer to the waves. I follow Whitman to the beach. It is easy to see why he spoke to the sea. Waves are always alive, ever ready to listen and talk back. Yet few of us walk along a deserted beach reciting poems. Young Walt clearly perceived life— and himself—in heroic proportions. Walk with me, Walt, and tell me what inner voices you heard. What was awakening inside you?

No answer can be found. The influence of his family seems limited. His mother read primarily religious publications. His father was rough and heavy drinking. Three of seven siblings suffered crippling emotional problems. Nor was school important: He quit at age 11. Yet Walt, borrowing books whenever possible, read *Arabian Nights* and novels by James Fenimore Cooper and Sir Walter Scott—all of which left him "simmering, simmering.". . .

LOOKING FOR WHITMAN IN MANHATTAN

New York's busiest street was Broadway. It stretched for about three miles from the ferry landing to 14th Street. Along the way were theaters, opera houses, hotels, restaurants. "I swim in it as in the sea," he wrote.

Whitman attended the opera often and loved to sing works by Rossini, Bellini, Mozart, and Verdi. His principal passion, however, was talking to men whose work gave them time to kill. He sat with Broadway stagecoach drivers, men with nicknames like Balky Bill and Old Elephant, and stopped to chat at the firehouse just off Broadway near Canal Street. . . .

I swim . . . into Broadway's sea, looking for Whitman in the crowds. Six feet tall. Thick chested. One hundred eighty pounds. Baggy trousers tucked into boots. Hands in pockets of calico jacket. Swagger. Shirt unbuttoned to expose muscular neck and hairy chest. Beard prematurely whitening. Freshly scrubbed face. Large, heavy-lidded eyes. Those eyes were key to his conversations. He asked questions, let you float up into sky-blue irises, and listened. You felt important. I am jealous of people who walked these same streets and got to meet him.

Whitman told no one when, at around age 30, he began writing *Leaves*. The Bible, classics, opera, patriotism, his experiences as a journalist, and love of nature all contributed to the song flowing from his fingers. Many people write from torment and misery. Walt's principal inspiration was what made him happiest, the people he said he "absorbed." He made his poems, more than anything else, a personal conversation.

Why did Whitman suddenly listen to his own voice? Most artists struggle, producing failed efforts with glimmers of future greatness. Whitman's transformation into a genius appears effortless. It seemed simply to happen. Whitman himself could offer no explanation. "I just did what I did because I did it—that's the whole secret," he said later. Photographs show that around this time his eyes become lighter, more inviting.

In 1855, after about five years, Walt published *Leaves of Grass*, setting some of the type himself. Twelve poems filled 83 pages. Whitman listed no author but ran a small picture of himself, jaunty, hand on hip. The absence of an author emphasized Whitman's belief that the voice in *Leaves* is Everyone.

Before Whitman, serious poems followed strict rules of rhyme and meter and generally addressed grandiose, romantic subjects. No poem in the original *Leaves* rhymes, and most focus on mundane concerns like earning a living. "Blacksmithing, glass-blowing, nail-making, coopering, tin-roofing, shingle-dressing," says "A Song for Occupations." Woven throughout is the proclamation that American democracy represents a new and irresistible force: "Unscrew the locks from the doors! / Unscrew the doors themselves from their jambs! /. . . I speak the password primeval. . . . I give the sign of democracy."

Whitman's ambition matched his audacity. He wanted the citizens of this democracy, the so-called common people, to incorporate *Leaves* into their daily rhythms.

Disappointment came quickly. Whitman's mother, with whom he still lived, found the book "muddled." Few bookstores would carry *Leaves* because of its content. Whitman said that poor people are as valuable as the rich and that women are the equals of men. Even worse, in an age that covered naked piano legs out of modesty, he praised the human body. Whitman, said one critic, "brought the slop-pail into the parlor.". . .

Never overly modest, Whitman wrote unsigned reviews of his own work, which various newspapers published. "An American bard at last!" read one; another proclaimed, "We announce a great Philosopher—perhaps a great Poet." But he achieved some of his fame because he was so easy to parody. In 1857 the London *Examiner* offered its version of a Whitman poem: "The teapot, five coffee cups, sugar basin and cover, four saucers and six cups."

How to Read *Leaves of Grass*

The *Leaves* that people ignored or mocked are now worth about $40,000 each. I stand in a Long Island bank vault with Barbara Mazor Bart, executive director of the Walt Whitman Birthplace Association, which stores its treasures here while constructing a visitors center. I have returned to read one of the fewer than 150 known survivors of the original 795 copies of *Leaves*.

Skimming Whitman's preface, I find a summary of his philosophy:

"Love the earth and sun and the animals, despise riches, give alms to every one that asks, stand up for the stupid and crazy, devote your income and labor to others, hate tyrants, argue not concerning God, have patience and indulgence toward the people, take off your hat to nothing known or unknown or to any man or number of men, go freely with powerful uneducated persons and with the young and with the mothers of families. . . . reexamine all you have been told at school or church or in any book, dismiss whatever insults your own soul, and your very flesh shall be a great poem."

Also in the preface are instructions about how to read *Leaves*. Go out in the open air, Whitman says. That night, I follow his advice, selecting "Song of Myself." You try it. Fold back the magazine, go outside, and read aloud with me.

"I celebrate myself, and sing myself, / And what I assume you shall assume, / For every atom belonging to me as good belongs to you.

"I loafe and invite my soul, / I lean and loafe at my ease observing a spear of summer grass.

"My tongue, every atom of my blood, form'd from this soil, this air, / Born here of parents born here from parents the same, and their parents the same, / I, now thirty-seven years old in perfect health begin, / Hoping to cease not till death."

The words are nice. They have melody. But I do not understand what I am reading, and I feel silly. Something keeps me going. "Creeds and schools in abeyance, / Retiring back a while sufficed at what they are, but never forgotten, / I harbor for good or bad, I permit to speak at every hazard, / Nature without check with original energy."

Please excuse me. I cannot read aloud anymore. The poem mentions houses and perfumes and then describes 28 young men. They are swimming. A young woman watches through a curtain. She finds them attractive. And then? An unrelated scene begins.

Even though I am discouraged, Joseph Brodsky, poet and winner of the 1987 Nobel Prize in Literature, tells me that reading aloud is indeed the best way to find Whitman. "Poetry *is* meant to be read aloud," he explains. "It's much more engaging than reading silently. You hear not only content, you hear the entire euphony of the words. Nothing beats the spoken word even if you are speaking to yourself."

According to Brodsky, who teaches at Mount Holyoke College, I went off course by expecting the poem to provide a story or drama that would keep my attention. Instead, he says, I should realize that poetry offers things available nowhere else: condensed scene, emotion, and story; a glimpse of something greater than ourselves; a stop sign that keeps us from rushing from moment to moment. "Poetry," he concludes, "is a mental accelerator that, if mastered, can cure anguish or cause joy.". . .

POETRY IN THE MOVIES

As I have learned, it can take more than a book and a motel room to get you to read poetry. I need the English teacher played by Robin Williams in the 1989 movie *Dead Poets Society*. He ordered students to rip the introduction from their poetry textbooks. "Learn to think for yourselves," Williams said. He told them that poetry can stimulate romance and captured Whitman's passion on the blackboard: "I sound my barbaric YAWP over the rooftops of the world."

"The movie is quite realistic," says Sam Pickering, the real teacher Williams was portraying. "I was 24 years old in 1965, teaching 15-year-olds at the Montgomery Bell Academy in Nashville, Tennessee. I was full of excitement. One of my students later used his notes for the movie screenplay."

I have reached Pickering by telephone in Perth, Australia, where he is on sabbatical from the University of Connecticut. Something in his voice creates the image of a man constantly looking around for fun. . . .

Pickering tells me that at age 53 he prefers [English poet Alfred, Lord] Tennyson's "rhythmic sleep-inducing 'Lotos-Eaters'" to Whitman's "yawp." He describes his daily routine: "I don't work. I'm a great wanderer. I walk the streets of the city or go into the bush carrying a magnifying lens. I get to know every tree, flower, and insect so I can celebrate them and help others celebrate."

He anticipates my next sentence and admits, "Yes, that does sound like Whitman."

"What advice do you have for people who want to find Whitman?"

"Remember that he made poetry celebrate things that aren't normally considered poetic. Take time to notice the world around you. See that the ordinary is extraordinary."

I mention my C in freshman English. "I got a C too," he says. "But I did not give up."

THE JOY OF WHITMAN

Pickering's advice is fun to follow. A list of objects visible from my front steps feels like the beginning of a Whitman poem. Instead of reading the newspaper while waiting for someone, I chat with strangers. We discuss topics, such as potholes and family visits, that are unimportant yet all-important. The next day I find myself at a crowded snack counter. Rather than ignoring the conversations around me, I listen as fragments float by. Such moments, I suspect, bring me closer to Walt.

Patch Adams, a 49-year-old clown, shows me that actually finding Whitman requires much more work. Adams greets me at his home in Arlington, Virginia. He is six feet four inches, with a handlebar mustache turned up at right angles and a long ponytail. He wears a brown velveteen jacket; one yellow and one orange sock; a purple shirt; baggy, green pants that—he soon shows me—can be easily pulled up to his chest, thus becoming shorts; and a square hat with a secret pocket containing his fake nose.

Adams's medical school diploma is somewhere in the basement, along with more than 12,000 books. "I'm pretty zealous about joy, and Walt showed me the way," Adams says. Although he is physically imposing, his soft voice makes me lean forward.

"Whitman," Adams continues. He lets the word trail away as though nothing more need be said. "How many of these other writers discuss joy?" he finally says. "Everyone else describes the size of the problem. Whitman is a neon sign for solutions. I try to spread his dust everywhere."

Adams wears his clown suit as we fly to Morgantown, West Virginia. About 200 health-care professionals join him in the ballroom of the West Virginia University student union for a workshop on joy. In one activity Adams has us sit, close our eyes, and make our bodies touch at least four strangers. Then we think of things that make us happy, hold them in as long as possible, and shout them out. The room soon sounds like one of Whitman's poems.

Much of Adams's message resembles Whitman's: Your body is nice. Only you can diminish yourself. Be curious instead of judgmental. Challenge accepted wisdom. But most important, he says, take what Whitman calls "the open road."

"That open road lies in front of everyone," Adams says. "Delight in your piece of it. Pursue your dreams. Find your road and take it."

Adams begins to recite Whitman's "Song of the Open Road": "Afoot and light-hearted I take to the open road, / Healthy, free, the world before me, / The long brown path before me leading wherever I choose." His voice becomes a whisper, sucking us toward him. "Henceforth I ask not good-fortune, I myself am good-fortune, / Henceforth I whimper no more, postpone no more, need nothing." For me this is the moment of discovery. To be Whitmanesque, I realize, is not to be poetic. It is taking your road and appreciating what you encounter along the way.

Adams's face reveals what is missing from my own reading of Whitman. Whether reading silently or aloud, you must participate. You cannot enter this territory as a tourist. Reading Whitman is not like reading a novel or seeing a movie. You cannot sit passively as a story sweeps you away. Rhythm and feeling must come from both you and the poet. Bring your hopes, frustrations, and fears. You are part of the art.

In many ways my search has ended. I have found *Leaves*, which is so personal, so intense, I have also found Whitman. No one can tell where the man ends and the creation begins. He talks to me. Other times he is me, talking to other people.

Some evenings I read Whitman for only five minutes. Even then, he leaves me simmering. . . .

In December 1862, 20 bloody months after the [Civil] war began, Whitman read in the newspaper that George Whitman—an officer of the 51st New York Regiment—had been wounded at Fredericksburg, Virginia. Although Walt often felt distant from his family—"Being a blood brother to a man," he once said, "don't make him a real brother"—he was always strongly loyal, and he immediately set out to find his brother.

FOLLOWING WHITMAN TO WASHINGTON

I retrace his steps, traveling south from Washington, D. C.— Walt went by boat and train—passing farms, low hills, and small towns. Between Washington and the Confederate capital of Richmond, nature offers only one major barrier: the Rappahannock River. As we near the river, the flow of the land shows how geography dictated military strategy. The Union Army tried to take the easiest crossing, which is at Fredericksburg.

Union commanders established headquarters in Chatham House, an estate overlooking the Fredericksburg crossing. When Whitman arrived, he learned that his brother had suffered only a superficial cheek wound. . . .

What Whitman saw, however, changed him forever. He accompanied the wounded to Washington, which already had more men in hospitals than the entire city population in 1850. He rented a room and found part-time work as a government clerk, doing what is now performed by photocopy machines. . . .

During free hours he visited Army hospitals. Wounded and sick soldiers often lay on dirty blankets next to pails of bloody bandages. Open sores and wounds festered. Men groaned and screamed. Some joked, barely noticing that others, boys as young as 15, were dying.

Whitman walked among these men, in his words, like a "great wild buffalo." Gray suit. Wide-brimmed sombrero. Immaculate shirt with flower or green sprig in lapel. Army boots with black morocco tops. Mostly he talked, sometimes throughout the night. The men, he wrote to his mother, "hunger and thirst for attention; this is sometimes the only thing that will reach their condition." For many homesick, lonely soldiers, Whitman's companionship and good cheer probably achieved more than the doctors did. . . .

WHITMAN IN CAMDEN

After the war Whitman stopped his regular hospital visits. His sleeplessness and distress resembled what is now called post-traumatic stress disorder. He was 46 years old and looked like an old man. "I would try to write, blind, blind, with my own tears," he later said.

Around this time Alfred, Lord Tennyson, the British poet laureate with whom Whitman corresponded, wrote "Charge of the Light Brigade"—"Flash'd all their sabers bare, / Flash'd as they turn'd in air. . . . / When can their glory fade? / O the wild charge they made!" Whitman, in contrast, said war is "nine hundred and ninety-nine parts diarrhea." He wrote that "the real war will never get in the books."

To tell true stories that capture war's brutality, Whitman turned to prose—most notably *Specimen Days*. One example: "After the battles at Columbia, Tennessee, where we repuls'd about a score of vehement rebel charges, they left a great many wounded on the ground, mostly within our range. Whenever any of these wounded attempted to move away by any means, generally by crawling off, our men without exception, brought them down by bullet. They let none crawl away. . . ."

Whitman also added new poems to *Leaves*, revised old ones, and continued to be an unembarrassed self-promoter. When he was scheduled to read a poem at the Dartmouth College commencement in 1872, one anonymous newspaper critic compared him to Homer and Shakespeare. You guessed it: Whitman wrote the story.

In 1873 Whitman, only 53, suffered a stroke and moved to Camden, New Jersey, to live with brother George and his wife, Louisa. George Whitman was a pipe inspector at the Camden Tool and Tube Works. Camden was an industrial suburb of Philadelphia, home to an unrelated Whitman family, famous since 1842 for manufacturing Whitman's Sampler chocolates. Walt never met them.

In the next few years Walt had more strokes and began to have trouble walking. Painful tubercular infections had invaded his bones. He sought to cure himself at nearby Timber Creek. The creek is now hidden among houses and highways, but I find where Whitman removed his clothes, covered himself with mud, and wrestled with oak and hickory saplings. "After you have exhausted what there is in business, politics, conviviality, love, and so on—have found that none of these finally satisfy, or permanently wear—what remains?" Whitman asked. "Nature remains."

The writings of a lifetime earned Whitman only a few thousand dollars. Low sales for *Leaves*, however, did not end his problems with censorship. In 1882 the Boston district attorney ordered him to delete "A Woman Waits for Me," "To a Common Prostitute," "The Dalliance of the Eagles," and lines from other poems. Whitman refused. "The dirtiest book," he said, "is the expurgated book."

During his lifetime, censors and critics focused on "I turn the bridegroom out of bed and stay with the bride myself" and other heterosexual lines. "I never read his book—but was told that he was disgraceful," Emily Dickinson wrote to a friend. Whitman's letters and poems, however, indicate a physical attraction to men. This has received considerable scholarly attention, reflecting, in large part, the intimacy of Whitman's writing. Readers feel they know him.

This interest in Whitman's sexuality is unusually intense. Who did Michelangelo or Mark Twain love? Few people know or care, yet Whitman's private life can stimulate bigotry. I wander into a bar on Camden's waterfront, much like those that Whitman frequented. It is dark at noon, and full of men with no pressing engagements. As I leave, the bartender stops wiping glasses. "You're not going to say Whitman's a faggot, are you?" he says. "I like his poetry, and I don't like people saying he's a faggot."

In Walt's day controversy over censorship brought him much needed attention, and he continued to reach the literati. *Leaves* "tumbled the world upside down for me," said Robert Louis Stevenson shortly after the publication of *Treasure Island*. Vincent van Gogh, then painting his apocalyptic *Starry Night*, read a French translation of *Leaves*. Whitman sees "a world of healthy, carnal love, strong and frank—of friendship —of work—under the great starlit vault of heaven," van Gogh told his sister. "It makes you smile, it is all so candid and pure."

A POET OF THE PEOPLE

But the people Whitman was writing for—ordinary people— did not read him. "O Captain! My Captain!" written after the death of Lincoln, was one of the few Whitman poems to become popular in his lifetime—"O Captain! my Captain! our fearful trip is done, / The ship has weather'd every rack, the prize we sought is won." It is also one of only two in *Leaves* that rhyme. Rather than enjoy its success, Whitman thought it too conventional, saying, "I'm almost sorry I ever wrote the poem."

Whitman's eyes stayed seductive. No angst or anger appears in later photographs. He remained optimistic. The last line in Whitman's final revision of *Leaves* is, "the strongest and sweetest songs yet remain to be sung." As his body declined—"the strange inertia falling pall-like over me"—he lost his roar but not his wisdom. "Have you learn'd lessons only of those who admired you, and were tender with you?" he asks. "Have you not learn'd great lessons from those who reject you, and brace themselves against you?". . .

By the 1880s Whitman had realized that *Leaves* would never attract a mass audience in his lifetime. He placed his faith in the future. The real test, he said, would come in a hundred years.

The hundred years have passed. Whitman's influence has been extraordinary. His persona—confidant, companion to the neglected, singer of human decency, advocate of equality, lover of nature—is part of our national landscape. "He is far more important than most Americans realize," Roger Asselineau, Sorbonne professor and author of *The Evolution of Walt Whitman*, explains as we sit in a café on Paris's Left Bank. "Students see in Whitman a metaphor into which they can read what they need. Equality for women. Sexual freedom. Freedom of expression."

Whitman, however, wanted to be in our hip pockets and on our nightstands. In this he is clearly still a failure.

The loss is ours. Go outside and read aloud. Adventure waits. You may also find a piece of yourself you didn't know was missing.

Whitman the Radical

Robert Martin

Robert Martin explores the background and implications of Walt Whitman's radical ideas. Never one to go along with the crowd, Whitman chose the road less taken poetically, philosophically, and sexually. Martin places Whitman in a long sequence of American radicals extending from early American philosophers Tom Paine and Ralph Waldo Emerson to twentieth-century poet Allen Ginsberg. Robert Martin has taught at the University of Montreal. He is the author of *The Continual Presence of Walt Whitman* (1992).

'I am as radical now as ever', Walt Whitman (1819–92) told his friend, the author Horace Traubel at the end of his life. A few months later he remarked to Traubel that 'there wouldn't be much wealth left in private hands—that is, if my say was final'. But Whitman's radicalism was individualistic; as he put it, he did not 'belong to any school'. In Whitman's earlier life he had been more willing to affirm party affiliations. In 1848 he had been a Brooklyn delegate to the Free-Soil convention, the anti-slavery coalition that split the Democrat Party, calling for unconditional backing for ex-President Martin Van Buren, and editing the new Free-Soil paper, *The Freeman*. He gave up the venture after the paper's office burned down, and after he had come to recognise the role of compromise in politics.

THE ROOTS OF WHITMAN'S RADICALISM

Whitman's radicalism had much in common with his age and his American roots. Radicals in America seem generally to have preferred the individual and the anarchistic to the collective and the socialist. Whitman might reject the idea of private property, but he cared too much about his sense of 'self' to be able to adapt to any political programme. Whitman's radical origins included the utopian movements that flourished in the American 1840s. He was a great admirer of Frances Wright, the British reformer (1795–1852), who had founded the Nashoba Community, an inter-racial utopia in West Tennessee, and collaborated with Robert Dale Owen on the New Harmony *Gazette*. Wright's talks on education, birth control, and the distribution of wealth, and her attacks on the church lie behind much of Whitman's poetry.

Another important formative influence on the young Whitman were the views of Quaker reformer, Elias Hicks. Hicks' transformation of American Quakerism brought it into line with a growing evangelism, replacing a strict code of unworldliness with an emphasis on the personal voice or 'inner light'. The appeal of Quakerism for Whitman was, as Newton Arvin put it, their 'spiritual independence and self-trust'.

The American 1848 [a revolutionary, utopian, politically active moment in America] was not a programme for political revolution, although it included a justification for resistance by individuals. It was instead a reaffirmation of American ideals of self-hood and individualism. Whitman imbibed these ideas above all from Ralph Waldo Emerson (1803–82), in essays such as 'Self-Reliance'. It was that joining of the celebration of the individual consciousness with the celebration of the young nation that appealed to Whitman, who saw himself as the national poet Emerson called for. Nevertheless, however much Whitman was a spiritual descendant of Emerson's, there were significant differences. Just as Whitman knew and admired the actual radicals and utopians of his day, and had himself participated in some of the moral/social crusades, such as the temperance movement, while Emerson remained aloof, so too Whitman saw himself as providing a place for the body that was strikingly absent, or derided, in Emerson's Platonism [philosophy of Plato].

Whitman's vision was not merely a product of the Concord philosophers (the group including Margaret Fuller, Henry Thoreau and Nathaniel Hawthorne that settled with Emerson in Concord, Massachusetts) of his time, but even more of an American radical tradition, an antinomianism (opposition to the obligatory nature of moral law) perhaps derived from the early Puritans and their dissenters, and from the revolutionary voice of Thomas Paine. For Whitman, America's 'radical human rights' were in large part the work of Paine. They were also the product of his own childhood and young adulthood. Whitman was the first major American writer to come from a working-class background that was far from the privileged élites of Boston, Philadelphia, or Virginia. He was born in West Hills, Long Island, into a family of English and Dutch farmers. His father was part of the first Revolutionary generation, and subscribed to the hopes of a democratic future. A few years after young Walter's birth in 1819, the family moved to Brooklyn, where they occupied a series of houses, as Walt's father built frame houses he hoped to sell at a profit. In an age of speculation, he failed. By the time he was twelve, Walt Whitman had begun work as a printer's apprentice. After completing his apprenticeship at sixteen, he was unable to find work as a printer, and turned to rural teaching (for which he had no training and scarcely any formal education) for several terms until returning to New York to work as a printer. Whitman had lived in democratic America, in practice as well as in theory, and knew first-hand the dangers of a free economy as well as the possibilities of self-creation. He was also a remarkable autodidact [a self-taught person], absorbing his reading and incorporating it into an eclectic, undisciplined body of heterogeneous knowledge. His poetry reflects his enormous storehouse of obscure information, as well as his disdain for 'official' knowledge: as he would write in his greatest poem, 'Song of Myself', 'I have no chair, no church, no philosophy'.

Whitman applied Emerson's theoretical democracy to the nation to the body, claiming a radical equality of body parts and functions. He expressed this not only as a statement of principle. 'Welcome is every organ and attribute of me, and of any man hearty and clean, / Not an inch nor a particle of an inch is vile, and none shall be less familiar than the rest', but in shockingly concrete terms, 'The scent of these armpits aroma finer than prayer'.

A FRANK VIEW OF SEXUALITY

The Concord philosophers sought to escape experience by a withdrawal into a world of pure idea; nature was the site of a disembodied experience (Emerson's 'transparent eyeball') of an eternal world of forms. Whitman's celebration of the radically new self was based on a recuperation of the body, and a breaking down of a body/soul hierarchy or binarism. A crucial arm in the struggle against Western philosophical idealism was the recuperation of 'lower' forms. In this struggle the resistance to Western philosophy ran parallel to a struggle against Victorian prudery. In the famous section 11 of 'Song of Myself' Whitman allied himself with the lonely woman observer who seeks to join in the erotic celebration of the young men bathing. The gender boundaries that normally enforce the image of the 'lady' in nineteenth-century culture break down in a vision of the men touched by 'an unseen hand' until they give in to the anonymous sexual encounter and 'souse with spray'.

That final image of an undirected seminality is crucial to Whitman's programme of resistance to the anti-masturbation campaign of his day. In a social context where masturbation was seen as an economic crime ('spending') as well as a moral transgression, Whitman celebrated the auto-erotic, as well as the homo- and heterosexual. Well aware that the status of women was connected to the cultural silence around sexuality, he argued that:

> only when sex is properly treated, talked, avowed, accepted, will the woman be equal with the man, and pass where the man passes, and meet his words with her words, and his rights with her rights.

A fervent believer in the equality of women, Whitman began the practice of inclusive language, insisting on 'the man or the woman' rather than the generic masculine. His adoption of such language also served to mask his own homosexual desires.

In his honesty about his physical sexual attraction to other men, Whitman found himself lacking a community. Sexual encounters were probably not difficult (his note books include many names of young men who spent the night with him), and 'bohemian' bars like Pfaff's may have provided some sort of place for fulfilment of homosexual desire, but Whitman found himself largely alone in his wish to understand his sexuality in a democratic culture. . . . It was in his sequence of 'Calamus' poems that he sought to give expression to his desires and to theorise their nature and possible social place.

The sequence begins with that most famous of classical homosexual allusions, [Roman poet] Virgil's second eclogue, but even here Whitman is making the landscape American and constructing a role for himself as the originator of 'athletic love' and the celebrator of 'the need of comrades'. Although 'athletic love' carries with it echoes of the Greek *gymnasium*, it is also being offered in opposition to a cultural assumption, both already existing and being constructed, of the homosexual as effete, decidedly unathletic dandy. Although Whitman's presentation of himself as the poet of homosexual love has made him a figure of enormous importance for later gay writers and readers, his position on desire between men has little in common with the 'minority' view taken by many sexual radicals in the 1960s. For Whitman homosexuals do not constitute a small group that requires equal rights; instead homosexuality is seen as the fundamental condition of a democratic society.

Whitman's influence has been enormous, and has always included a recognition of his part in the redefinition of sexual desire. Homosexual writers including Garcia Lorca, Pessoa, Hart Crane, Jack Spicer, Allen Ginsberg, and many others have felt themselves enabled by Whitman's example. Women writers, too, although sometimes troubled by the almost exclusively male world of Whitman's imagination, have often responded enthusiastically to his affirmation of female desire and his insistence upon sexual equality. Kate Chopin's *The Awakening* (1899), in particular, derives its heroine's sexual awakening from Whitman's model. And black writers have found Whitman's influence on the novelist Richard Wright (1908–60) and poet Langston Hughes (1902–67) was considerable. Such writers saw beyond the sentimental adaptations of Whitman that had been offered by American liberals such as Carl Sandburg or Sherwood Anderson, and tried to enlist Whitman in a radically engaged struggle against racism and economic privilege.

RADICAL POETICS

In matters of poetic form Whitman was even more of a radical, although his transformations have turned out to be so lasting that it may now be difficult to recognise the magnitude of his accomplishment. As [American poet] Ezra Pound put it, Whitman 'broke the back' of conventional metre, thus putting into practice Emerson's famous dictum that 'it is not metre but a metre-making argument' that defines poetry. There were other radical attempts at redefining English metre in this period, including notably [British poet] Gerard Manley Hopkins' 'sprung rhythm', but they failed to take. Whitman invented the long unmetrical line that allows him to expand, to dilate. Avoiding prose by paratactic structures and parallelism, Whitman is able to shift the spine of the poem to its left-hand margin. Only such an open form could give voice to his inclusiveness, his refusal of principles or order and subordination. His famous 'catalogue' technique, or enumerative style, allows him to celebrate the thing itself, without a surrounding fabric of hierarchies of value. At the same time the very act of inclusion, in the genteel world of verse, amounts to a confrontation of the reader with the reality and diversity of experience, unfiltered by 'art'. His poetry is, as he put it in 'Song of Myself':

> the meal equally set, . . . the meat for natural hunger, / It is for the wicked just the same as the righteous, I make appointments with all, / I will not have a single person slighted or left away.

THE POET'S PERSONA

Whitman's self-presentation, as in the famous frontispiece to the first edition of *Leaves of Grass,* the book coterminous with the life that Whitman constantly rewrote and revised, was that of a worker in open-necked shirt, with hand jauntily on the hip. The poems, too, try to break away from the power of the *salon,* offering instead the outdoors of adventure and freedom. 'Song of Myself' proclaims the natural man of Romantic origins, now physically present in an American landscape. To go outdoors was also to liberate the self, to 'come out': 'I will go to the bank by the wood and become undisguised and naked'. Conventional life, like conventional sexuality was a disguise: nakedness was the condition of truth. 'Song of the Open Road' brought together Whitman's love for the natural world with his sense of political mission, as he adapted the French Revolutionary call, '*Allons*', into a call for a 'greater struggle' of the self for freedom from the fixed paths. Whitman's 'open road' created American space and possibility, later to be claimed by the Beats in the fifties, and it associated it with what Whitman called 'adhesiveness', adopting a term from the nineteenth century pseudo-science of phrenology and making it into a name for a love of men that was casual, spontaneous, and omnipresent, the talk of those turning eye-balls'.

Although Whitman's indifference to the proprieties alarmed many of his literary colleagues, he found a warm response among many readers. His work as a nurse in the Civil War brought out his qualities of friend and care-giver. The letters between him and the wounded soldiers are an extraordinary testimony to the power of his sympathy to cross lines of class, and in an age before the sharp demarcation of kinds of desire, to offer loving affection to the men in his care. These men, often barely literate, were moved by Whitman's attention and kept in touch with the poet even after they returned to civilian life and, in most cases, marriage. The war tested Whitman's faith in the power of the American democratic vision, but he emerged from it convinced that liberty cannot be obtained by legal documents, but only with 'manly affection' that can tie the states with 'the love of lovers'.

WHITMAN'S SOCIAL INFLUENCE

Whitman's dream of national unity and his vision of friendship across class lines made him a powerful attraction for English socialists of the late nineteenth century. The poet and reformer Edward Carpenter (1844–1929) did more than anyone to apply Whitman's ideas and poetic practice, and tried to develop a community of lovers devoted to social and sexual equality. In his Whitman-like poem 'Towards Democracy' and in essays such as 'Love's Coming of Age' and 'The Intermediate Sex', Carpenter developed a social critique based on the adaptation of feminist and socialist theory. The views of Carpenter and his colleagues in Sheffield, joining as they did, multiple reform movements and utopian strains, looked back to the same kind of radical impulse that had given rise to Whitman, but they were increasingly removed from a socialist movement now linked to trade unionism and uninterested in sexual reform. The last gasp of this line of influence, at least during this period, came in E.M. Forster, whose final novel *A Passage to India* records the impact of Carpenter on the young Forster and the novelist's attempt to imagine the power of an inter-racial, intercultural male friendship to overcome imperialism and racism.

But Whitman's India, apparently untouched by the colonial experience, seemed unattainable. So too the poets of the 1950s could only look back to Whitman with a sense of loss. Allen Ginsberg could find 'the older man' only in 'a supermarket in California', the American dream gone sour. It would take a still later generation of poets such as Marlon Riggs to recapture something of Whitman's original sense of possibility. In his 'Tongues Untied' the ability to find a voice, to speak for the speechless and silenced, which Whitman had taken as his task, becomes real again. Whitman's lasting power has remained one of enablement, of allowing the excluded to speak:

I act as the tongue of you, / Tied in your mouth, in mine it begins to be loosen'd.

Whitman's Disguised Sexuality

Alan Helms

In the Victorian society of nineteenth-century America, exploring sexuality in literature was taboo. According to Alan Helms, Whitman broke through this barrier in his writings, but the poet had to zealously guard the secret of his homosexuality. Such modesty is reflected in the subtly disguised sexual passages that appear in the early editions of *Leaves of Grass*. Whitman often avoided gender-specific pronouns so that the reader could not tell if the object of the narrator's desire was male or female. Helms argues that after 1860, Whitman's desire for widespread acceptance caused him to abandon his most explicit topics altogether. Alan Helms has taught at the University of Massachusetts at Boston.

In 1882, a young Oscar Wilde in a brown velvet suit paid a call on Walt Whitman in Camden. Afterward, Wilde told the friend who had taken him that if the elderberry wine he'd been offered "had been vinegar, I would have drunk it all the same, for I have an admiration for that man which I can hardly express." Oscar Wilde at a loss for words? What did the quick-witted dandy find so admirable about the lumbering, home-spun, Good Gray Poet? For one thing, an illustration of his favorite theory: life imitates art. Wilde found a consciously crafted man who had become his own ideal version of himself. For another, Wilde discovered what he had expected to find ever since he had read an early edition of *Leaves of Grass*: a fellow queer, or a fellow Uranian [slang for "gay"], or however else it was homosexual men saw themselves in the public eye in those days (and how very conscious Wilde and Whitman were of the public eye). Next day, Whitman told a Philadelphia reporter: "We had a very happy time together. I think him genuine, honest, and manly," and later: "He is so frank, and out-spoken, and manly. I don't see why such mocking things are written of him."

WHITMAN'S CAUTION

Whitman's insistence upon Wilde's "manliness" suggests a cautionary tactic designed to dispel suspicion by appropriating the standards by which most nineteenth century American men judged other men. Whitman was, in fact, an extremely cautious man, for he was a homosexual writing in a homophobic society. In the Preface to the first *Leaves of Grass* he starts a list of "parts of the greatest poet" with the item "Extreme caution or prudence," an odd requirement for a poet, especially when stipulated by someone who kept wanting to "undrape" himself, to become "undisguised and naked," although it is true he only does so cautiously—only "in paths untrodden," or only "apart from other men,"

> Or else, only by stealth, in some wood, for trial, or back of a
> rock, in the open air . . .

or

> . . . just possibly with you on a high hill—first watching lest any
> person, for miles around, approach unawares. . . .
> Here to put your lips upon mine I permit you,
> With the comrade's long-dwelling kiss, or the new husband's
> kiss,
> For I am the new husband, and I am the comrade.

What is strikingly homosexual here is not so much the phrase "I am the new husband" or even the image of that lingering kiss, but rather the sense of extreme caution expressed in "first watching lest any person, for miles around, approach unawares"—a caution born of a fear of exposure, since exposure as a homosexual in a homophobic society generally guarantees some form of abuse, judgment, condemnation, even violence. In 1860 Whitman published an epigram which, superficially odd, goes far toward explaining a basic feature of his nature and his style:

> He is wisest who has the most caution,
> He only wins who goes far enough.

How can one be extremely cautious and at the same time go far enough? Whitman tells how in *Calamus* 44, the penultimate [second to last] poem of that sequence and the one in which Whitman is explicit about his need for caution and his fear of exposure:

Here my last words, and the most baffling,
Here the frailest leaves of me, and yet my strongest-lasting,
Here I shade down and hide my thoughts—I do not expose
    them,
And yet they expose me more than all my other poems.

A SYSTEM OF DISGUISES

Whitman will go far enough, cautiously. He will expose his homosexuality through the agency of his poems; but since he is afraid of exposure, he will do so cautiously—by shading down and hiding his thoughts, by speaking in what he refers to, in "When I Read the Book," as, "hints . . . faint clews and indirections."

Granted that the word "indirection" has played an important role in American poetics ([American poets] Emily Dickinson, Robert Frost, and T.S. Eliot all speak of its importance in their work), and granted that writers of a mystical tendency sometimes speak in indirection, through metaphor or allegory. Granted even the contemporary argument that all literature is to some degree a form of indirection, it is nevertheless true that Whitman's homosexuality gave him an additional reason for employing a mode which for a century and a quarter has thrown most readers off the track of his most intimate meanings. Unable to speak directly of his homosexuality, this extremely sexual poet must employ an elaborate system of disguises—hints, clues, and indirections—to convey his meaning; in order to become "undisguised and naked," he must first disguise himself.

One of Whitman's most successful disguises takes a form of that linguistic invention which is such a prominent feature of his style and such an important part of his excitement. In passages of sexual content, Whitman often creates a verbal surface of such density that it interposes itself between us and our comprehension of what we are reading. Language is normally used to aid comprehension; in the following lines, it is used to prevent it:

Is this then a touch? quivering me to a new identity. . . .
On all sides prurient provokers stiffening my limbs,
Straining the udder of my heart for its withheld drip,
Behaving licentious toward me, taking no denial,
Depriving me of my best as for a purpose,
Unbuttoning my clothes and holding me by the bare waist,
Deluding my confusion with the calm of the sunlight
    and pasture fields,
Immodestly sliding the fellow senses away,

> They bribed to swap off with touch, and go and graze at the
>   edges of me,
> No consideration, no regard for my draining strength or my
>   anger,
> Fetching the rest of the herd around to enjoy them awhile,
> Then all uniting to stand on a headland and worry me.

Although this passage is clearly sexual in content, it is not altogether clear who is doing what to whom. Distractions abound: the startling image of "the udder of my heart," that freight train of principles loaded with ambiguous meanings, the fuzz of syntax toward the end, the incredibly confusing notion of "deluding my confusion." Whitman is capable of being plain-spokenly clear when it suits his purpose—even as here, where a line like "unbuttoning my clothes and holding me by the bare waist" is startlingly clear, and thus performs as a ruse to keep us reading. But our urgent questions about this passage—Who are the provokers? Why is the speaker angry? How is the sex illicit?—these never get answered. The variety of interpretations that have been "stucco'd all over" this passage attests to Whitman's success here in shading down and hiding his thoughts.

Another obvious disguise occurs in "Song of Myself," section 11, wherein the shy lonely woman who desires the twenty-eight bathers joins them in imagination:

> An unseen hand . . . passed over their bodies,
> It descended tremblingly from their temples and ribs.
> The young men float on their backs, their
>   white bellies swell to the sun. . . .
>   they do not ask who seizes fast to them,
> They do not know who puffs and declines with
>   pendant and bending arch,
> They do not think whom they souse with spray.

Critics point out that an amazing feat of this passage is Whitman's identification with both subject and object, the woman and the bathers, but by that same means it is the speaker who vicariously performs the masturbation so beautifully described at the end. To my mind, a more interesting example of Whitman's identification with subject and object occurs in *Calamus* 29. The poem begins:

> One flitting glimpse, caught through an interstice,
> Of a crowd of workmen and drivers, in a barroom,
>   around the stove, late of a winter night

and we assume that the speaker is the observer who looks with us into the barroom; but no, for the poem continues: "—And / I unremarked, seated in a corner." Whitman is watching himself, as if to see how he might appear to a passing stranger glimpsing a middle-aged man holding hands with "a youth who loves me, and whom I love." He defuses judgment of this scene by appropriating to himself the role of outside observer.

The experience of being simultaneously an observer and the observed is a common one for homosexuals, and in this, the passage just quoted is characteristic of the gay sensibility. In Whitman's poetry, this experience takes on emblematic significance in the activity of cruising [seeking out lovers] which appears so prominently in the early work—an activity that would seem to be anything but a disguise, since in cruising we find ways to make our sexual desires undisguised. Those *ways* are disguised, however, in that we only show our desires to a selected few, usually by communicating them through the eyes:

> Among the men and women, the multitude, I
>   perceive one picking me out by secret and
>   divine signs. . . .
> Some are baffled—But that one is not—
>   that one knows me.
>
> Lover and perfect equal!
> I meant that you should discover me so, by my
>   faint indirections,
> And I, when I meet you, mean to discover you
>   by the like in you.

Cruising is a complicated activity which signifies many things. It is a disguised exposing; it is also a blatant hinting, and in that sense it is related to the many hints at a secret which occur throughout Whitman's early poetry:

> This hour I tell things in confidence
> I might not tell everybody, but I will tell you,

Whitman says, luring us on through a rhetoric of seduction which guarantees that we will wonder about this confidence he hints at but never fully shares. Some things he promises to tell us in private, cautiously: " . . . I swear I never will translate myself at all, only to him or her who privately stays with me in the open air." Some things he simply will not tell us: "My final merit I refuse you. . . . I refuse putting from me the best I am." And some things he cannot tell us, as in *Calamus* 36:

> . . . there is something fierce and terrible
>   in me, eligible to burst forth,
> I dare not tell it in words—not even in
>   these songs.

Since "these songs" are the Calamus poems, the remark "not even in these songs" becomes a clue that *Calamus* would normally be an appropriate place for speaking of "something fierce and terrible in me." By means of such hints, Whitman makes sure we will try to penetrate to the meaning of his secret: "My words itch at your ears till you understand them" ("Song of Myself," 1246).

AVOIDING GENDER WORDS

Once we come into possession of the entire system of hints, clues, and indirections which permeates so much of Whitman's writing through the first three editions of *Leaves of Grass*, we are obliged to reassess our understanding of that writing in the light of Whitman's homosexual disguises. One result of such a reassessment is to force upon our attention what is probably the most obvious of all the disguises: Whitman's frequent avoidance of gender words, a tactic allowing him to treat sexual matters in poetry that lends itself to contrary interpretations, as if the content were androgynous. The most interesting example of such a disguise occurs in the famous description of transcendence at the beginning of "Song of Myself":

> I mind how we lay in June, such a transparent
>   summer morning;
> You settled your head athwart my hips and
>   gently turned over upon me,
> And parted the shirt from my bosom-bone, and
>   plunged your tongue to my barestript heart,
> and reached till you felt my beard, and
>   reached till you held my feet.

This passage gives us a description of homosexual love, but the sexuality is so thoroughly disguised that it is impossible to prove its homosexual nature without reference to the whole system of disguises which provides the context for such an interpretation. The passage therefore serves as an example of what until recently was the ultimate triumph for a homosexual writer—a disguising of homosexuality so complete that it becomes invisible, thereby saving straight readers from the discomforts of fag meanings.

Whitman's style is thus what [literary critic] Wolfgang Iser calls "overdetermined," which is to say that the very style of the writing lends itself to widely varying interpretations. As soon as you think you have sighted a clear meaning, it turns into something else in the view of a different reader. For some readers, Whitman's homosexuality turns into "adhesiveness"; for others, a figure of transcendence; for still others, a program of political action. But for those who read Whitman most fully and most clearly, it is all these things, while remaining at the same time fundamentally homosexual, and all these things—adhesiveness, transcendence, political action—can only be fully understood in the light of Whitman's homosexuality.

WHITMAN CENSORING HIMSELF

Whitman himself would surely have us read him so at long last, for anyone who hints repeatedly at a secret wants to be found out. This exciting tension in Whitman's poetry between the impulse toward disguise and the impulse toward exposure explains why it is that *Leaves of Grass* creates the impression of cruising the reader, a book in search of lovers. The remarkable thing is probably not so much the elaborate disguises Whitman employs to hide his homosexuality than the enormous risk he takes in speaking as openly about it as he does, with an ingenuousness only possible to someone who lived before Freud. Yet the risk became too great when it threatened Whitman's cherished dream of widespread public acceptance, so after the 1860 *Leaves of Grass* this extremely sexual poet simply removed the sex from his poetry, with disastrous consequences for the poetry. It seems an odd choice, yet what else could Whitman do? He could either write openly about his sexuality and thereby surrender any hope of public acceptance, like Cavafy, or he could remain a public poet only by sublimating his sexuality out of his art, like Auden. Given Whitman's enormous desire for fame, and his time and place, he really had no other choice than to remove the sex. This haunting lyric poet whose genius was moved by "cries of unsatisfied love" sings no such cries after 1860. The rest is one of the most disappointing and self-destructive chapters in our literary history.

Whitman's Treatment of Homosexuality

Gregory Woods

In this excerpt from his book *A History of Gay Literature*, English poet Gregory Woods discusses how Whitman's homosexuality affected his writings. While Whitman was not, Woods asserts, an intimate writer when it came to discussing physical relationships, this was not because he associated love plots with bad romance novels so much as it reflected his need to be careful about depicting gay love. The truth about Whitman and his poetry still makes mainstream America uncomfortable today, which is one measure of the poet's continued success. Gregory Woods has taught at Norttingham Trent University in England.

The successive editions of Walt Whitman's *Leaves of Grass* (1855, 1856, 1860, 1867, 1871, 1881 and the so-called 'Deathbed Edition' of 1891) have turned out to be the most influential of the American homo-erotic texts, and indeed influential *as* homo-erotic texts. David Reynolds has pointed out that the erotic agenda of Whitman's work was to a large extent reactive to a context in popular culture. Reynolds writes: 'a primary reason heterosexual love does not have more prominence in *Leaves of Grass* is that Whitman above all wanted to avoid the deceit, the artificiality, the amorality that he associated with the heterosexual love plot of popular novels'. This is reasonably convincing, but it cannot override what I take to be *the* 'primary reason', namely Whitman's own homosexuality. And yet, writing in an environment where any 'miserable sodomite' might run the risk of being 'rashly dealt with', Whitman was both astonishingly outspoken and expediently circumspect. His natural morality of male comradeship *had to* avoid deceit, but bodily safety probably depended on it to some extent. Lynch law is no respecter of fine distinctions.

A GEOGRAPHICAL WRITER

Whitman's dream of democratic comradeship was, perforce, as much influenced by his actual experience of the city of New York as by his fantasies about the open prairie, or the Rocky Mountains, or the Great Lakes. Even if the geography is often based on secondary sources, he is essentially a geographical writer whose versions of personal relations are strongly determined by his (and his culture's) perceptions of space, both private and public. It is [literary critic] Michael Moon who most usefully addresses this topic. He writes: 'In engaging directly in the furor of the times over the increasing availability to young men in cities of novel spaces, both private and public, in which to enjoy the opportunities for pleasure ("dissipation") afforded by the brothel, the tavern, and the extrafamilial privacy of boarding-house rooms, Whitman was exceptional among American Renaissance writers.' This question of spaces, as Moon so rightly perceives, is crucial to Whitman's perception of other men. Representing American democracy as they so often have to, these men are always carefully placed in significant American spaces, whether urban or rural, generally out of doors. (It is, of course, woman who presides over the domestic spaces in the *Leaves*.) Each man's attractiveness is assessed in relation to his physical setting. Indeed, there is a strong association between physicality and space in everything that Whitman wrote, perhaps even stronger in him than in other nineteenth-century male American writers. The American individual and the American continent are one; together they constitute the nation.

Like other writers of the same period, Whitman makes some effort to demonstrate that the urban industrial revolution cannot obliterate the virility of the pioneering spirit. Much depends on his portrayals of urban manhood. The city has to be as amenable a location, when it comes to love, as the prairie or the open road. The relation between the urban crowd and the pair of individuals is central to both versions of 'Once I Pass'd through a Populous City', the straight and the gay. This is the poem which commemorates Whitman's 1848 trip to New Orleans, where he appears to have had a brief affair with, in the version most often published, a 'woman who passionately clung to me', or in the original version, another man:

Once I passed through a populous city, imprinting my
    brain, for future use, with its shows, architecture,
    customs and traditions,
But now of all that city I remember only the man who
    wandered with me, there for love of me,
Day by day and night by night, we were together—all else
    has been long forgotten by me,
I remember, I say, only one rude and ignorant man who,
    when I departed, long and long held me by the hand,
    with silent lips, sad and tremulous.

This evocation of an uneducated man so fascinating as to
have distracted the poet from his self-educative tourism
through New Orleans is meant to impress us with a sense of
the poet's overriding dedication to matters of the heart
rather than to those of the intellect; but, more importantly, it
emphasises Whitman's constant argument that the culture
of the United States exists in the hearts of the people rather
than in institutions. That is how the poet feels he came to
know the 'populous city' so well—through one of its citizens,
not as a tourist but as a peripatetic [walking about] lover.

NOT AN INTIMATE WRITER

I find it hard to disagree with [American social critic]
Camille Paglia's view that 'There is no true intimacy in
Whitman. His poetry is a substitute for intimacy and a
record of the swerve *from* it.' Many of his more 'private'
poems (like this one) actually appear to have public, political points to make. The better-known voice of Whitman is,
of course, far from being an intimate one. The 'barbaric
yawp' is self-consciously brazen and public, addressing itself to a much wider audience than the poet could ever plau-
sibly have expected his work to reach. It is aimed at the
generic category of *strangers*, as if Whitman needs above all
to believe that he can use his poetry as a medium through
which actually to *meet* every other American. In these public poems there is indeed, as Paglia suggests, an affectation
of intimacy which is wholly bogus. For example, there is the
famous moment in the poem 'So Long!' when Whitman addresses the reader as follows:

Camerado, this is no book,
Who touches this touches a man,
(Is it night? are we here together alone?)
It is I you hold and who holds you,
I spring from the pages into your arms[.]

The association of poem and flesh was not new, of course; and Whitman's insistence that he himself was manifest between the pages of his book is entirely in harmony with his overall strategy. But it is when he actually starts to imagine the space in which the reader and he hold each other (dark or light? public or private?) that his strategy becomes intrusive—particularly, I guess, to women readers—and even imperialistic. He is intent on colonising the reader, body and soul, without prior consultation. If there is any intimacy in this kind of gesture, it is the limited intimacy of anonymous sex. Contact is established—and that is enough.

In 'Whoever You Are Holding Me Now in Hand', with impressive presumption, Whitman engages the unknown reader as his comrade or wife:

> Here to put your lips upon mine I permit you,
> With the comrade's long-dwelling kiss or the new husband's
> kiss.
> For I am the new husband and I am the comrade.

He imagines engaging in this kiss on a high hill, or out at sea, or on a beach or a quiet island, 'lest any person for miles around approach unawares'. The openness of nature is invoked as a closed, private space—even a guilt-ridden one. The reader is thus inveigled into an uncomfortable conspiracy of kisses which ill accords with the avowal of openness which occurs in virtually all of the poems. That open spaces are used as closets is a deeply disruptive trope [metaphor] throughout *Leaves of Grass*.

It is true that Whitman does not write love poems of the sort in which the first person singular addresses the second person singular in tones of private avowal. (One reason for this may be that the men he loved were, above all, men he loved *talking* to, and men who were not normally comfortable with books.) But a poem like 'When I Heard at the Close of the Day', if not really a direct expression of true intimacy (as how many poems ever are?), does at least record such intimacy. Its dismissal of public honours ('how my name had been receiv'd with plaudits in the capitol') is rather a grand gesture, to be sure; but as the poem enacts the wait for the approaching loved one, it also performs the move away from the public arena (and the city) into an emphatically natural intimacy beneath shared bed covers, within hearing distance of the sea. It is here that, contrary to Camille Paglia, by shifting the locus of the poem from capitol to bed, Whitman

most convincingly swerves *towards* intimacy. This is one of
the most beautiful of gay love poems. It dismisses the for-
malities of democratic civics as an irrelevance—albeit, perhaps, temporarily—to the free play of sexual closeness. In
doing so, it fires a shot across the bows of interventive politi-
cians.

When Whitman writes, in 'In Paths Untrodden', 'in this
secluded spot I can respond as I would not dare elsewhere',
he is referring not only to an imagined landscape of over-
grown paths and the reedy banks of ponds, a place where
one might 'celebrate the need of comrades' in the most obvious way without fear of interruption, but also to the site of
the poem itself. The poem, that is to say, is a safe space, for
all that it is so manifestly public. This is possibly because he
feels he can control the reception of his desires better when
publishing them in a poem than, say, when cruising the
streets (not that he ever expressed any difficulty in this latter
respect). The somewhat mischievous irony with which he
thus declares his blaring poetry to be a 'secluded spot', set
apart from the democratic multitudes he is so famous for
celebrating, is a further example of his attempt to draw the
reader into a private space with a promise of public friendship. It is important to remember, also, that Whitman's version of pastoral is often associated with the male body. In
section 24 of the 'Song of Myself, not only does he celebrate
his own body as a landscape, but he then imagines himself
inhabited by the kinds of men he is inclined to love. If, he
writes, he will ever worship one thing more than another,
'You sweaty brooks and dews it shall be you! / Winds whose
soft-tickling genitals rub against me it shall be you! / Broad
muscular fields, branches of live oak, loving lounger in my
winding paths, it shall be you!'

THE CIVIL WAR POEMS

The Civil War poems present adhesiveness in practice. It so
often takes a war to persuade men to love each other at all
demonstratively. Like so many homosexual writers before
and since, Whitman found his war as erotic as it was tragic.
This is not to accuse him of insensitivity; on the contrary.
There is little inhibition about *Drum-Taps*. From the start,
the poet invests his faith in the men in Yankee blue. In 'First
O Songs for a Prelude' he enthuses: 'How good they look as
they tramp down to the river, sweaty, with their guns on

their shoulders! / How I love them! how I could hug them, with their brown faces and their clothes and knapsacks cover'd with dust!' Many of the poems that follow celebrate purposeful groups of men; indeed, in 'Eighteen Sixty-One', the year itself is praised as having a 'masculine voice'. But as soon as Whitman comes to the effects of war, the injuries and deaths, he starts to focus on individuals: in 'Vigil Strange I Kept on the Field One Night' a killed boy ('dearest comrade', 'boy of responding kisses'); in 'A Sight in Camp in the Daybreak Gray and Dim' a 'sweet boy with cheeks yet blooming' although dead; in 'As Toilsome I Wander'd Virginia's Woods' a soldier's grave bearing the scrawled inscription 'Bold, cautious, true, and my loving comrade'. They are (or were) individuals, but they are many. When Whitman ends 'The Wound-Dresser' with the lines

> Many a soldier's loving arms about this neck have cross'd and
>   rested,
> Many a soldier's kiss dwells on these bearded lips

he sounds like a prolific lover, boasting of his promiscuity. His point is more than the usual one in war poetry—that the bodies of potential lovers have been wasted as corpses. The loveliness and the lovingness of the Union soldiers is a significant factor in their subsequent victory; it is also a substantial part of what they are fighting for. Given that Whitman proposes in 'For You O Democracy' (in the 'Calamus' section of the *Leaves*) to 'make the continent indissoluble' by instituting the 'manly love of comrades' wherever he turns, it is clear that he associates a Union victory, and hence the very existence of the States as one nation, with his own prolific experience of male love, both at war and in time of peace.

A Mixed Tribute

In December 1994 the *National Geographic* magazine published a 'photo essay' feature on Whitman. The opening double-page spread, on which the title 'America's Poet: Walt Whitman' is overlaid, consists of a photograph captioned as follows: 'Bucking stormy seas, a [young, male] lifeguard rides the surf off Montauk, New York—Walt Whitman's youthful swimming grounds'. Twenty pages later, another seashore photograph is captioned: 'Towed by a plane, an underwear ad hails a [naked, male] sunbather on Long Island. Whitman's odes to sex and homoeroticism shocked many

19th-century ears—but not all'. The ad in question is the famous photograph of [singer and actor] Marky Mark Wahlberg dressed in nothing but his pristine Calvin Klein underpants. The accompanying essay by Joel Swerdlow eventually comes round to the topic of gayness by a circuitous route. Having described Whitman's nursing and visiting work during the Civil War, Swerdlow adds: 'If Walt were alive today, we would probably find him with those dying "amid strangers" at facilities such as those that care for people with AIDS'. The poet's own sexuality is not broached until the penultimate page of the essay, as follows:

> During his lifetime, censors and critics focused on 'I turn the bridegroom out of bed and stay with the bride myself' and other heterosexual lines. 'I never read his book—but was told that he was disgraceful,' Emily Dickinson wrote to a friend. Whitman's letters and poems, however, indicate a physical attraction to men. This has received considerable scholarly attention, reflecting, in large part, the intimacy of Whitman's writing. Readers feel they know him.

> This interest in Whitman's sexuality is unusually intense. Who did Michelangelo or Mark Twain love? Few people know or care, yet Whitman's private life can stimulate bigotry. I wander into a bar on Camden's water-front, much like those that Whitman frequented. It is dark at noon, and full of men with no pressing engagements. As I leave, the bartender stops wiping glasses. 'You're not going to say Whitman's a faggot, are you?' he says. 'I like his poetry, and I don't like people saying he's a faggot.'

This odd sequence of *non sequiturs* and half-truths makes for a rather mealy-mouthed tribute. Its messages are mixed. It blames any discomfort connected with Whitman's gay status on anonymous 'bigotry', but never attempts an argument against that position. The national bard is thus protected in an international forum—the *National Geographic*—by recourse to the passing opinion of a New Jersey bartender, who is allowed to stand in for all those Americans who remain uneasy when the Good Gray Poet is said to have been gay. Not a word of the homo-erotic poetry is ever quoted. I offer this text as exemplifying the extent to which Whitman's homosexuality both must and yet cannot be acknowledged in the United States. Manifestly, his destiny is to be treated as the embarrassment which, for much of his career, he sought to become. In that sense, the unease he still causes is a measure of his continuing success.

CHAPTER 2

Themes

READINGS ON
WALT WHITMAN

Whitman's Themes and Images

Martin S. Day

Whitman's writing stems from the everyday experience of American life, and his themes reflect these experiences. Chief among them are the greatness of America, democracy, individualism and brotherhood. To suggest these themes, Whitman employed frequently occurring imagery that assumed symbolic value. Martin S. Day compares Whitman with other Romantic poets such as British writers William Wordsworth and Samuel Taylor Coleridge, who often celebrate nature, the individual, and the simple life. Day points out both where Whitman's themes coincide with other Romantics and where they differ (for example, in his positive attitude toward the city). Martin S. Day has taught at the University of Houston as well as in Canada, Australia, and in a number of Asian countries.

The greatest influence upon Whitman was the actual experience of American life. The chief intellectual influences were: American Transcendentalism, European philosophy (particularly German Idealism), and Oriental mysticism (mostly Hindu and mostly through the New England Transcendentalists). His major themes are:

One great America. The geographic immensity and the rich diversity of peoples in the U.S.A. thrilled Whitman. The earlier editions are chauvinistic, but by the later editions he conceived of America as a supreme example to all mankind. He interpreted all history as shaping toward the American dream. America was the fresh start, unfettered by the dead hand of the European past, free to soar beyond all man's previous achievement .

Democracy. Liberty and Equality were perennial watchwords with Whitman. A thoroughgoing egalitarian, he op-

Reprinted from *A Handbook of American Literature*, by Martin S. Day. Copyright © Martin S. Day, 1975. Reprinted by permission of the University of Queensland Press.

posed any tyranny, any discrimination; hence he was an abolitionist and a feminist. Recognizing the shortcomings of contemporary America, he maintained absolute confidence in the average man and believed that the ideal of democracy would ultimately triumph. In the Jeffersonian tradition he considered the least government the best.

Individualism. For Whitman the highest praise of democracy was its opportunity for the fullest development of the self. His glorification of individualism springs from the Romantic-Protestant ethic.

Brotherhood. "Comradeship" was Whitman's preferred term for the brotherhood of man. To reconcile his plea for individualism with the necessity of social order, he evolved his theory of "personalism", a condition in which each human is a distinct personality but also a part of the whole. Politically, each person is a separate "identity" and simultaneously an inseparable citizen .

Industry and labour. Romantic poets had ecstatically addressed nature but even when most rhapsodic about progress had cold-shouldered the obstreperous industrialism of the nineteenth century. From the verses of the New England poets a reader cannot ascertain that there ever was an Industrial Revolution. No other of the world's poets matches Whitman in lyric tributes to this new economy. In his verse Whitman delighted in the new machine ("the many-cylinder'd steam printing press") and the new terminology ("daguerreotyping"). Modernizing his text, he altered "sail'd" of the earlier editions to "steam'd". He strung out litanies of the trades and tools; he hymned the glories of technology. No other American poet has so voiced the American thirst for renovation and change, the eagerness to drive ahead, doing and making. The rapid pace of industrial development symbolized eternal renewal and inevitable advancement to Whitman. The American mechanical drive seemed to him the spirit dominating matter, a passionate explosion of vibrant energy. The mystic in Whitman construed the new industrialism as continuous evolution, as the emblem of a universe eternally becoming. In later editions he especially cautioned against materialism that forgets the broader purpose of industrialism—buttress of democracy, raw material for the exercise of the soul.

Sex. No previous poet in the English language so celebrates all manifestations of sex. In transferring the focal point of sensibility from the heart to the genitals, Whitman prefigured Freud and profoundly shocked his own age. Whitman's main attack is against the asceticism and puritanism in the American psyche. He calls for the sexual exploration as it gives full throttle to natural and individual development, as it promises a ripe and rich future to America, and as it contains the vital principle of life and growth.

Mysticism. Whitman recapitulates in much of his verse the oft-trodden path of many of the world's noted mystics. Apparently he experienced extraordinary mystic ecstasy in June of 1853. Thereafter his mysticism was less convulsive but nonetheless sustained. Beyond mundane objects he constantly perceived spiritual presences so that he always felt himself a dedicated voice of divinity. In the first edition he proclaimed himself a successor and reincarnation of the Christ. More modestly in later editions he announced himself as a precursor of the "sacerdotal bards" of future democracy and spirituality. Always he insisted that the divine inspiration of the poet is to bear the

---

FREEDOM AND OPENNESS IN WHITMAN'S POETRY

One of Whitman's themes is freedom. According to Theodore Gross, Whitman urged that one should be radical in its pursuit, and in his early, more daring work, he comes closest to the heroic quest for freedom.

Song of Myself—and I would add "Song of the Open Road" and "Crossing Brooklyn Ferry" as other obvious examples—is a song of freedom and openness. Inspired by Emerson, Whitman expressed his belief in the infinitude of the private man: "I know I have the best of time and space, and was never measured and never will be measured." His belief in the common American compelled him to deny all forms of authority except that of the individual himself and this Whitman, who believed deeply in the heroic ideal, is most effectively dramatized in *Song of Myself;* it is this aspect of his multi-faceted personality that spans the century and speaks of an important trait within the American character itself. This Whitman—and there are other Whitmans, there are many Whitmans—is the one who has been raised to the role of patron saint by our contemporary generation. Yet it would be misleading—it would be a distortion of his total achievement—to present Whitman as a poet who sought only to deny authority. "Be radical, be radical, be not too damned radical," he warned Americans; and we ought to remember his words to Horace Traubel whenever we think

reader's soul into union with the world soul.

Pantheism. Unlike most Romantics, such as Wordsworth and Coleridge, Whitman never fell back [late in life] into orthodox faith. His religion (and all his work is fundamentally religious) is perhaps best labeled "materialistic spirituality", i.e. an assertion of the absolute equality of body and soul. In turn, all is part of God, the great Oversoul that includes every particle of the cosmos. Following one's own innate nature is not to become a mere eccentric but to reveal the divine personality, the pantheistic All, within the specific soul.

The Soul Becoming. Birth is the receiving of "identity" by some of the soul-stuff pervading the universe. The entire cosmos is an irresistible torrent without beginning or ending, ceaselessly propelling and evolving "identities" toward the future. Death is not an extinction but an indispensable arc of the great cyclic death-and-resurrection pattern of the universe. Whitman wavered between absorption into the universal soul and the persistence of individuality, but he

---

of this early phase of his career: "I am not afraid of conservatism, not afraid of going too slow, of being held back: rather I often wonder if we are not going ahead too swiftly—whether it's not good to have the radicalities, progress, reforms, restrained. The fact remains that we must hold our horses, that we must not rush aimlessly ahead." Whitman did grow more conservative, as Milton Hindus has suggested, by the time he wrote *Democratic Vistas* (1871) and his later poetry. But his lyrics of the seventies and eighties—even his ambitious poem, *A Passage to India*—do not have the moral urgency or the striking imagery of *Song of Myself.* Behind his first poem lies the implicit authority of the past, those religious strictures and cultural attitudes that imprison the American imagination—Whitman is so bold because his readers have been so timid, and his boldness strengthens the verse itself. Not only is *Song of Myself* more relevant to the American tradition of the heroic ideal and thus to the contemporary American; the poem is intrinsically superior to the later work because it expresses the tension, on the personal as well as the cultural level, that is locked within Whitman and that finds its release in the affirmative burst of language that caused Emerson—and causes the modern reader—to rub his eyes "a little, to see if this sunbeam were no illusion."

Theodore Gross, *The Heroic Ideal in American Literature.* New York: The Free Press, 1971.

never wavered in his certitude of eternal life and eternal becoming. Suffusing all is the conviction that the life force and
the universe are totally good. Evil is a sickness, an incomplete good, a stimulus to the forward thrust.

WHITMAN'S IMAGES

His major images (in addition to those specified above, e.g.
grass, machinery):

Water. As immemorially to poets, water to Whitman is an
image of life, apparently from the amniotic fluid. The rest-
lessness of the sea suggests the evolutionary surge. Especially, "the seas of God" represent to Whitman the spiritual
world. The sea whispers "Death", for its constant movement
is archetypal of the cycle that brings life, death, and more life.

Trees. Frequently used by Whitman as a phallic symbol,
trees also logically symbolize the great wilderness, the untapped resources of the continent. Further, trees are life symbols, like the grass, with the added virtue of aspiration and
reaching upward.

Birds. Like all Romantics, Whitman dotes on the soaring of
birds as symbolic of the outward thrust, the escape from the
mundane. Bird-flights suggest to him the promise of future
perfection embodied in the imperfect present. Though dis-
playing many different facets, every bird image in Whitman
partakes of the spiritual ideal.

The City. Most Romantic poets, rhapsodic about Nature,
flee the city as they would the plague. Probably no other of the
world's poets has been so lyrically touched by the urban symbol as was Whitman. Man for him is the supreme focus, and
the crowded city is therefore the greatest concentration of
comradeship and creativity. Its energy and rapid change seem
to Whitman the truest symbol of evolutionary movement.

Celestial objects. Whitman's cosmic symbology is probably
his most conventional. The sun is fruitful fulfilment, while the
moon is the somber concomitant of death; the recurrence of
both is linked to the life-death-life cycle. Another handling of the
cycle is the death-like obscuration by the cloud followed by the
reappearance of the star; thus illusory is death. The starry ex-
panse of the heavens familiarly assures a cosmic harmony. Like
Milton or perhaps the space-poets yet to come, Whitman creates
striking effects by poising afar off to see the globe of Earth
awhirl. From such a vantage point the human assumes a mag-
nified position in the cosmos as observer and participant.

Whitman's Use of the American West

Henry Nash Smith

Henry Nash Smith explores the theme of westward movement in Whitman's works. Despite Whitman's limited travels, his poetry foresaw the inevitable movement of American pioneers across the continent, a concept often referred to as "manifest destiny." Whitman's later poems, such as "A Passage to India," go even farther, suggesting a brotherhood of man that will reach across the Pacific Ocean. Henry Nash Smith has taught at the University of California at Berkeley. He has written books on Mark Twain in addition to *Virgin Land*, a study of the American West in literature, from which this excerpt is taken.

Walt Whitman, the poet who gave final imaginative expression to the theme of manifest destiny, was a native and lifelong resident of the Atlantic seaboard. He was drawn into contact with the Western intellectual tradition not through firsthand experience—for he had not even traveled beyond the Mississippi when he wrote his principal poems—but through his burning conviction that the society and the literature of the United States must be adapted to the North American continent. This obsession led him to declare with [U.S. congressman Thomas Hart] Benton (and of course also with Emerson) that America must turn away from the feudal past of Europe to build a new order founded upon nature:

> I swear there is no greatness or power that does not emulate those of the earth!
> I swear there can be no theory of any account, unless it corroborate the theory of the earth!

He wrote in the preface to the first edition of *Leaves of Grass* in 1855 that the poet of America "incarnates its geography and natural life and rivers and lakes":

Reprinted by permission of the publisher from *Virgin Land*, by Henry Nash Smith, Cambridge, Mass.: Harvard University Press. Copyright © 1950 by the President and Fellows of Harvard College; © 1978 by Henry Nash Smith.

Mississippi with annual freshets and changing chutes, Missouri and Columbia and Ohio and Saint Lawrence with the falls and beautiful masculine Hudson, do not embouchure where they spend themselves more than they embouchure into him. . . . When the long Atlantic coast stretches longer and the Pacific coast stretches longer he easily stretches with them north or south. He spans between them also from east to west and reflects what is between them.

As this statement implies, Whitman originally set out to sing the whole continent, East and West, North and South; and intermittently throughout his life he returned to the impartial celebration of all the regions. But the Atlantic seaboard after all represented the past, the shadow of Europe, cities, sophistication, a derivative and conventional life and literature. Beyond, occupying the overwhelming geographical mass of the continent, lay the West, a realm where nature loomed larger than civilization and where feudalism had never been established. There, evidently, would grow up the truly American society of the future. By 1860 Whitman had become aware that his original assumptions logically implied the Western orientation inherent in the cult of manifest destiny. "These States tend inland, and toward the Western sea," he wrote, "and I will also." He made up his mind that his future audience would be found in the West: "I depend on being realized, long hence, where the broad fat prairies spread, and thence to Oregon and California inclusive." It was in inland America that he discovered the insouciance, the self-possession, the physical health which he loved. He declared that his *Leaves* were made for the trans-Mississippi region, for the Great Plains and the Rocky Mountains and the Pacific slope, and dwelt with ecstasy upon "a free original life there . . . simple diet, and clean and sweet blood, . . . litheness, majestic faces, clear eyes, and perfect physique there. . . ." Above all, he foresaw "immense spiritual results, future years, inland, spread there each side of the Anahuacs."

EXPANDING THE VISION

At the same time, Whitman had become interested in the conception of a fated course of empire leading Americans to the shores of the Pacific and bringing them into contact with Asia. In "Enfans d'Adam" he gives the ancient idea a vivid restatement:

Inquiring, tireless, seeking that yet unfound,
I, a child, very old, over waves, toward the house of maternity,

the land of migrations, look afar,
Look off over the shores of my Western sea—having arrived
at last where I am—the circle almost circled;
For coming westward from Hindustan, from the vales of
Kashmere,
From Asia—from the north—from the God, the sage, and the
hero;
From the south—from the flowery peninsulas, and the spice
islands,
Now I face the old home again—looking over to it, joyous, as
after long travel, growth, and sleep;
But where is what I started for, so long ago?
And why is it yet unfound?

The plaintive question at the end of this passage does not belong to the jubilant Western tradition and indeed represents but a passing moment of melancholy in Whitman himself. Three poems in the collection *Drum-Taps*, published in 1865, return to the course of empire with an optimism more appropriate to Whitman's philosophy as a whole and to the intimations of manifest destiny. "Pioneers! O Pioneers," his most celebrated although not his best poem about the westward movement, depicts the march of the pioneer army. . . . The peoples of the Old World are weakening; the youthful and sinewy pioneers take up the cosmic burden. Having conquered the wilderness and scaled the mighty mountains, they come out upon the Pacific coast. Their advent inaugurates a new era in the history of mankind: "We debouch upon a newer, mightier world . . ."

"Years of the Unperform'd" . . . launches the westward-moving pioneer out upon the waters of the Pacific and equips him with the weapons of a developing technology:

Never was average man, his soul, more energetic, more like
a God;
Lo, how he urges and urges, leaving the masses no rest;
His daring foot is on land and sea everywhere—he colonizes
the Pacific, the archipelagoes;
With the steam-ship, the electric telegraph, the newspaper,
the wholesale engines of war,
With these, and the world-spreading factories, he interlinks
all geography, all lands. . . .

And the idea of an American empire in the Pacific is carried even farther in "A Broadway Pageant," celebrating the arrival of the first Japanese embassy in New York in 1860:

I chant the world on my Western Sea; . . .
I chant the new empire, grander than any before—As in a vision
it comes to me;

I chant America, the Mistress–I chant a greater supremacy;
I chant, projected, a thousand blooming cities yet, in time, on
    those groups of sea-islands; . . .
I chant commerce opening, the sleep of ages having done its
    work—races, reborn, refresh'd. . . .

For the long circuit of the globe is drawing to its close: the
children of Adam have strayed westward through the cen-
turies, but with the arrival of the American pioneers in the
Pacific a glorious millennium begins.

Passage to India

Elaborate as these ideas are, Whitman was not yet done with
the theme of the course of empire. He returned to it in 1871
in "Passage to India," which he said was an expression of
"what, from the first, . . . more or less lurks in my writings,
underneath every page, every line, every where." Again he
depicts the myriad progeny of Adam and Eve moving westward around the globe, "wandering, yearning, curious . . .
with questionings, baffled, formless, feverish—with never-
happy hearts. . . ." God's purpose, hidden from men through
countless ages, is revealed at last when the Suez Canal, the
Atlantic submarine cable, and especially the Pacific railway
connect the nations of the earth with a single network:

The people [are] to become brothers and sisters,
The races, neighbors, to marry and be given in marriage,
The oceans to be cross'd, the distant brought near,
The lands to be welded together.

But the new era begun with the closing of the cycle of history meant even more than the mingling of peoples: it was to
restore man's lost harmony with nature. The secret of impassive earth was to be uttered at last. The "strong, light
works of engineers" encircling the globe were to lead man
into a full understanding of nature and a permanently satis-
fying communion with her:

All these hearts, as of fretted children, shall be sooth'd,
All affection shall be fully responded to—the secret shall be
    told:
All these separations and gaps shall be taken up, and hook'd
    and link'd together;
The whole earth—this cold, impassive, voiceless Earth, shall
    be completely justified; . . .
Nature and Man shall be disjoin'd and diffused no more,
The true Son of God shall absolutely fuse them.

This is a mysticism difficult for the twentieth century to

follow, but it moves in a straight line from Benton's first intimation that the course of empire would lead the American people westward to fabulous Asia. In view of the less attractive inferences that other thinkers have drawn from the notion of an American empire in the Pacific, one is grateful for the intrepid idealism that so triumphantly enabled Whitman to see in the march of the pioneer army a prelude to peace and the brotherhood of nations.

Whitman Makes a Religion of Himself and His Poetry

Alfred Kazin

In this excerpt from his book *God & the American Writer*, Alfred Kazin, one of America's leading literary critics, discusses Walt Whitman's concept of God and religion. While nineteenth-century America was suffused with various modes of organized and unorganized religion, Whitman belonged to no church outside of himself and his own poetry. He considered all of nature and life holy and blessed, and sought to express this philosophy through his poetry. These radical ideas never caught on with the average American, whom Whitman truly wished to reach. Instead his followers were rebels, progressives and intellectuals on both sides of the Atlantic. Alfred Kazin has taught at Harvard, Smith College, and numerous other colleges. His first book, *On Native Grounds*, published in 1942, is considered a landmark study in American literature.

Like so many of his countrymen in the nineteenth century, Whitman was drenched in religion; he positively swam in it, without having to believe in much of it. There was no personal God. He was not a Christian. He was to add nothing to the many public "revivals" of faith storming around him. Even in his childhood among Long Island Quakers, he owed his spiritual aloofness, his independence from orthodoxy, to his father's admiration for [American radical philosopher] Tom Paine and the father's adherence to [Quaker leader] Elias Hicks, whose belief in the sufficiency of the "inner light" separated him from most Quakers. On the other hand, Whitman *fils* [the son] was no eighteenth-century Deist; in his easy embrace of the universe (and of its diverse creeds) he was the

From *God and the American Writer* by Alfred Kazin. Copyright © 1997 by Alfred Kazin. Reprinted by permission of Alfred A. Knopf, Inc.

most fervid example imaginable of what Whitehead meant when he said that "Romanticism is spilled religion." "Religion" was in Whitman's blood, as in all his American generation (and after), but it was not central to his attempt to incarnate himself as the "divine literatus" (as he would call himself in *Democratic Vistas*)—the poet as world-embracing witness to all that was now profane in America but still sacred because of the limitless progress it embodied. Whitman, personifying this American optimism, presented himself at the center of everything material and "spiritual." In old age, when he was still fighting for recognition, he called religion essential to the ultimate design of *Leaves of Grass.*

A RELIGION OF POETRY

There would be wholeness but no intended "design" to his final edition. Everything in Whitman's thirties followed from personal appetite, ambition, and the strident radicalism of both his political and religious background, which promoted the faith in universal benevolence that carries one along in "Song of Myself"—Here Comes Everybody! [an allusion to *Finnegan's Wake* by Irish writer James Joyce]. This was before the Civil War, before the Gilded Age, and before the worship of a few heated disciples cast him in his last role—as "the Good Gray Poet," the elegist of Lincoln and of the democracy that had never recognized him as its most fervent apostle. But "young" or old—and as a writer he made the most of both—he never had as much interest in "God" as he did in replacing conventional religion with himself as all-seeing poet. "The priest departs, the divine literatus comes."

Why "divine" and why "literatus"? Because, lordly as Whitman paraded himself in "Song of Myself," the metaphor that opens the poem, insinuates itself everywhere back into the poem, and recurs at the end leads to a conclusion perfect in tenderness:

Failing to fetch me at first keep encouraged,
Missing me one place search another,
I stop some where waiting for you.

When Whitman says "I," there is always another in wait. He said it in the most comprehensive way, the most loving. There is never a direct reference to the other he seeks, loves, is making love to. The "nigh young men" who boisterously, familiarly greet him in the street remain just that. In the unusually intimate poem "Out of the Cradle Endlessly Rocking" the boy on the beach recognizes himself as a poet-to-be, "uniter of here and hereafter," in the mating songs of "Two feather'd guests from Alabama, two together." But one disappears, forsakes the other, so that it must be in loss and loneliness, the boy weeping yet ecstatic, that the emerging poet recognizes.

> Now in a moment I know what I am for, I awake,
> And already a thousand singers, a thousand songs, clearer,
>   louder and more sorrowful than yours,
> A thousand warbling echoes have started to life within me,
>   never to die.
> O you singer solitary, singing by yourself, projecting me,
> O solitary me listening, never more shall I cease perpetuating
>   you.

Whitman in "Song of Myself,". . . was never so true, for once truly personal, as when he ended the "solitary singer" passage with

> Never more shall I escape, never more the reverberations,
> Never more the cries of unsatisfied love be absent from me,
> Never again leave me to be the peaceful child I was before
>   what there in the night,
> By the sea under the yellow and sagging moon,
> The messenger there arous'd, the fire, the sweet hell within,
> The unknown want, the destiny of me.

That first arousal is backed up by the mother-sea, "the fierce old mother incessantly moaning," and the maternal breasts represented by "The yellow half-moon enlarged, sagging down, drooping, the face of the sea almost touching." The mother as the everlasting sea, the sorrowfully "moaning" sea, is the only other human person—represented as a force of nature—in the poem. One wonders if, after all the parading of his masculine charms, Whitman as *seeker* of love was not more real than the lover he portrays as so publicly irresistible that

> I am satisfied. . . . I see, dance, laugh, sing;
> As God comes a loving bedfellow and sleeps at my side all
>   night and close on the peep of the day.

However that was, Whitman the lover in general was at first sufficiently recognized by Emerson when he said that Whitman's book "has the best merits, namely of fortifying and encouraging." Emerson turned his back on Whitman when it became clear with "Children of Adam" and "Calamus" that the poet was "fortifying," all right, but not in the direction that Concord thought worthy of public print. "It was as if the beasts spoke," said Thoreau (who was charged up by the book for reasons his purity did not recognize). In Amherst, Emily Dickinson, who never saw a line by Whitman, was told he was "disgraceful." It was all too early for anyone to tell her that some of her poems, silently seething in her bedroom drawer, were in a sense more "sexual" than his, since they were fed by a direct passion for one particular man after another. It was more *natural* for Whitman (not just more discreet) to embrace the universe. To name a "hugging and loving bed-fellow" as "God."

In the 1881 version of "Song of Myself" "God" got replaced by someone we know as little—"the hugging and loving bed-fellow sleeps at my side through the night, and withdraws at the peep of the day with stealthy tread." Whitman in the overflowing heedless spontaneity of the first version (before "Song of Myself" became so overladen an epic journey through America that the original sexual connection was submerged in inventory) was in such rapture of self-creation that "God" was just as lovable and nameable as anything else. Perhaps that is the real point of naming God, including God in his many personae. The whole world of existent phenomena is open to Whitman's general lovingness, which is boundless affirmation. Nothing may be excluded; nothing is higher or lower than anything else. He is the perfect democrat, in religion as in love and politics. There is no hierarchy in his determination to love everything and everyone in one full sweep.

The essential point is that almost despite himself, Whitman made something infinitely precious of *Leaves of Grass.* The essence of it is a call for infinite harmony, harmony relating all things to the poet at the center. It is remarkable: every great Whitman poem grows out of itself, *on* itself as nature does. What runs through *Leaves of Grass* and turns a collection of poems into a *book* (a word Whitman always insisted on; it was his American testament) is his genius for evoking love, sympathy, "comradeship" and for receiving them in turn. Starting with the acceptance of homosexual love for himself, he transformed individual love into a love for everything natural that finally made not "God" sacred but the world. . . .

BECOMING A RELIGION

One did not need to posit a supernatural Deity—Whitman did not—to be a "religious" poet. It was enough to *become* a religion. The more in his time he languished for attention as a poet, the more he presented himself as a unique example, the prophet of a wholly new age to come, an American of Americans. A "screamer" as he might be to the Establishment, something vaguely sacred, a touch of authority clung to someone who was, as a poet, so many things at once. Perhaps the "nigh young men" he describes in "Crossing Brooklyn Ferry" flirtatiously calling to him as he crossed Broadway helped form his idea of himself as irresistible. But crucial as liberated sex was to his self-developing legend, it was only a prelude to the comprehensive "vision" he gained from sex:

> Swiftly arose and spread around me the peace and joy and
>   knowledge that pass all the art and argument of the earth;
> And I know that the hand of God is the elder hand of my own,
> And I know that the spirit of God is the eldest brother of my
>   own,
> And that all the men ever born are also my brothers . . .
> And the women my sisters and lovers,
> And that a kelson of the creation is love;
> And limitless are leaves stiff or drooping in the fields,
> And brown ants in the little wells beneath them,
> And mossy scabs of the worm fence, and heaped stones, and
>   elder and mullen and pokeweed.

Pokeweed! A perennial herb better than its name, but it was a name that only a truly folk poet would have come up with to conclude the most exalted passage in "Song of Myself." So the rough earth and true personal spirituality (our American genius) came together. Not altogether, even in Whitman's old age. No other American writer made such a thing of being "old" at forty-six. With his great beard and the various slouches to which he put his hat, he was such a favorite of photographers that he was virtually a professional model. He willingly posed holding a "butterfly" on one finger. (It was wood, a contraption.)

Of course the "average" Americans Whitman was always calling to paid no attention. Nothing was farther from the reality of Whitman's emerging reputation than the resounding conclusion of his preface to *Leaves of Grass.*

> The soul of the largest and wealthiest and proudest nation
> may well go half-way to meet that of its poets. The signs are
> effectual. There is no fear of mistake. If the one is true the
> other is true. The proof of a poet is that his country absorbs
> him as affectionately as he has absorbed it.

WHITMAN'S DISCIPLES

Whitman's appeal was to the young, to rebels and "progressives," the sexually liberated, the freethinkers and socialist utopians (especially in Germany) who anticipated that the twentieth century would at last be "theirs." He was admired in England by Tennyson, Swinburne, Hopkins, Edward Dowden, W. M. Rossetti, Edward Carpenter, and John Addington Symonds, and in Germany by young radicals and poets who were fated to die in the "Great War" [World War I] with pocket editions of Whitman in their uniforms. Of course the "real" Whitman had to tell the German Jewish socialist Horace Traubel, who in 1873 became an intimate friend of Whitman's and who meticulously recorded every last thought of the great man after 1888 in the six volumes of *With Walt Whitman in Camden,* "Be radical, be radical, be not too damned radical!"

But Whitman happily agreed with everything his admirers and disciples said about him. His time had come, his life was finally crowned. By 1872, summing up his career in "As a Strong Bird on Pinions Free," he generously admitted that in his poetry "one deep purpose underlay the others, and has underlain it and its execution ever since—and that has been the religious purpose." "Purpose" was certainly yielding to convention in a way that undercut the actual subtlety of his "purpose" as an *artist.* And he did not have to declare his faith in "immortality" when all his greatest poems, especially his one triumph as a truly "old" man, "Passage to India," made "immortality" less a password than a vision:

> All these hearts as of fretted children shall be sooth'd,
> All affection shall be fully responded to, the secret shall
>   be told,
> All these separations and gaps shall be taken up and hook'd
>   and link'd together,
> The whole earth, this cold, impassive, voiceless earth, shall
>   be completely justified,
> Trinitas divine shall be gloriously accomplish'd and
>   compacted by the true son of God, the poet. . . .
> . . . .
> Nature and Man shall be disjoin'd and diffused no more,
> The true son of God shall absolutely fuse them.

Of course the poetry was not enough for those who wanted to be not admirers but disciples. How Whitman, the supposedly broken and half-paralyzed Whitman in Camden, actually furthered his legend as a cosmic figure is shown in the way he took over the adoring biography of him by the Canadian alienist [psychiatrist] Dr. Richard Maurice Bucke. Bucke, on encountering *Leaves of Grass* in 1867, became an instant "convert" thanks to the divine capabilities he saw in Whitman. Bucke's *Walt Whitman* (1883) is so rapturous in celebrating *Leaves of Grass* as "revealer and herald" of a religious era not yet reached that one sees in its most enthusiastic form the Romantic belief that poetry would rescue religion by replacing it.

> With the incoming moral states to which it belongs, certain cherished social and religious forms and usages are incompatible; hence the deep instinctive aversion and dread with which it is regarded by the ultra-conventional and conservative. Just so, in their far-back times, was Zoroastrianism, Buddhism, Mohammedanism, Christianity, and every new birth received. . . . So also our churchgoing, bible-reading, creeds, and prayers, will appear from its vantage-ground mere make-believes of religion. . . . *Leaves of Grass* . . . is the preface and creator of a new era. . . . What the Vedas were to Brahmanism, the Law and the Prophets to Judaism, the Avesta and Zend to Zoroastrianism, the Kings to Confucianism and Taoism, the Pitakas to Buddhism, the Quaran to Mohammedanism, will *Leaves of Grass* be to the future of American civilization.

Whitman, after his best work was done, never tired of summing up self and career, interpreting both in weary but friendly new perspectives. He never tired of self-portraits, especially when he discovered readers who thought him as wondrous as he did himself. A year before his death he wrote to Dr. Bucke likening himself to [Shakespeare's King] Lear as he went over the complete *Leaves of Grass* once again. "From my own point of view I accept without demur its spurty (old Lear's irascibility)—its offhandedness, even evidence of decrepitude & old fisherman's seine character as part of the *artism* (from my point of view) & as adherent as the determined cartoon of personality that dominates or rather stands behind all of *L. of G.* like the unseen master & director of the show. W. W."

THE CHURCH OF WHITMAN

Not without his blessing, he became a church. In Bolton, Lancashire, a group of "adherents" met weekly to read his poems aloud. This was a great source of cheer to people who habitually suffered from "despondency." On May 29, 1891, he wrote to one of its leaders, J.W. Wallace, that he was "badly prostrated, horrible torpidity" but went on to say, "I guess I have a good deal of the feeling of Epictetus & stoicism—or tried to have. They are specially needed in a rich & luxurious, & even scientific age. But I am clear that I include & allow & probably teach some things stoicism would frown upon & discard. One's pulses & marrow are not *democratic & natural* for nothing."

Whitman as the American Adam

R.W.B. Lewis

Early American theology was dominated by the concept of original sin, which stated that mankind was born into a fallen state. In this excerpt from his book, *The American Adam*, R.W.B. Lewis contends that Whitman provided an antidote for this philosophy. The Whitman protagonist was a man born into a new world, who, like Adam in *The Bible*, had the task of naming the world's creations. But Whitman went beyond Adam: his hero was both the creator as well as the namer, for in the very act of naming he was creating the world as if for the first time. Thus the America that Whitman celebrates truly becomes a new world. R.W.B. Lewis has taught at Yale University. He has authored and edited numerous books on American literature. His biography of the novelist Edith Wharton won a Pulitzer Prize in 1976.

The fullest portrayal of the new world's representative man as a new, American Adam was given by Walt Whitman in *Leaves of Grass*—in the liberated, innocent, solitary, forward-thrusting personality that animates the whole of that long poem. *Leaves of Grass* tells us what life was made of, what it felt like, what it included, and what it lacked for the individual who began at that moment, so to speak, where the rebirth ritual of [Henry David Thoreau's] *Walden* leaves off. With the past discarded and largely forgotten, with conventions shed and the molting season concluded, what kind of personality would thereupon emerge? What would be the quality of the experience which lay in store for it?

Leaves of Grass was not only an exemplary celebration of novelty in America: it also, and perhaps more importantly, brought to its climax the many-sided discussion by which—

over a generation—innocence replaced sinfulness as the first attribute of the American character. . . .

A NEW MAN IN A NEW WORLD

It is, in fact, in the poems gathered under the title *Children of Adam* (1860) that we have the most explicit evidence of [Whitman's] ambition to reach behind tradition to find and assert nature untroubled by art, to re-establish the natural unfallen man in the living hour. Unfallen man is, properly enough, unclothed as well; the convention of cover came in with the Fall; and Whitman adds his own unnostalgic sincerity to the Romantic affection for nakedness:

> As Adam, early in the morning,
> Walking forth from the bower refresh'd with sleep,
> Behold me where I pass, hear my voice, approach,
> Touch me, touch the palm of your hand to my body
>   as I pass,
> Be not afraid of my body.

For Whitman, . . . the quickest way of framing his novel outlook was by lowering, and secularizing, the familiar spiritual phrases: less impudently than Thoreau but more earnestly, and indeed more monotonously, but with the same intention of salvaging the human from the religious vocabulary to which (he felt) it had given rise. Many of Whitman's poetic statements are conversions of religious allusion: the new miracles were acts of the senses . . . ; the aroma of the body was "finer than prayer"; his head was "more than churches, bibles and all creeds." "If I worship one thing more than another," Whitman declaimed, in a moment of Adamic narcissism, "it shall be the spread of my own body." These assertions gave a peculiar stress to Whitman's seconding of the hopeful belief in men like gods: "Divine am I, inside and out, and I make holy whatever I touch." Whitman's poetry is at every moment an act of turbulent incarnation.

But although there is, as there was meant to be, a kind of shock-value in such lines, they are not the most authentic index to his pervasive Adamism, because in them the symbols have become too explicit and so fail to work symbolically. Whitman in these instances is stating his position and contemplating it; he is betraying his own principle of indirect statement; he is telling us too much, and the more he tells us, the more we seem to detect the anxious, inflated utterance of a charlatan. We cling to our own integrity and will not be thundered at. We respond far less willingly to Whitman's frontal assaults than we do to his dramatizations; when he is enacting his role rather than insisting on it, we are open to persuasion. And he had been enacting it from the outset of *Leaves of Grass.* . . .

THERE IS ONLY THE PRESENT

The "self" in the very earliest of Whitman's poems is an individual who is always moving forward. To say so is not merely to repeat that Whitman believed in progress; indeed, it is in some sense to deny it. The young Whitman, at least, was not an apostle of progress in its customary meaning of a motion from worse to better to best, an improvement over a previous historic condition, a "rise of man." For Whitman, there was no past or "worse" to progress from; he moved forward because it was the only direction (he makes us think) in which he could move; because there was nothing behind him—or if there were, he had not yet noticed it. There is scarcely a poem of Whitman's before, say, 1867, which does not have the air of being the first poem ever written, the first formulation in language of the nature of persons and of things and of the relations between them; and the urgency of the language suggests that it was formulated in the very nick of time, to give the objects described their first substantial existence.

Nor is there, in *Leaves of Grass,* any complaint about the weight or intrusion of the past; in Whitman's view the past had been so effectively burned away that it had, for every practical purpose, been forgotten altogether. In his own recurring figure, the past was already a corpse; it was on its way out the door to the cemetery; Whitman watched it absent-mindedly, and turned at once to the living reality. He did enjoy, as he reminds us, reciting Homer while walking beside the ocean; but this was just because Homer was exempt from tradition and talking at and about the dawn of time. Homer was the poet you found if you went back far enough; and as for the sea, it had (unlike Melville's) no sharks in it—no ancient, lurking, indestructible evil powers. Whitman's hope was unspoiled by memory. When he became angry, as he did in *Democratic Vistas* (1871), he was not attacking his generation in the Holgrave manner for continuing to accept the old and the foreign, but for fumbling its extraordinary opportunity, for taking a wrong turn on the bright new highway he had mapped for it. Most of the time he was more interested in the map, and we are more interested in him when he was.

It was then that he caught up and set to music the large contemporary conviction that man had been born anew in the new society, that the race was off to a fresh start in America. . . . It was there that the hope that had enlivened spokesmen from Noah Webster in 1825 ("American glory begins at the dawn") to the well-named periodical, *Spirit of the Age* in 1849 ("The accumulated atmosphere of ages, containing stale ideas and opinions . . . will soon be among the things that were")—that all that stored-up abundance of hope found its full poetic realization. *Leaves of Grass* was a climax as well as a beginning, or rather, it was the climax of a long effort to begin.

This was why Emerson . . . made a point of visiting Whitman in New York and Boston; why Thoreau, refusing to be put off "by any brag or egoism in his book," preferred Whitman to [American writer and fellow Concord, Massachusetts, resident] Bronson Alcott; and why Whitman, to the steady surprise of his countrymen, has been regarded in Europe for almost a century as unquestionably the greatest poet the New World has produced: an estimate which even [American novelist] Henry James would come round to. European readers were not slow to recognize in Whitman an authentic rendering of their own fondest hopes; for if much of his vision had been originally imported from Germany and France, it had plainly lost its portion of nostalgia en route. While European romanticism continued to resent the effect of time, Whitman was announcing that time had only just begun. He was able to think so because of the facts of immediate history in America during the years when he was maturing: when a world was, in some literal way, being created before his eyes. It was this that Whitman had the opportunity to dramatize; and it was this that gave *Leaves of Grass* its special quality of a Yankee Genesis: a new account of the creation of the world—the creation, that is, of a new world; an account this time with a happy ending for Adam its hero; or better yet, with no ending at all; and with this important emendation, that now the creature has taken on the role of creator.

It was a twofold achievement, and the second half of it was demanded by the first. We see the sequence, for example, in the development from section 4 to section 5 of "Song of Myself." The first phase was the identification of self, an act which proceeded by distinction and differentiation, separating the self from every element that in a traditional view might be supposed to be part of it: Whitman's identity card had no space on it for the names of his ancestry. The exalted mind which carried with it a conviction of absolute novelty has been described by Whitman's friend, the Canadian psychologist, Dr. R.M. Bucke, who relates it to what he calls Whitman's "cosmic consciousness." "Along with the consciousness of the cosmos [Dr. Bucke wrote], there occurs an intellectual enlightenment which alone would place the individual on a new plane of existence—would make him almost a member of a new species.". . .

Whitman achieves the freedom of the new condition by scrupulously peeling off every possible source of, or influence upon, the "Me myself," the "what I am." As in section 4 of "Song of Myself":

> Trippers and askers surround me
> People I meet, the effect upon me of my early life, or the
>   ward and the city I live in or the nation. . . .
> The sickness of one of my folks, or of myself, or the ill-
>   doing or loss or lack of money, or depressions or
>   exaltations,
> Battles, the horror of fratricidal wars, the fever of doubtful
>   news, the fitful events,
> These come to me days and nights and go from me again,
> But they are not the Me myself.
> Apart from the pulling and hauling stands what I am;
> Stands amused, complacent, compassionating, idle, unitary;
> Looks down, is erect, or bends an arm on an impalpable
>   certain rest,
> Looking with side-curved head curious what will come next,
> Both in and out of the game, and watching and wondering
>   at it.

There is Emerson's individual, the "infinitely repellent orb." There is also the heroic product of romanticism, exposing behind the mass of what were regarded as inherited or external or imposed and hence superficial and accidental qualities the true indestructible secret core of personality. There is the man who contends that "nothing, not God, is greater to one than one's self."

THE NEW ADAM

There, in fact, is the new Adam. If we want a profile of him, we could start with the adjectives Whitman supplies:

amused, complacent, compassionating, idle, unitary; especially unitary, and certainly very easily amused; too complacent, we frequently feel, but always compassionate—
expressing the old divine compassion for every sparrow that
falls, every criminal and prostitute and hopeless invalid,
every victim of violence or misfortune. With Whitman's help
we could pile up further attributes, and the exhaustive portrait of Adam would be composed of a careful gloss on each
one of them: hankering, gross, mystical, nude; turbulent,
fleshy, sensual, eating, drinking, and breeding; no senti-
mentalist, no stander above men and women; no more modest than immodest; wearing his hat as he pleases indoors
and out; never skulking or ducking or deprecating; adoring
himself and adoring his comrades; afoot with his vision,

> Moving forward then and now and forever,
> Gathering and showing more always and with velocity,
> Infinite and omnigenous.

And announcing himself in language like that. For an actual
illustration, we could not find anything better than the styl-
ized daguerreotype [early photograph] of himself which
Whitman placed as the Frontispiece of the first edition. We
recognize him at once: looking with side-curved head, bending an arm on the certain rest of his hip, evidently amused,
complacent, and curious; bearded, rough, probably sensual;
with his hat on.

Whitman did resemble this Adamic archetype, according
to his friend John Burroughs. "There was a look about him,"
Burroughs remembered, "hard to describe, and which I
have seen in no other face, —a gray, brooding, elemental
look, like the granite rock, something primitive and Adamic
that might have belonged to the first man." The two new adjectives there are "gray" and "brooding"; and they belong to
the profile, too, both of Whitman and of the character he dramatized. There was bound to be some measure of specula-
tive sadness inherent in the situation. Not all the leaves
Whitman uttered were joyous ones, though he wanted them
all to be and was never clear why they were not. His ideal
image of himself—and it is his best single trope for the new
Adam—was that of a live oak he saw growing in Louisiana:

> All alone stood it and the mosses hung down from the
>   branches,
> Without any companion it grew there uttering joyous
>   leaves of dark green,

> And its look, rude, unbending, lusty, made me think of
> myself.

But at his most honest, he admitted, as he does here, that the
condition was somehow unbearable:

> I wondered how it could utter joyous leaves standing alone
> there without a friend near, for I knew I could not. . . .
> And though the live-oak glistens there in Louisiana solitary
> in a wide flat space,
> Uttering joyous leaves all its life without a friend a lover
> near,
> I knew very well I could not.

Adam had his moments of sorrow also. But the emotion
had nothing to do with the tragic insight; it did not spring
from any perception of a genuine hostility in nature or lead
to the drama of colliding forces. Whitman was wistful, not
tragic. We might almost say that he was wistful because he
was not tragic. He was innocence personified. It is not difficult to marshal a vast array of references to the ugly, the
gory, and the sordid in his verses; brought together in one
horrid lump, they appear as the expression of one who was
well informed about the shabby side of the world; but
though he offered himself as "the poet of wickedness" and
claimed to be "he who knew what it was to be evil," every
item he introduced as vile turns out, after all, to be merely a
particular beauty of a different original coloration. "Evil propels me and reform of evil propels me, I stand indifferent." A
sentiment like that can make sense only if the term "evil"
has been filtered through a transfiguring moral imagination,
changing in essence as it passes.

That sentiment, of course, is not less an expression of
poetic than of moral motivation. As a statement of the poetic
sensibility, it could have been uttered as easily by Shakespeare or [Italian poet] Dante as by Whitman. Many of the
very greatest writers suggest, as Whitman does, a peculiar
artistic innocence, a preadolescent wonder which permits
such a poet to take in and reproject whatever there is,
shrinking from none of it. But in Whitman, artistic innocence merged with moral innocence: a preadolescent ignorance of the convulsive undertow of human behavior—
something not at all shared by Dante or Shakespeare. Both
modes of innocence are present in the poetry of Walt Whitman, and they are not at any time to be really distinguished.
One can talk about his image of moral innocence only in
terms of his poetic creation.

"I reject none, accept all, then reproduce all in my own forms." The whole spirit of Whitman is in the line: there is his strategy for overcoming his sadness, and the second large phase of his achievement, following the act of differentiation and self-identification. It is the creative phase, in that sense of creativity which beguiles the artist most perilously into stretching his analogy with God—when he brings a world into being. Every great poet composes a world for us, and what [Henry] James called the "figure in the carpet" is the poet's private chart of that world; but when we speak of the poet's world—of [Russian novelist Fyodor] Dostoevski's or [French novelist Honore de] Balzac's—we knowingly skip a phrase, since what we mean is Dostoevski's (or Balzac's) selective embodiment of an already existing world. In the case of Whitman, the type of extreme Adamic romantic, the metaphor gains its power from a proximity to the literal, as though Whitman really were engaged in the stupendous task of building a world that had not been there before the first words of his poem.

The task was self-imposed, for Whitman's dominant emotion, when it was not unmodified joy, was simple, elemental loneliness; it was a testimony to his success and contributed to his peculiar glow. For if the hero of *Leaves of Grass* radiates a kind of primal innocence in an innocent world, it was not only because he had made that world, it was also because he had begun by making himself. Whitman is an early example, and perhaps the most striking one we have, of the self-made man, with an undeniable grandeur which is the product of his manifest sense of having been responsible for his own being—something far more compelling than the more vulgar version of the rugged individual who claims responsibility only for his own bank account.

And of course he was lonely, incomparably lonely; no anchorite [a woman who lives in seclusion for religious purposes] was ever so lonely, since no anchorite was ever so alone. Whitman's image of the evergreen, "solitary in a wide, flat space . . . without a friend a lover near," introduced what more and more appears to be the central theme of American literature, in so far as a unique theme may be claimed for it: the theme of loneliness. . . . The only recourse for a poet like Whitman was to fill the space by erecting a home and populating it with companions and lovers.

Whitman began in an Adamic condition which was only too effectively realized: the isolated individual, standing flush with the empty universe, a primitive moral and intellectual entity. In the behavior of a "noiseless, patient spider," Whitman found a revealing analogy:

A noiseless, patient spider
I mark'd, where, on a little promontory, it stood out, isolated,
Mark'd how, to explore the vacant, vast surrounding,
It launched forth filament, filament, filament, out of itself,
Ever unreeling them—ever tirelessly speeding them.

"Out of itself." This is the reverse of the traditionalist attitude that, in [poet T.S.] Eliot's phrase, "home is where one starts from." Whitman acted on the hopeful conviction that the new Adam started from himself; having created himself, he must next create a home. The given in individual experience was no longer a complex of human, racial, and familial relationships; it was a self in a vacant, vast surrounding. Each simple separate person must forge his own framework anew. This was the bold, enormous venture inevitably confronted by the Adamic personality. He had to become the maker of his own conditions—if he were to have any conditions or any achieved personality at all.

There were, in any case, no conditions to *go back to*––to take upon one's self or to embody. There is in fact almost no indication at all in *Leaves of Grass* of a return or reversion, even of that recovery of childhood detected in *Walden*. Whitman begins after that recovery, as a child, seemingly self-propagated, and he is always going *forth;* one of his pleasantest poems was constructed around that figure. There is only the open road, and Whitman moves forward from the start of it. Homecoming is for the exile, the prodigal son, Adam after the expulsion, not for the new unfallen Adam in the western garden. Not even in "Passage to India" is there a note of exile, because there is no sense of sin ("Let others weep for sin"). Whitman was entirely remote from the view of man as an orphan which motivated many of the stories of [American novelist Nathaniel] Hawthorne and Melville and which underlay the characteristic adventure they narrated of the search for a father. Hawthorne, an orphan himself and the author of a book about England called *Our Old Home,* sometimes sent his heroes to Europe to look for their families; Melville dispatched his heroes to the bottom of the sea on the same mission. This was the old way of posing the problem: the way of mastering life by the recovery of home, though it might require descent to the land of the dead; but Whitman knew the secret of his paternity.

CREATOR OF HIS WORLD

Whitman was creating a world, even though he often sounds as though he were saluting a world that had been lying in wait for him: "Salut au monde." In one sense, he is doing just that, welcoming it, acknowledging it, reveling in its splendor and variety. His typical condition is one of acceptance and absorption; the word which almost everyone who knew him applied to his distinguishing capacity was "absorptive." He absorbed life for years; and when he contained enough, he let it go out from him again. "I . . . accept all, then reproduce all in my own forms." He takes unflagging delight in the reproductions: "Me pleased," he says in "Our Old Feuillage"; it is the "what I am." But the pleasure of seeing becomes actual only in the process of naming. It is hard to recall any particular of life and work, of men and women and animals and plants and things, of body and mind, that Whitman has not somewhere named in caressing detail. And the process of naming is for Whitman nothing less than the process of creation. This new Adam is both maker and namer; his innocent pleasure, untouched by humility, is colored by the pride of one who looks on his work and finds it good. The things that are named seem to spring into being at the sound of the word. It was through the poetic act that Whitman articulated the dominant metaphysical illusion of his day and became the creator of his own world.

Whitman's Transcendentalism

Russell Blankenship

Influenced by the revered American writer and philosopher Ralph Waldo Emerson, Walt Whitman was a proponent of transcendentalism. Transcendentalists had a generally optimistic view of life and believed in the importance of the individual and the mystical oneness of God and nature, and by extension, God and man. Russell Blankenship details Whitman's relationship with such New England transcendentalists as Emerson and Henry David Thoreau. He shows how Whitman adapted transcendental concepts in *Leaves of Grass*. Russell Blankenship has taught at the University of Washington.

The influence of Emerson upon Whitman was deep and enduring, and Emerson was the chief of American transcendentalism. *Leaves of Grass* shows unmistakably transcendental paternity in its conception of human nature, its optimism, its idea of nature, its tolerant individualism that created democracy, and especially in the mystical background of its whole thought. Both Emerson and Whitman acknowledged the relationship of their ideas. In a record of Whitman's conversations covering only a little more than a year, Emerson is mentioned about two hundred times. Writing once of the Concord teacher the poet said: "He pierces the crusts that envelop the secrets of life. He joins on equal terms the few great sages and original seers. He represents the freeman, America, the individual." Again he said: "Emerson is great—oh! very great: he was a far reaching force; a star of the first, the very first magnitude, maybe; without a doubt that." In the 1856 edition of the *Leaves of Grass* he spoke of Emerson's work in awakening a new social conscience in America: "Those shores you found. I say

Reprinted from *American Literature as an Expression of the Mind*, by Russell Blankenship (New York: Holt, Rinehart and Winston, 1958). Copyright, 1958, by Russell Blankenship.

you have led the States there—have led me there. I say that none has ever done or ever can do a greater deed for the States than your deed."

EMERSON'S INTELLECTUAL OFFSPRING

Writing to Whitman in July, 1855, the month of the publication of the first edition, Emerson said:

> I am not blind to the worth of the wonderful gift of *Leaves of Grass*. I find it the most extraordinary piece of wit and wisdom that America has yet contributed. I am very happy in reading it, as great power makes us happy . . . I give you joy of your free and brave thought. . . . I find incomparable things said incomparably well, as they must be . . . I greet you at the beginning of a great career. . . . The solid sense of the book is a sober certainty. It has the best merits, namely of fortifying and encouraging.

In the height of his rapture over *Leaves of Grass*, Emerson exclaimed: "Americans who are abroad may now return: unto us a man is born." Emerson probably was never so enthusiastic about another book; well might he be enraptured, for he was applauding his own intellectual offspring. Such lines as the following are undiluted Emersonian doctrine:

> I do not trouble my spirit to vindicate itself or be understood,
> I see that the elementary laws never apologize,
> (I reckon I behave no prouder than the level I plant my house by, after all)
>
> Whimpering and truckling fold with powders for invalids, conformity goes to the fourth-remov'd,
> I wear my hat as I please indoors or out.

It is perfectly true that Whitman might have reached his distinctive views without having read Emerson, for transcendentalism was rife in the very air of America during the forties, but the fact remains that he did not. He read Emerson and acknowledged his indebtedness to him in a public utterance, and Emerson acknowledged his approval of the doctrine in *Leaves of Grass* by a letter of warm appreciation.

HENRY DAVID THOREAU'S ADMIRATION

In Thoreau, Whitman had even a more intense admirer than he found in Emerson. For this there was a reason. Thoreau was much more of a natural man than Emerson was, more like a wild animal, more in love with the ecstasy of living. He was enough of a child of nature not to be frightened by a catalog of anatomical names, and he was enough of a practicing transcendental individualist to recognize his kind when he saw it. Emerson once wrote in his journal: "Perhaps his [Thoreau's] fancy for Walt Whitman grew out of his taste for wild nature, for an otter, a woodchuck, or a loon." Whitman's poems are filled with lines that, but for their rhetorical peculiarities, might easily fit into [Thoreau's] *Walden* or the *Week* [*A Week on the Concord and Merrimac Rivers*]. Thoreau's disdain for money and the material things of life are echoed in: "And you or I pocketless of a dime may purchase the pick of the earth."

The intense individualism which found the whole universe in a Concord bean-field, even under one's very hat-brim, would be satisfied with this declaration of the importance of self:

> I exist as I am, that is enough,
> If no other in the world be aware I sit content,
> And if each and all be aware I sit content.
> One world is aware and by far the largest to me, and that is
> myself.

He who came into the world "to live in it, not to make it over" would find a congenial spirit in Whitman, who declared himself to be "the caresser of life wherever moving," and all transcendentalists in New England and elsewhere must have found epitomized in the following lines their mistrust of formal learning, their joy in simple life and occupations, and their abounding egotism:

> And to glance with an eye or show a bean in its pod confounds the learning of all times,
> And there is no trade or employment but the young man following it may become a hero,
> And there is no object so soft but it makes a hub for the wheel'd universe,
> And I say to any man or woman, Let your soul stand cool and composed before a million universes.

Whitman's Mysticism

Like all the transcendentalists Whitman based his whole workaday philosophy on a profoundly mystical basis. From his mother, a good Quaker, he received the belief that "the unseen is proved by the seen," that the inner light, the intuition, is the safest guide to conduct, and that God dwells in all men and all men in Him.

> Swiftly arose and spread around me the peace and knowledge that pass all arguments of the earth,
> And I know that the hand of God is the promise of my own,
> And I know that the spirit of God is the brother of my own,
> And that all the men ever born are also my brothers, and the

women my sisters and lovers,
And that a kelson of the creation is love. . . .

Again:

Why should I wish to see God better than this day?
I see something of God each hour of the twenty-four, and
each moment then,
In the faces of men and women I see God, and in my own face
in the glass,
I find letters from God dropt in the street, and every one is
sign'd by God's name,
And I leave them where they are, for I know that wheresoe'er
I go,
Others will punctually come forever and ever.

God Is in All of Us

The mystical aspects of transcendentalism could not be
more clearly stated, for the lines acknowledge the constant
and immediate presence of God in every human being and
the ability of each to receive messages directly from the
Deity at all times. To the person who holds such a view and
allows it to others, as Whitman did, equalitarian democracy
is not a vague possibility or a desirable though remote ideal
but rather a necessity based upon the sacred duty of allowing each man to follow and express the divinity that is
within him.

Twenty years after the first edition of *Leaves of Grass*
Whitman again uttered his belief in the divine origin of the
inner light, the still small voice of the conscience:

O I am sure they really came from Thee,
The urge, the ardor, the unconquerable will,
The potent, felt, interior command, stronger than words,
A message from the Heavens whispering to me even in sleep,
These sped me on. . . .
. . . Thou O God my life hast lighted,
With ray of light, steady, ineffable, vouchsafed of Thee. . . .

Such a mystical conception of the union of God and man
can hardly be treated as a practical consideration; it is an attitude of mind which colors all facts that come into its influence. The mystical union is not regarded as the exclusive
prerogative of any one man or group of men. It is a universal possibility, and if man errs it is simply because he does
not follow the plain guidance of the light within. By bringing
the individual into direct communication with God, it
creates a tremendous individualism, but by allowing to all
men the same relations with God it makes a complete spiri-

tual equalitarianism, a firm and sure basis for equalitarian democracy, both spiritual and political.

Whitman does not allow his estimate of human nature to be implied in a general statement of his mysticism. Again and again he explicitly declares his faith in the indwelling presence of God, and beseeches all men to remember that their bodies are temples of the divine spirit.

None has begun to think how divine he himself is.

Upon a battle field the body of his slain enemy moves him to pity.

My enemy is dead, a man as divine as myself is dead.

Nowhere does the seen mirror the unseen more accurately than in the relations of the soul and body.

Was somebody asking to see the soul?
Behold the body includes and is the meaning, the main concern, and includes and is the soul;

HENRY DAVID THOREAU'S ADMIRATION FOR WHITMAN

In a letter to a friend, Henry David Thoreau, author of Walden, *expresses his admiration for Whitman.*

That Walt Whitman, of whom I wrote to you, is the most interesting fact to me at present. I have just read his second edition [of *Leaves of Grass*] (which he gave me), and it has done me more good than any reading for a long time. Perhaps I remember best the poem of Walt Whitman, an American, and the Sun-Down Poem. There are two or three pieces in the book which are disagreeable, to say the least; simply sensual. He does not celebrate love at all. It is as if the beasts spoke. I think that men have not been ashamed of themselves without reason. No doubt there have always been dens where such deeds were unblushingly recited, and it is no merit to compete with their inhabitants. But even on this side he has spoken more truth than any American or modern that I know. I have found his poem exhilirating, encouraging. As for its sensuality,—and it may turn out to be less sensual than it appears,—I do not so much wish that those parts were not written, as that men and women were so pure that they could read them without harm, that is, without understanding them. One woman told me that no woman could read it,—as if a man could read what a woman could not. Of course Walt Whitman can communicate to us no experience, and if we are shocked, whose experience is it that we are reminded of?

On the whole, it sounds to me very brave and American, after whatever deductions. I do not believe that all the sermons,

Whoever you are, how superb and how divine is your body, or any part of it.

Again:

I have said that the soul is not more than the body,
And I have said that the body is not more than the soul,
And nothing, not God, is greater to one than one's self is.

This close interlinking of the soul and the body and the rapture over the divinity of man's physical structure led to the fleshliness and primitiveness that have repelled so many from Whitman's poetry. In the closing section of the "Song of Myself" the poet says:

I too am not a bit tamed, I too am untranslatable,
I sound my barbaric yawp over the roofs of the world.

Many, many critics of Whitman seem to have read no other lines of his poetry. The genteel [upper class], impressed by the wildness of his "barbaric yawp," have set him

---

so called, that have been preached in this land put together are equal to it for preaching.

We ought to rejoice greatly in him. He occasionally suggests something a little more than human. You can't confound him with the other inhabitants of Brooklyn or New York. How they must shudder when they read him! He is awfully good.

To be sure I sometimes feel a little imposed on. By his heartiness and broad generalities he puts me into a liberal frame of mind prepared to see wonders,—as it were, sets me upon a hill or in the midst of a plain,—stirs me well up, and then—throws in a thousand of brick. Though rude, and sometimes ineffectual, it is a great primitive poem,—an alarum or trumpet-note ringing through the American camp. Wonderfully like the Orientals, too, considering that when I asked him if he had read them, he answered, "No: tell me about them."

I did not get far in conversation with him,—two more being present,—and among the few things which I chanced to say, I remember that one was, in answer to him as representing America, that I did not think much of America or of politics, and so on, which may have been somewhat of a damper to him.

Since I have seen him, I find that I am not disturbed by any brag or egoism in his book. He may turn out the least of a braggart of all, having a better right to be confident.

He is a great fellow.

Henry David Thoreau, *Familiar Letters of Henry David Thoreau.* F.B. Sanborn, ed. Boston: Riverside, 1894, pp. 345–347.

down as the defiant apologist of sheer animalism, and with this estimate have condemned his verses to the limbo of unspeakable indecencies. In his self-characterization Whitman was guilty of poetic exaggeration, for he is perfectly translatable, and his most barbaric passages are merely glorifications of the physical body as the divine home of the soul. Whitman is no more indecent than a book on physiology is indecent. He only permitted to "speak at every hazard nature without check with original energy." Concerning this aspect of *Leaves of Grass* Thoreau makes the best criticism: "As for the sensuality of Whitman's *Leaves of Grass* I do not so much wish that it was unwritten, as that men and women were so pure that they could read it without harm."

In short, Whitman had the transcendental view of human nature. He considered it divine, and he went one step beyond the New Englanders in insisting that the body, the home of the soul, is equally divine with the spirit. The individual considered alone is divine, and no less divinity attends him in the democratic mass, the congregation of the common man. Furthermore, the best moral guide of man is the individual conscience, the voice of God, which always attends every man, whether he be a solitary figure or one of a huge society.

CHAPTER 3

Analyses of Individual Poems

The Structure of "Song of Myself"

John M. Nagle

At first glance Whitman's longest individual poem, "Song of Myself," may seem to be a loosely collected series of reflections on virtually every topic in the universe. John M. Nagle attempts to find an order in this chaos, breaking the poem into eight main sections that Whitman organized into a unified whole. Nagle discusses the many organizational principles the poet used to bind his poem. John M. Nagle has taught at the University of Pittsburgh.

'Song of Myself,' the longest poem in Walt Whitman's collection of poems *Leaves of Grass*, presents any reader with a considerable challenge. The poem consists of a total of 1346 lines of poetry, and though Whitman has divided those 1346 lines into 52 'sections' or 'paragraphs' or 'chants,' their marked variations in length and scope tend to add to the puzzle that is the poem rather than help to clarify it. The shortest of these sections is six lines long while the longest contains more than 150 lines. The scope of ideas treated throughout the poem is practically impossible to describe, for there is little either within or beyond the universe that does not at some point come under the close scrutiny of the poet. Body, soul, life, death, earth, sea, time, space, God, man—all, and more too, are dealt with by Whitman at various times and to various degrees throughout the 1346 lines. The poem ranges in tone from the almost ecstatic and graphic account of the sexual union of body and soul to the narrative summary of a futile and disastrous sea battle, from the dispassionate listing of a multitude of sense impressions to the exultant and triumphant experiencing of the Unknown.

It is little wonder then that a first reading of 'Song of Myself' leaves the uninitiated Whitman student gasping for

Reprinted from "Toward a Theory of Structure in 'Song of Myself,'" by John M. Nagle, *Walt Whitman Review*, vol. 15, no. 3, September 1969. Reprinted by permission of Wayne State University Press. © Wayne State University Press.

breath and explanation, frustrated by what he knows he has missed and exhausted by what he thinks he has understood. After several subsequent readings, however, this same student may begin to see some interrelationships within the total poem and he may very well ask the following question: 'Did Walt Whitman deliberately structure his poem, or is it really the amorphous mass of fleeting sense impressions and inexplicable abstractions that it seemed to be after my first reading?' It is this exact question, 'Is there deliberate structure in "Song of Myself"?' and its expansion, 'If so, what *is* the structure and how does Whitman maintain it?' that will provide focus for the discussion which follows.

A CAREFULLY STRUCTURED POEM

Several hypotheses will guide that discussion's development: first, that Whitman's 'Song of Myself' is a carefully structured poem, made up of distinguishable parts or phases joined to form a unified whole (as used in the remainder of this discussion, the term 'section' will refer to one of Whitman's fifty-two divisions; the term 'phase' will refer to the grouping of several sections); second, that Whitman's repetition of themes and symbols and his clear transitional signals enable the reader to follow the poem's movement from section to section and phase to phase; and third, that each section, including the so-called 'catalogues,' has a definite structure and movement. Without attempting to view the poem as anything but what it is, a sensitive reader should be aware of Whitman's conscious structure and organization. To get at these more precisely, I should like to look first at the structure of a single phase, then to apply the same sort of analysis to the total poem, and finally to move back again to examination of several other parts of the poem which reflect Whitman's conscious effort to structure the 1346 lines of 'Song of Myself.'

WHITMAN INTRODUCES HIS THEMES

There is undoubtedly no more meaningful place to start in an analysis of a single phase of the poem than to look carefully at Sections 1–5, for these sections not only introduce many of the themes and ideas that pervade the rest of the poem, but they also illustrate nicely Whitman's concern for organization and his careful use of transitions. Basically, this first phase provides the focus for the rest of the poem.

For instance, within the first five lines of the poem, Whitman focuses attention upon 'I' the poet, 'you' the reader, the inter-existence of all men, the material atom and body, the soul, and the 'spear of summer grass,' that all-important and unifying symbol in the poem. To indicate further its focusing characteristics, a list of other themes introduced in these first five sections will perhaps suffice:

—the evolutionary nature of the Self
—infinity of all, including time, heaven, hell, perfection
—the dialectic of life
—'creeds and schools in abeyance'
—'nature without check with original energy'
—an acceptance of all, good and bad
—the union of the Self with nature
—the Self's ability to interpenetrate all
—the everpresent 'procreant urge' of the world
—the perfect fitness and equanimity of all things
—the 'Me myself' apart from 'the pulling and hauling'
—the essential and beautiful union of body and soul
—love, 'a kelson of the creation'
—and the omnivorous nature of the poet

How often the remainder of the poem echoes these themes!

In terms of organization, Sections 1–5 are a unified whole, having conflict, climax and fulfillment. Sections 1–4 represent a reaching out, a grappling by the poet; Section 5 climaxes this search and concludes with the poet's undeniable assertions of what he knows to be true. The basic conflict between 'creeds and schools' and 'nature without check with original energy' is clearly presented in the first section of the phase and then is continually kept in view as the poet moves toward his climax in Section 5. In Section 2, for instance, Whitman contrasts the 'houses and rooms' which are full of perfumes to the 'atmosphere' which is not and the ability to read and 'get at the meaning of poems' to the possession of 'the origin of all poems.' In Section 3, this conflict is represented on one side by the 'talkers' who 'talk of the beginning and the end' and on the other by Whitman who talks not of beginning and end but of now as the time of greatest fulfillment. In Section 4, the 'talkers' become 'the trippers and askers' and in contrast to their 'pulling and hauling stands what I am,' the poet's 'Me myself.' Finally, after that climactic physical union of body and soul in Section 5, the poet brings out the conflict once more when he speaks of 'the peace and knowledge that pass all the argument of the earth.'

To recapitulate, on one side can be grouped the 'creeds and schools,' 'houses and rooms,' reckoning, reading and getting at poems, talkers talking, 'trippers and askers,' 'pulling and hauling,' and 'the argument of the earth'; on the other side, one can easily group 'nature without check with original energy,' 'the atmosphere,' 'the origin of all poems,' the completeness of 'now,' 'this mystery,' 'the perfect fitness and equanimity of things,' 'Me myself,' and 'peace and knowledge.' The climax of this conflict, that physical union of body and soul, enables the 'I' to assert with complete conviction his place in relation to the world around him. These assertions that end Section 5 are so all-inclusive and so sharply fixed that they automatically signal conclusion not only for Section 5 but for the total movement of this first phase.

In addition to his use of the organizational pattern of conflict-climax-fulfillment and his numerous illustrations of that conflict, Whitman maintains unity in the first phase by use of careful transitions within and between sections. This can be seen by once again tracing Whitman's development. Section 1 ends with the stated conflict between 'creeds and schools' and 'nature without check.' Section 2 is spaced by Whitman into five parts. In the first and fourth, he amplifies on 'creeds and schools'; in the second and fifth he amplifies on 'nature without check'; in the third, he enumerates with images that appeal to the senses of touch, sight, smell, and sound exactly what he means by his madness to be undisguised, naked and in contact with the atmosphere. Section 3 begins with another example of the basic conflict, this time focusing on 'talkers.' Contrasting himself to these 'talkers,' the poet launches into a discussion of the 'procreant urge,' the dialectic of life, and the unity and equality of all, and he concludes with the rhetorical question of whether or not he should postpone his 'acceptation and realization' of 'this mystery' and turn to the petty, limited concerns of life. Section 4 immediately enumerates some of those petty concerns. At the conclusion of this brief listing, the poet actively answers the question previously raised when he divorces the 'Me myself' from the enumerated items of 'pulling and hauling.' Section 4 ends with the poet witnessing and waiting, and Section 5 presents that for which the poet has waited, the sexual union of body and soul. That fulfillment has been the result is evident in those final assertions already mentioned that clearly and powerfully drive the first phase to a close.

THE POEM AS A WHOLE

Let us now broaden our view and look to the total poem, for here too can be found indications of Whitman's deliberate structure and form. Focusing almost completely upon the poem itself and its transitional signals, and looking for organizational signals similar to those evident in the poem's first five sections, we find that the fifty-two sections seem to divide themselves into some eight unified phases. The first phase, consisting of Section 1–5, has already been discussed at some length. It, in effect, introduces the major themes of the whole poem and successfully focuses attention upon the self, the soul and body, and the artificial and real. The second phase begins with the question 'What is the grass?' and switches the focus for the moment from the poet to the child and his query. Conjecturing some answers to that question, the poet talks in Section 7 of his oneness with all of life and death and commands at the end of Section 7 that the world 'undrape' itself. Sections 8–16 reflect the poet's 'undraping' of life and death and his interpenetration of all. Section 17 asserts the universality of all the poet has presented in the prior sections and concludes with this strong, declarative answer to the original question raised in Section 6 (note that emphasis naturally falls on the first word):

> This is the grass that grows wherever the land is and the
>   water is,
> This is the common air that bathes the globe.

Carrying this theme of equality and universality into Section 18, the poet asserts that he sings of all and to all, victors and vanquished; and on that note, the second phase—constructed totally within the framework of the question 'What is the grass?'—draws to a close.

Some of this commonality, however, spills over into the first half of Section 19, at which point the poet asks the question 'Do you guess I have some intricate purpose?' and, with that question, he makes his transition to his next topic: Who is this 'I' who speaks so astonishingly and what is he about? In almost whispered tones, Whitman concludes Section 19 with a personal assurance and invitation:

> This hour I tell things in confidence,
> I might not tell everybody, but I will tell you.

The first of these 'things' told in confidence is introduced in the first lines of Section 20 with another series of questions:

Who goes there? hankering, gross, mystical, nude;
How is it I extract strength from the beef I eat?
What is man anyhow? what am I? what are you?

From Sections 19–25, the poet attempts to find answers to these questions, to identify himself and his reason for being. In Section 20, he is sound, solid, deathless and august; in 21, he is the poet of body and soul; in 21 and 22, he is at one with the night, earth and sea; in 23, he is the poet of En Masse, accepter of all. Finally in Section 24, he is able to name himself and his identity in the climactic assertion to which he has been building:

Walt Whitman, a kosmos, of Manhattan the son,
Turbulent, fleshy, sensual, eating, drinking and breeding . . .

From this point until the end of Section 25, the poet asserts the nobility of the body, attaches to nature the physical characteristics of humans, and affirms his abilities to impart. The definition of Self, introduced with the question, 'Who goes there?' back in Section 20 has been at least partially achieved by the end of Section 25, the end of the third phase.

Whereas the poet imparted in Sections 24–25, the first line of Section 26 indicates that he will now receive, and, by means of this shift, he launches into the fourth phase.

Now I will do nothing but listen,
To accrue what I hear into this song, to let sounds contribute
    toward it.

As he *listens* now rather than *expresses*, he becomes aware by the end of Section 26 of 'the puzzle of puzzles, / And that we call Being.' and for the next six sections he tries to resolve that puzzle. He undergoes an almost sexual climax and fulfillment with the sense of touch, he explores the relationship of the world to the self, and he discovers that because 'All truths wait in all things,'

I find I incorporate gneiss, coal, long-threaded moss, fruits,
    grains, esculent roots,
And am stucco'd with quadrupeds and birds all over,
And have distanced what is behind me for good reasons,
But call any thing back again when I desire it.

Section 32 climaxes this fourth phase when the poet rides the 'gigantic beauty of a stallion,' whose 'well-built limbs tremble with pleasure,' for it is this stallion which best symbolizes the primitive innocence and being which the poet has sought; he has found at least a partial answer to the 'puzzle of puzzles.'

The poet's exultation over his new found knowledge is initially expressed in the first lines of Section 33,

Space and Time! now I see it is true, what I guess'd at,
What I guess'd when I loaf'd on the grass,
What I guess'd while I lay alone in my bed,
And again as I walk'd the beach under the paling stars
    of the morning,

and this jubilation carries him through the first half of this longest of sections in which he once again interpenetrates all, though this time with increased insight:

My ties and ballasts leave me, my elbows rest in sea-gaps,
I skirt sierras, my palms over continents,
I am afoot with my vision.

Somewhat imperceptibly, as the poet skirts afoot with his vision, the nature of the interpenetration changes. Instead of sense impressions that call forth joy and exultation, they begin to call forth misery and woe, and by the end of Section 33, the poet is heading into what James E. Miller, Jr calls 'the dark night of the Soul.' Sections 34–37 reflect this dark night superbly, and in the final lines of Section 37 the poet not only identifies with but actually is in quick succession a convict in jail, a mutineer handcuffed, a larcener, a cholera patient, and a beggar sitting shamefaced with hat projected.

Having arrived at the utter depths of despair and misery in the final lines of Section 37, the poet has no where to go but up, and he projects himself forth with this undeniable exclamation in the first lines of Section 38:

Enough! enough! enough!
Somehow I have been stunn'd. Stand back!
Give me a little time beyond my cuff'd head, slumbers,
    dreams, gaping,
I discover myself on the verge of a usual mistake.

Exactly what that usual mistake is becomes the topic of the sixth phase of the poem, Sections 38–43, as the poet talks of faith in love, faith in the primitive and innocent, and finally faith in 'what is untried and afterward.' Uniting himself with Christ and with 'the friendly and flowing savage,' this poet-Christ-savage becomes the 'I' who in Sections 38–43 enunciates his faith as 'the greatest of faiths and the least of faiths.' Whereas the questions asked earlier in the third phase of the poem were 'What is a man anyhow? what am I? what are you?' the questions now asked in this sixth phase become 'And what is reason? and what is love? and what is life?' Certainly the poet's definition of himself, his total involvement with both the joys and miseries of existence, and his awakening to the significance of an omnivorous faith—all of which have occurred between the two sets of questions—have contributed to the increased depth of his understanding. The poet concludes Section 43, the last in this sixth phase, with another unquestionable assertion, this time that his faith in 'what is untried and afterward' can never fail.

In Section 44, the poet clearly begins the next phase of the poem and even more clearly defines its subject:

> It is time to explain myself—let us stand up.
>
> What is known I strip away,
> I launch all men and women forward with me into the
> Unknown.

From here to Section 50, the poet launches us all forth into the Unknown, into that faith which is 'untried and afterward.' Temporal and spatial limitations disappear as all become involved in the perpetual journey to the Unknown, the inevitable meeting with the great Camerado. In Section 46, the poet involves the reader directly when he echoes the self-reliance theme of the Transcendentalists:

> Not I, not any one else can travel that road for you,
> You must travel it for yourself . . .
>
> You are also asking me questions and I hear you,
> I answer that I cannot answer, you must find out for yourself.

As the poem moves toward its conclusion, the poet reaffirms the power of the self over all—God, body, soul, death, life—when he writes that 'nothing, not God, is greater to one than one's self is.' This seventh phase, the journey to the Unknown, ends with a final three-line assertion:

> I ascend from the moon, I ascend from the night,
> I perceive that the ghastly glimmer is noonday sunbeams
> reflected,
> And debouch to the steady and central from the offspring
> great or small.

In contrast to the strength of assertion and absoluteness in the last lines of Section 49, nearly all of Section 50 seems tentative and hesitant. These last three sections represent the final phase of the poem as the poet, exhausted but satisfied, attempts to conclude his lines without concluding their movement, Section 50 appears to be a halting effort to explain what has happened in the preceding sections, but it ends unsuccessfully in an almost 'I give up' explosion of explanations:

> It is not chaos or death—it is form, union, plan—it is eternal life—it is Happiness.

HOW TO READ "SONG OF MYSELF"

A noted Whitman scholar offers suggestions to beginning readers of "Song of Myself."

When I introduce Walt Whitman to students, in France or in the United States, I ask them first to read "Song of Myself"—all of it or as much as they can bear, for one must keep in mind Poe's warning that the common reader cannot read more than one hundred lines of poetry at a sitting.

The reason I choose this poem is that I want to jolt students by exposing them to poetry for which they probably have not been prepared, "pure" poetry, poetry laid bare, divested of its traditional trappings, stripped of all adornments, equally contemptuous of storytelling and moral didacticism, indifferent to prosodical conventions, in short, singing the self without recourse to extraneous matters, as in these lines near the beginning of section 2:

> The atmosphere is not a perfume, it has no taste of the
>   distillation, it is odorless,
> It is for my mouth forever, I am in love with it,
> I will go to the bank by the wood and become undisguised
>   and naked,
> I am mad for it to be in contact with me.
>
> The smoke of my own breath,
> Echoes, ripples, buzz'd whispers, love-root, silk-thread,
>   crotch and vine,
> My respiration and inspiration, the beating of my heart, the
>   passing of blood and air through my lungs,
> The sniff of green leaves and dry leaves, and of the shore and
>   dark-color'd sea-rocks, and of hay in the barn,
> The sound of the belch'd words of my voice loos'd to the
>   eddies of the wind,
> A few light kisses, a few embraces, a reaching around of
>   arms,
> The play of shine and shade on the trees as the supple
>   boughs wag,
> The delight alone or in the rush of the streets, or along the
>   fields and hill-sides,
> The feeling of health, the full-noon trill, the song of me
>   rising from bed and meeting the sun. (*LG* 29–30)

By Section 52, the poet, now less hesitant, has come to asso-
ciate himself with the spotted hawk, for neither is tame or
translatable. All of which substantiates what the poet has already affirmed, that 'Not I, not any one else can travel that
road for you.' Though the last lines focus on 'you' and though

... The Italian essayist Giovanni Papini defined this essential
quality of "Song of Myself" very aptly when he wrote:

> I must confess that I, a Tuscan, an Italian, a Latin, have not felt
> what poetry really means through [Italian epic poets] Vergil or
> Dante—and still less through Petrarch and Tasso, luxury poets
> and consequently men of letters rather than poets—but, on the
> contrary, through the childish enumerations and impassioned
> evocations of the kindly harvester of *Leaves of Grass.*

After letting my students follow the apparently erratic course
of Whitman's self shooting across the sky like a comet, I show
them the underlying structure of the poem, its hidden logical
pattern. Then I try to bring out its "paraphrasable content," to
take up [American literary critic] Kenneth Burke's phrase, its
implicit metaphysics, that is, Whitman's transcendentalism,
pantheism, optimistic faith in the fact that the world "is not
chaos or death" but "form, union, plan . . . eternal life . . . happiness" (sec. 50). But it is important not to reduce the poem to a
mere paraphrase. I therefore underscore the poet's sense of the
infinity of space and "amplitude of time" and refer my students
to "A Noiseless Patient Spider," which describes the poet lost in
the middle of measureless oceans of space" but nevertheless
trying to anchor the web of his poems by launching forth "filament, filament, filament" out of himself.

Then we come back to earth. So far we have studied only
the universal features of the poet, and while Whitman, as
[French author] André Gide noted, could have written *Leaves
of Grass* anywhere, or at least what is essential in it, he was
also an American and must be studied as such with the help
of a good biography (Gay W. Allen's, Justin Kaplan's, or mine)
and reattached to the literature of his time with the help of
books like F.O. Matthiessen's *American Renaissance,* Newton
Arvin's *Whitman,* or Allen's *New Walt Whitman Handbook.*
Then poems besides "Song of Myself"—*Drum-Taps,* "Memo-
ries of President Lincoln," "Passage to India," "Prayer of
Columbus," and so on—become accessible to students in
ever-widening circles.

Roger Asselineau, "Some Contexts for 'Song of Myself' in *Approaches to Teaching Whitman's* Leaves of Grass." Donald D. Kummings, ed. New York: Modern
Language Association, 1990, pp. 64–66.

the identity of the poet dissolves, the movement of the poem
continues ever onward and upward:

> You will hardly know who I am or what I mean,
> But I shall be good health to you nevertheless,
> And filter and fibre your blood.

> Failing to fetch me at first keep encouraged,
> Missing me one place search another,
> I stop somewhere waiting for you.

ORGANIZATION OF THE POEM

To review very, very briefly this organizational scheme
based nearly solely upon Whitman's transitional signals:

Phase I	(1–5):	Focus upon the self, the grass, the body and soul; introduction of recurrent themes in the poem.
Phase II	(6–18):	The poet's initial penetration of the world out there as he attempts to answer the question, 'What is the grass?'
Phase III	(19–25):	Identification of the poet, beginning of those things to be told in confidence.
Phase IV	(26–32):	The poet's attempt to solve the 'puzzle of puzzles' by listening carefully to the 'sounds' of the world.
Phase V	(33–37):	The 'puzzle' solved, Being revealed; the poet actively participating in all, good and bad, joyful and distressing.
Phase VI	(38–43):	The importance of faith, the power of the poet-Christ-savage, the 'untried and afterward.'
Phase VII	(44–49):	Flight to the Unknown.
Phase VIII	(50–52):	The poet exhausted but satisfied, stopping 'somewhere waiting for you.'

Certainly the earlier discussion of the first five sections of
'Song of Myself' and the structural analysis just presented indicate definite attempts by Whitman to organize carefully the
total poem. Attention should be given to several additional
structural techniques. Foremost among these is the poet's repetition of significant themes and symbols—in much the same
way that he handled 'creeds and schools' and ' nature without
check with original energy' in the first five sections. The relationships between body and soul and between life and death
exemplify two of the many recurrent themes in the poem. The
grass, probably the poem's central and outstanding symbol, is
mentioned at least seven times. In Section 1, the poet leans and

loafes at his ease 'observing a spear of summer grass,' and in Section 5 he asks the soul to join him while he loafes on the grass; in Section 6, the poet asks the question 'What is the grass?' and eleven sections later, he asserts, 'This is the grass that grows . . .'; in Section 31, he remarks that 'a leaf of grass is no less than the journey-work of the stars,' and in Section 33 he exults that what he had guessed earlier when he loafed on the grass is actually true; and in the final section, the poet again returns to the grass when he writes, 'I bequeath myself to the dirt to grow from the grass I love."

Whitman's organization of individual sections also contributes to the total unity of the poem. Eight of the sections are introduced by questions, and, in nearly every case, the poet attempts to answer in either that section or following sections the questions which he has raised. Nearly fifteen of the sections begin with clear-cut assertions about the self's identity, its beliefs or its knowledge, and Whitman then goes on in the same section to illustrate or expand that assertion. Examples of such assertions might include, 'I am the poet of the Body and I am the poet of the Soul' (Section 21); 'All truths wait in all things' (Section 30); or 'I know I have the best of time and space, and was never measured and never will be measured' (Section 46). Sometimes the poet will discuss in two back-to-back sections two contrasting subjects. For instance, in Section 25, he focuses on speaking and writing, means of *expression*; in the next section, he shifts the focus to listening and absorption, means of *impression.* Or in Section 8, the poet focuses on urban images; in 9, on rural images. Often Whitman will suggest a topic in the last lines of one section and will amplify on that subject at length in the next section. For instance, in the last line of Section 6, he suggests the luck of dying, and then he deals directly with it in 7; in Section 27, he mentions the sense of touch and then focuses on it exclusively in 28–29.

One of Whitman's unique transitions occurs between Sections 24 and 25. At the end of 24, he focuses on a morning-glory, on daybreak, and on the erotic urge of the sunrise. His first line of Section 25 focuses on this same sunrise, but then in the second line, the poet changes the meaning of sunrise and it becomes something which goes out of himself; by the fifth line he has defined that sunrise going out of himself as his voice and the twirl of his tongue. In effect, it would seem that Whitman successfully turns the subject of one section (the sunrise) into a metaphor for the subject of the next section (his voice). Here are the lines that do it (Section 25):

> Dazzling and tremendous how quick the sun-rise would kill me,
> If I could not now and always send sun-rise out of me.

> We also ascend dazzling and tremendous as the sun,
> We found or own O my soul in the calm and cool of the daybreak.

> My voice goes after what my eyes cannot reach,
> With the twirl of my tongue I encompass worlds and volumes of worlds.

WHITMAN'S CATALOGUES

Finally, let's look briefly at Whitman's so-called 'catalogues.' These comprise a topic in themselves and what follows can hardly do justice to them; however, selected observations about the three longest 'catalogues,' Sections 15, 16 and 33, would seem to indicate a deliberate ordering or disordering on the part of Whitman. The first of these enumerates particular people, all of whom are doing something in the present tense. There is no obvious connection between any of them; in fact, they seem almost to be deliberately disordered. Several juxtapositions are most interesting: the duck shooter hunts and the deacons are ordained; the newly-come immigrants cover the wharf and the wooly-pates hoe in the sugar-field; the bride unrumples her white dress and the opium-eater reclines; the prostitute draggles her shawl and the president holds a cabinet meeting. As for the poet, he is simply a detached observer who does not appear until the final three lines:

> And these tend inward to me, and I tend outward to them,
> And such as it is to be of these more or less I am,
> And of these one and all I weave the song of myself.

Throughout the entire section, there is a slight hint that a calendar year is passing, for we move from the children riding to a Thanksgiving dinner to a First-day loafe to the hoeing of a sugar-field to a band concert to the Fourth of July to a pike-fisher fishing through the ice. There is, however, a more definite indication that night has come by the end of the section. It would almost seem as if Whitman has superimposed a yearly cycle upon a daily one.

The second of these three 'catalogues,' Section 16 of the poem, is introduced by the word 'I' and thereby focuses attention on the poet rather than on others. This time the poet is less the detached observer and more the involved and transcendent participant. This time, groups of people rather than individuals are named, and these groups seem organized into contrasting pairs: the old and young, the Southerner and the Northerner, the learner and the teacher. As the poet clearly indicates in the first and last lines of the section, he is no longer simply 'tends' toward those he presents, but he now is simultaneously a part of all of them. If time governs somewhat the organizational pattern in Section 15, then space serves a similar function in 16.

The final 'catalogue,' Section 33, consists of over 150 lines and comes during that moment of ecstatic revelation when the poet feels he has solved the 'puzzle of puzzles.' Somewhat ironically addressed to Space and Time, the lines defy these, emphasizing that the poet is no longer limited by anything—time, space, body, soul, sex. Rather, he is now able to interpenetrate all, not as a dispassionate observer of individuals or as an omnivorous part of groups, but as the people themselves, able to assume their activities and places. The focus of this section, therefore, is totally upon the poet and upon what he himself is doing. There is no chronological or spatial ordering of items now, for time and space are limitless. Rather, the items can be divided into those in the first half which inspire rejoicing [and] those in the second half which inspire distress. Whereas the first lines relate back to the 'common air that bathes the globe' and to the poet's incorporation of all, the last lines lead nicely into the murder in cold blood and the disastrous sea battle portrayed so dramatically in Sections 34–36. If in fact there is definite structure and organization in these three sections, it hardly seems valid to label them loosely as 'catalogues.'

The original questions raised for discussion were, 'Is there deliberate structure in "Song of Myself"?' and its expansion, 'If so, what *is* that structure and how does Whitman maintain it?' The preceding discussion ought to suggest some definite answers to those questions—answers which seem to move progressively forward toward a theory of structure in 'Song of Myself.'

A Song of Many Selves

Richard Chase

To Richard Chase, Whitman's "Song of Myself" is a
playful, paradoxical look at the many sides of the
poem's protagonist. While Whitman's other poems often create a protagonist who journeys toward self-
fulfillment, in "Song of Myself" the self continually
changes, avoiding any attempts the reader may make
to define it and thereby limit its lively spontaneity. The
structure of the poem coincides with this theme: there
is no discernable plot or movement. The poem is as diverse and varied as the self. Richard Chase has taught
at Columbia University. He is the author of numerous
books on American literature, including *Walt Whitman
Reconsidered*, from which this excerpt is taken.

The main item of the 1855 edition of *Leaves of Grass* was, of
course, "Song of Myself," the profound and lovely comic
drama of the self which is Whitman's best poem and contains in essence nearly all, yet not quite all, there is to *Leaves
of Grass*. The comic spirit of the poem is of the characteristic American sort, providing expression for a realism at once
naturalistic and transcendental, for the wit, gaiety, and fes-
tive energy of all good comedy, and also for meditative solil-
oquy, at once intensely personal and strongly generic.

One circumstance that contributes to the general spontaneity of "Song of Myself" is, in fact, Whitman's unsuccess-
ful attempt to be an Emersonian [after American writer
Ralph Waldo Emerson] or Wordsworthian [after English
poet William Wordsworth] moralist. In his preface, he wrote
that "of all mankind the poet is the equable man. Not in him
but off from him things are grotesque or eccentric or fail of
their sanity . . . He is the arbiter of the diverse and he is the
key. He is the equalizer of his age and land." Whitman tries,
indeed, to install himself in his poem on this high moral
ground: he will, he says, first regenerate himself by leaving

the fallacious artificialities of modern life and getting back to fundamentals; then, having perfected himself as the norm, he will summon all the world to him to be freed of its abnormalities. But although in the poem the self remains pretty much at the center of things, Whitman finds it impossible to accept the idea that it is a norm. To the sententious prophet who "promulges" the normative self, the comic poet and ironic realist keep introducing other, disconcertingly eccentric selves.

Who goes there? hankering, gross, mystical, nude. . . .

Whoever he is, he is not in a position to utter morality. The self in this poem *is* (to use [English writer D.H.] Lawrence's phrase) "tricksy-tricksy"; it does "shy all sorts of ways" and is finally, as the poet says, "not a bit tamed," for "I too am untranslatable." So that as in all true, or high, comedy, the sententious, the too overtly insisted-on morality (if any) plays a losing game with ironical realism. In the social comedy of [French playwright Jean] Molière, [English playwright William] Congreve, or Jane Austen, moral sententiousness, like other deformities of comportment or personality, is corrected by society. But this attitude is, of course, foreign to Whitman, who has already wished to invite society to correct itself by comparing itself with him and who, furthermore, cannot even sustain this democratic inversion of an aristocratic idea. Whitman's comic poetry deflates pretensions and chides moral rigidity by opposing to them a diverse, vital, indeterminate reality.

A POEM OF MANY SELVES

"I resist anything better than my own diversity," says Whitman, and this is the characteristic note of "Song of Myself.". . . The poem is full of odd gestures and whimsical acts; it is written by a neo-Ovidian [after the Roman poet] poet for whom self-metamorphosis is almost as free as free association, who can write "I am an old artillerist" or "I will go to the bank by the wood, and become undisguised and naked" as easily as he can write:

Askers embody themselves in me and I am embodied
   in them,
I project my hat, sit shame-faced, and beg.

The sense of incongruous diversity is very strong in "Song of Myself," and although one does not know how the sly beggar projecting his hat or the martial patriot is transformed into the "acme of things accomplish'd," and "encloser of things to be" who suddenly says:

> I find I incorporate gneiss, coal, long-threaded moss,
>   fruits, grains, esculent roots,
> And am stucco'd with quadrupeds and birds all over,

one is nevertheless charmed with the transformation.

Whitman conceives of the self, one might say, as [American novelist Henry] James conceives of Christopher Newman in *The American*—as having the "look of being committed to nothing in particular, of standing in an attitude of general hospitality to the chances of life." In other words, the "self" who is the protagonist of Whitman's poem is a character portrayed in a recognizable American way; it illustrates the fluid, unformed personality exulting alternately in its provisional attempts to define itself and in its sense that it has no definition. . . .

A NOVELISTIC POEM

The very scope of Whitman's universe and the large freedom he assumes to move about in it allowed him to appropriate new areas of experience and thus to make of "Song of Myself" the original and influential poem it is. For one thing, this is the first American poem to invade that fruitful ground between lyric verse and prose fiction that so much of modern poetry cultivates, and one may suppose that "Song of Myself" has had at least as much effect on the novel as, let us say, [Herman Melville's] *Moby Dick* or [Henry James's] *The Golden Bowl* have had on poetry. The famous lines in Section 8 are, at any rate, both "imagistic" and novelistic:

> The little one sleeps in its cradle;
> I lift the gauze and look a long time, and silently brush
>   away flies with my hand.
> The youngster and the red-faced girl turn aside up the
>   bushy hill;
> I peeringly view them from the top.
> The suicide sprawls on the bloody floor of the bed-
>   room;
> I witness the corpse with its dabbled hair, I note where
>   the pistol has fallen.

It is probably true that more than anyone else, more than [English poet William] Blake or [French poet Charles] Baudelaire, Whitman made the city poetically available to literature:

> The blab of the pave, tires of carts, sluff of boot-soles,
>   talk of the promenaders,
> The heavy omnibus, the driver with his interrogating
>   thumb, the clank of the shod horses on the granite
>   floor . . .

Such lines as these have been multitudinously echoed in modern prose and poetry, they have been endlessly recapitulated by the journey of the realistic movie camera up the city street. One might argue that Whitman's descriptions of the city made possible T.S. Eliot's *Waste Land.* The horror of Eliot's London, as of Baudelaire's "*cité pleine de rêves,*" is unknown in *Leaves of Grass,* but was not Whitman the first poet, so to speak, who put real typists and clerks in the imaginary city?

SEXUALITY IN "SONG OF MYSELF"

There can be no doubt that "Song of Myself" made sex a possible subject for American literature, and in this respect Whitman wrought a great revolution in, for example, his beautiful idyllic scene in which the "handsome and richly drest" woman imagines herself to join the "twenty-eight young men" who "bathe by the shore." In such a passage as this . . . American literature was moving toward the freedom and inclusiveness that came more naturally to Europeans. . . . It is sex, too, although of an inverted kind, that allows Whitman to write the following unsurpassable lines in which love is at once so sublimely generalized and perfectly particularized:

> And [I know] that a kelson of the creation is love,
> And limitless are leaves stiff or drooping in the fields,
> And brown ants in the little wells beneath them,
> And mossy scabs of the worm fence, and heap'd stones,
>   elder, mullein and poke-weed.

WHITMAN'S POETIC PRECISION

No summary view of "Song of Myself" would be complete without reference to the elegiac tone of the concluding lines. If, as we have been saying, Whitman's poem is remarkable for its gross inclusive scope, his elegiac verse is a great act of discrimination and nicety. Where else, in the generally grandiose nineteenth-century melodrama of love and death shall we find anything like the delicate precision of these incomparable lines?

> The last scud of day holds back for me;
> It flings my likeness after the rest and true as any, on
>   the shadow'd wilds,
> It coaxes me to the vapor and the dusk.
>
> I depart as air, I shake my white locks at the runaway
>   sun,
> I effuse my flesh in eddies, and drift it in lacy jags.
>
> I bequeathe myself to the dirt, to grow from the grass
>   I love;
> If you want me again look for me under your boot-
>   soles.
>
> You will hardly know who I am or what I mean,
> But I shall be good health to you nevertheless,
> And filter and fibre your blood.
>
> Failing to fetch me at first keep encouraged,
> Missing me one place, search another,
> I stop somewhere, waiting for you.

As every poet does, Whitman asks us provisionally to accept the imagined world of his poem. It is a fantastic world in which it is presumed that the self can become identical with all other selves in the universe, regardless of time and space. Not without precedent in Hindu poetry, this central metaphor is, as an artistic device, unique in American literature, as is the extraordinary collection of small imagist poems, versified short stories, realistic urban and rural genre paintings, inventories, homilies, philosophizings, farcical episodes, confessions, and lyric musings it encompasses in "Song of Myself." Yet as heavily taxing our powers of provisional credence, as inventing a highly idiosyncratic and illusory world, "Song of Myself" invites comparison with other curious works of the American imagination—*Moby Dick,* let us say, and [Nathaniel Hawthorne's] *The Scarlet Letter* and [Henry James's] *The Wings of the Dove.* It is of the first importance at any rate to see that Whitman's relation of the self to the rest of the universe is a successful aesthetic or compositional device, whatever we may think of it as a moral assertion.

THE PARADOX OF IDENTITY

If we look at Whitman's implicit metaphor more closely, we see that it consists in the paradox of "identity." The opening words of *Leaves of Grass,* placed there in 1867, state the paradox:

> One's-self I sing, a simple separate person,
> Yet utter the word Democratic, the word En-Masse.

In more general terms the opening lines of "Song of Myself" state the same paradox:

I celebrate myself and sing myself;
And what I assume you shall assume;
For every atom belonging to me, as good belongs
    to you.

Both politically and by nature man has "identity," in two senses of the word: on the one hand, he is integral in himself, unique, and separate; on the other hand, he is equal to, or even the same as, everyone else. . . .

In some of his best as well as in some of his worst poems, Whitman actually conceives of the self as making a journey —for example, "Song of the Open Road," "Crossing Brooklyn Ferry," and "Passage to India." In others the self journeys, as it were, not forward and outward but backward and inward, back to the roots of its being, and discovers there a final mystery, or love, comradeship, or death—for example, the *Calamus* and *Sea Drift* poems. (Notably among the latter are "Out of the Cradle Endlessly Rocking" and "As I Ebb'd with the Ocean of Life".) In "Song of Myself," however, the self is not felt to be incomplete; it has no questing odyssey to make. It stands aggressively at the center of things, "Sure as the most certain sure, plumb in the uprights, well entretied, braced in the beams." It summons the universe, "syphons" universal experience through its dilating pores, calls "anything back again when I desire it." Or the self imagines itself to be infinitely expandable and contractible (like the web of the spider in Whitman's little poem called "A Noiseless Patient Spider"), so that there is no place where at any moment it may not be, no thing or person with whom it may not merge, no act in which it may not participate. Of great importance is the fact that most of "Song of Myself" has to do not with the self searching for a final identity but with the self escaping a series of identities which threaten to destroy its lively and various spontaneity. This combination of attitudes is what gives "Song of Myself" the alternately ecstatic and gravely musing, pastoral-godlike stability one feels at the center, around which, however, the poet is able to weave the most astonishing embellishments of wit and lyric song.

AN UNSTRUCTURED POEM

This is perhaps a valid way of feeling the shifting modes of sensibility in the poem. Yet it would be wrong to attribute any clear cut structure to "Song of Myself." "The United States themselves are essentially the greatest poem," wrote Whitman in his preface. A Jacksonian Democrat [after President Andrew Jackson, who upheld the common man], Whitman was not an admirer of federal unity, either in a nation or a poem. He was content to make his poem a loose congeries of states and half-settled territories. He was content that his poem should mirror that "freshness and candor of . . . physiognomy," that "picturesque looseness of carriage," and that "deathless attachment to freedom" which, in his preface, he attributed to his countrymen. His style would be organic; he would "speak in literature with the perfect rectitude and insouciance" of animals and growing things. Although capable of finely pictorial images, Whitman composed more by ear than by eye, and his ear being attuned to music of the looser, more variable sort, such as the Italian operas, he strung his poems together on a free melodic line and by means of motifs, voices, recapitulations, recitatives, rests, *crescendi* [rising] and *diminuendi* [falling].

The motif of "Song of Myself" is the self taking on a bewildering variety of identities and with a truly virtuoso agility extricating itself from each one. The poem begins with the exhortation to leave the "rooms full of perfume," the "creeds and schools." Apart from conventions,

Apart from the pulling and hauling stands what I am,
Stands amused, complacent, compassionating, idle, unitary.

Having put society and convention behind, "What I am" finds itself in an Edenlike, early-morning world, wherein one easily observes the portentous dialectics of the universe:

Urge and urge and urge,
Always the procreant urge of the world.
Out of the dimness opposite equals advance, always
    substance and increase, always sex,
Always a knit of identity, always distinction, always a
    breed of life.

But of more importance is the fact that in this idyllic world the veil is lifted from the jaundiced eye, the cramped sensibility is set free, the senses and pores of the body receive the joyful intelligences dispatched to them by a friendly and providential nature. The self appears to be the offspring of a happy union of body and soul; sublime and delightful thoughts issue from the mind in the same miraculous way as the grass from the ground. Death itself is seen to be "lucky." And, in short, "what I am" can well afford to be complacent, to be certain that it is "unitary." Nor is the feeling of power denied to the self. It derives power from nature, as does the horse—"affectionate, haughty, electrical"—with which the poet compares himself. It derives power, too, from identification with others—the "runaway slave," "the butcher-boy," the "blacksmiths," "the boatmen and clam-diggers," the "trapper," the "red girl"—and finally with America itself.

> In me the caresser of life wherever moving, backward
>   as well as forward sluing,
> To niches aside and junior bending, not a person or
>   object missing,
> Absorbing all to myself and for this song.

Sections 24–28, though in places rather obscure, contain the essence of Whitman's drama of identity. The poet begins by proclaiming himself a Kosmos, and commanding us to "unscrew the locks from the doors! / Unscrew the doors themselves from their jambs!" so that the universe may flow through him—"through me the current and index" (that is, the undifferentiated flux and the "identities" that emerge therefrom). This proclamation announces not only the unshakable status and palpable reality but also the redemptive powers of the self. In a world which has been created by banishing social sanctions and social intelligence, what will keep man from being lost in idiocy, crime, squalor? What of that underground realm inhabited by

> . . . the deform'd, trivial, flat, foolish, despised,
> Fog in the air, beetles rolling balls of dung?

The threat of madness, crime, and obscenity is to be allayed by the curative powers of that Adamic world where wisdom consists in uttering "the pass-word primeval," "the sign of democracy." Siphoned through the haughty, electrical self or discussed frankly by persons not inhibited by prudery (the discourses seem perilously interchangeable), the crimes and obscenities will be redeemed:

> Voices indecent by me clarified and transfigur'd.

The poet then records a dreamlike idyl of auto-erotic experience, in which the parts of the body merge mysteriously with natural objects, and a great deal of diffuse and wistful love is generated. And, when dawn comes, the redemption is symbolized in these astonishing metaphors:

Hefts of the moving world at innocent gambols silently
   rising, freshly exuding,
Scooting obliquely high and low.

Something I cannot see puts upward libidinous prongs,
Seas of bright juice suffuse heaven.

The poem then speaks anew of how the self may be distorted
or destroyed. The poet's "identity" is said to be assailed and
warped into other "identities" by agents referred to as "traitors,"
"wasters," and "marauders." Somewhat elusive in particular,
these appear to have in common a quality of aggressiveness
and imperiousness. They act as a radical individualist conceives society to act. They break down the self, they swagger,
they assert convention, responsibility and reason, they domi-
nate and impose passivity and furtiveness on the individual.

The beautiful, diffuse, kindly dawn is succeeded by a
more formidable, a more imperious, apparition. The "dazzling and tremendous" sun leaps over the horizon and cries,
"See then whether you shall be master!" The poet replies to
this challenge by saying that the sunrise would indeed "kill
me / If I could not now and always send sunrise out of me."
The power with which the poet defeats what seeks to destroy
him is asserted to be "my vision" and "my voice."

My voice goes after what my eyes cannot reach,
With the twirl of my tongue I encompass worlds.

In Section 26 both the metaphorical effects and the subject matter shift from the visual to the auditory. The
"bravuras of birds, bustle of growing wheat, gossip of
flames, clack of sticks cooking my meals"—these and myriad other sounds amplify into a symphonic orchestration.
The crescendo and dying fall of the conclusion are rendered
with full tone and exquisite wit.

I hear the train'd soprano (what work, with hers, is this?)
The orchestra whirls me wider than Uranus flies,
It wrenches such ardors from me I did not know I
   possess'd them,
It sails me, I dab with bare feet, they are lick'd by the indolent
   waves,
I am cut by bitter and angry hail, I lose my breath,
Steep'd amid honey'd morphine, my windpipe throttled
   in fakes of death,
At length let up again to feel the puzzle of puzzles,
And that we call Being.

But again the poet is confronted with "Being"—that is,
form or identity—and is not certain that this is the Being he

wants to be. It is therefore dissipated and generalized, in Section 27, into a universal process of reincarnation.

In Section 28 there occurs the famous auto-erotic pastoral dream in which "prurient provokers," like nibbling cows, "graze at the edges of me." The "provokers," conceived as symbolic of the sense of touch, arouse and madden the dreaming poet and then they all unite "to stand on a headland and worry me." After touch has "quivered" him "to a new identity"—has left him confused, vexed, self-reproachful, and isolated—he proceeds in the following sections to resume a "true," "real," or "divine" identity. This act of restoration is accomplished through love, natural piety, pastoral and cosmic meditations, symbolic fusions of self with America, . . . ritual celebrations, and fatherly preachments, and finally, in the last Section, by the assertion that death is also merely an extrication of the self from an identity.

Life and Death in "Out of the Cradle Endlessly Rocking"

James E. Miller Jr.

In this excerpt from his book, *A Critical Guide to Leaves of Grass*, James E. Miller Jr. interprets Whitman's complex poem, "Out of the Cradle Endlessly Rocking." This is a memory poem, as the accomplished writer looks back to his youth to recall the moment at which he first became a poet. Miller explains that the poem, with its songs and symbols, never explicitly states a meaning, but instead suggests the young boy's understanding of the life cycle, and how spiritual awakening may follow a physical death.

"Out of the Cradle Endlessly Rocking" is a vivid, imaginative re-creation by the mature poet of the primary childhood experience that determined him to be a poet and granted him poetic (or spiritual) insight. In understanding the structure of the poem it is important to note the "time" frame within which the action of the drama is set. The poet is "A man, yet by these tears a little boy again" and he is "borne hither," back to the scene of the unforgettable boyhood experience by recollection of all the images of nature that played such important roles in the experience. But in addition the poet remembers the experience so vividly because he recalls "the thousand responses of my heart never to cease," the "myriad thence-arous'd words," and "the word stronger and more delicious than any." All the poet's poems are reminders of that one crucial experience and carry him back, almost against his will. Indeed, with the onrush of all the lines of the opening section, lines tumbled onto each other by the swiftly moving "out of," "over," "down," "up from," "out from," "from," the poet is apparently overwhelmed with recollections that spring

Reprinted from *A Critical Guide to "Leaves of Grass,"* by James E. Miller Jr. © 1957 by The University of Chicago. Reprinted by permission of The University of Chicago Press.

out at him from all directions at once. Possessed by an insistent memory, the poet finds himself helpless as he is transported imaginatively back into the past of his childhood. He curiously looks upon the words of this poem as somehow detached from and uncontrolled by him:

> From such as now they [the words] start the scene revisiting,
> As a flock, twittering, rising, or overhead passing.

The metaphor of the flock itself suggests that the poet's will has been subverted by his overpowering memory and the experience is, in a sense, forcefully re-creating itself.

A POEM OF MEMORY

Although the poem in the main is the boy's experience, the reader is not allowed to forget throughout that that experience is re-created out of a man's memory, the recollection of a mature poet, and the experience has its greatest significance in relation to the man as poet. When the he-bird first discovers his mate missing and sends forth his first anguished cry, the poet confides, "He pour'd forth the meanings which I of all men know." And when the poet reveals, "I have treasur'd every note," he is suggesting to the reader that the bird's song has a significance far beyond what is apparent in the dramatic incidents of the poem. At the end of the poem, too, the poet reminds the reader that the experience of the poem is not immediate but recalled, and recalled primarily because the experience reveals the source of the mature man's poetic vision. As the bird sang to the boy "in the moonlight on Paumanok's gray beach," the song evoked, like that "flock, twittering, rising," a "thousand responsive songs at random"; the poet says simply, "My own songs awaked from that hour." In this line lies the key to the primary meaning of "Out of the Cradle Endlessly Rocking."

This frame, of the adult poet re-creating in his imagination a boyhood experience, serves not only to inclose and give form to that experience but also to endow it with its primary significance. The boy is not just an ordinary boy but an "outsetting bard." The man recalling the boy is the accomplished bard. The "meaning" of the poem, if it is to have a meaning separate from the drama, is the "meaning" of the experience for the poet's songs. What are the "meanings" that the poet "of all men" knows? Why were his songs "awaked from that hour"? Perhaps one of the secrets of the triumph of this poem is that its "meaning" is nowhere explicitly stated but is imaginatively and emotionally evoked. The reader, like the boy in the poem, lives the experience and through that experience comes intuitively to *know*.

MEANING THROUGH ACTION

In order to discover the meaning closest to that intended by the poet, it is perhaps best to examine closely the dramatic action of the poem. The characters of the action as well as the setting function symbolically, and the action itself becomes ultimately symbolic. There are three stages in the drama of the re-created experience. In the first the dominant characters are the two mockingbirds, the "two feather'd guests from Alabama," who in their carol of bliss sing the song of ideal love and happiness. In the second stage, introduced with the sudden disappearance of the she-bird, the male mockingbird becomes the central character and sings his powerful, anguished lament for his lost love, a carol of "lonesome love." In the final stage of the experience, the ocean becomes the main character and sings its song. Compared to the preceding carols, the ocean's song is barren, for it has only one word—death. But that word is the missing "clew."

Though these "characters" successively assume center stage in the drama, it must be remembered that what is happening is doubly seen and heard. It is filtered first through the consciousness of the boy who is there; it is filtered next through the memory of the boy become man and poet. The reader is thus twice removed from the actual experience. It is this indirect point of view in the poem that constitutes its realism. Only the brilliant imagination of the boy could translate the music of the birds and the sound of the sea into words; only the poet could fuse these "messages" into a profound insight into the nature of man's fate. In reality, then, the central character throughout is the boy, shadowing forth the man-poet he is to become, and attention is focused not on the birds and sea but on the boy-man's deepening understanding wrought by the impingement of these elements of nature on his sensitive consciousness. Each of the stages outlined above broadens the boy-poet's awareness of the nature of life and death. In the first stage the protagonist learns something of the nature of fulfilled love. While the two mockingbirds are together, they sing "all time" and mind "no time" in their bliss; out of their transfiguring love they create their own eternity. After the she-bird becomes lost, "may-be kill'd, unknown to her mate," the protagonist gains insight into "lonesome love," a love deprived of its beloved, an anguished love of the spirit, a love that has nothing to sustain it except the spiritual.

Finally, after the aria of the he-bird "sinks," the protagonist cries out: "O if I am to have so much, let me have more!" And as the sea sends forth its single word, "death," as the ocean chants the word "death," the protagonist responds with the emotional fervor of a deep and intuitive insight. He "fuses"

> . . . the song of my dusky demon and brother,
> That he sang to me in the moonlight on Paumanok's [Long Island's] gray beach,
> With the thousand responsive songs at random,
> My own songs awaked from that hour,
> And with them the key, the word up from the waves.

This fusion is not a fusion of logic in the intellect but rather a fusion of the emotions in the soul. The meaning of the aria of the bird has been "deposited" in his soul ("the ears, the soul, swiftly depositing"), and the sea's word has been a response to the "boy's soul's questions." The fusion, then, of his songs, the bird's carol, and the sea's chant is a fusion in which the soul acts as catalyst. The poetry of this "outsetting bard" is to be forever spiritually tinged with the lament of lonesome love and the "strong and delicious word," death. There is the inevitable suggestion of the spiritual fulfilment of lonesome love in death, a concept dominant in the "Calamus" poems. The sea is described as "hissing melodious" its word of death. Such a phrase, a conscious juxtaposition of words whose connotations clash, suggests the paradoxical nature of death: "hissing" connotes all the horror aroused at the thought of death; "melodious" connotes all the happiness and harmony resulting from the spiritual fulfilment of death. It is an intuitive understanding of this paradox, an insight into the relationship of death and love, death as the spiritual fulfilment of love, that is the "meaning" of the poem and that informs the "thousand responsive songs" forged in the soul of the mature poet.

ELEMENTS OF THE POEM

But the most important elements in "Out of the Cradle Endlessly Rocking" have so far gone almost unnoticed; these are the elements that bring about or "precipitate" the protagonist's insight into love and death. Whether they are regarded as mere elements of the setting or as highly charged symbols, surely there can be no doubt that the sun and moon, the day and night, the land and sea, the stars and waves play significant roles in convincing or persuading through the logic of emotion. At least there can be no disagreement that the *poetry* of "Out of the Cradle Endlessly Rocking" exists primarily in the dramatic use of these vividly created images.

It is no accident that in the first part of the poem, when the two mockingbirds are described in their wedded bliss, Paumanok is pictured in brilliant colors. The "lilac-scent" is in the air and "Fifth-month grass" is growing. In the bird's nest among the briers are "four light-green eggs spotted with brown." Amid all this color and all these images suggestive of life, fertility, and love, the two birds together sing out their paean of joy:

> Shine! shine! shine!
> Pour down your warmth, great sun!
> While we bask, we two together.

The sun is the great life-giver, and to it the birds pay tribute for their supreme happiness. But the tone of the joint song of the birds is one of defiance—

> Winds blow south or winds blow north,
> Day come white or night come black

—a defiance of the elements as long as the birds remain "two together."

Those very winds defied by the two birds in their song of happiness are invoked by the he-bird as he searches for his lost mate: "Blow! blow! blow!" The meter of the stark line, recalling the opening of the previous carol ("Shine! shine! shine!"), brings into dramatic focus not only the change of fortune of the singer but also the transformed setting. Instead of the sun pouring down its great warmth, now the stars glisten, the waves slap the shore, and the moonbeams intertwine with the shadows. Day has become night. Attention is gradually shifted from the land (the sea is not even mentioned in the bird's opening carol) to the ocean. And such images as "the white arms out in the breakers tirelessly tossing," suggestive of unassuageable grief, reflect the tragic turn that events have taken.

THE HEART OF THE POEM

The he-bird's carol of lonesome love, which forms in more senses than one the real heart of the poem, is justly celebrated for its incomparable marriage of sound and image. The three heavy beats of the previous songs are repeated not only in the opening line ("Soothe! soothe! soothe!") but also at intervals throughout, strong reminders of the tragic transformation. As the he-bird in his song scans the ocean, the land, and the sky for any sign of his beloved, he re-creates a world after his own emotional image. The breakers and waves of the sea, the brown-yellow, sagging moon, the land, and the rising stars— all reflect the he-bird's dejected and despairing state. These objects of the setting emerge vividly as symbols. When the bird cries out—

> *O brown halo in the sky near the moon, drooping upon the sea!*
> *O troubled reflection in the sea!*

—both moon and sea are symbols. But it is well to remember that they are not functioning directly as such for the reader. The reader sees both moon and sea as the man-poet remembers, when a boy, having imagined their appearance to the grieving bird. From this circuitous route these natural objects emerge charged with complex meanings by the minds through which they have filtered. The very universe comes to reflect like a mirror the emotional turbulence disturbing the bird, the boy, and the poet.

The opening duet of bliss and the he-bird's lament introduce a series of opposites suggestive of the duality of nature: sun and moon, day and night, land and sea. These pairs indicate not only a dual but also a rhythmical universe, a universe whose patterned unfolding must be, the result of some unrevealed purpose. But there is additional significance to these symbols. The sun, day, and land are associated with the blissful, fulfilled life of the birds—"two together." The moon, night, and sea are associated with unfulfilled, lonesome love, a love deprived of its object. In short, one set of these symbols is associated with physical love, the body, and life; the other with spiritual love, the soul, and death. Out of these associations comes the suggestion that life and death too, like day and night, are merely a part of the rhythmical evolution of the universe.

When the he-bird in his anguished lament cries out—

> *O madly the sea pushes upon the land,*
> *With love, with love*

—it is, surely, with some understanding of the land and sea as symbols of body and soul. The sea "loves" the land as the spirit is attracted to the body, gains its identity through the body, finds its fulfilment only through the physical. With the land and sea established as symbols of the material and spiritual (they have been established as such in earlier sections of *Leaves of Grass*), the point of contact, the shore, inevitably develops special significance. It is symbolic of death itself, that point where the material life ends and the spiritual begins. The poet has exploited this special symbolic significance by using as the setting for his drama the seashore, with the he-bird singing his lament from the land to the she-bird lost over the sea. The poet makes explicit use of this symbolic significance of the seashore near the end of the poem, when he portrays the boy as crying out for the "clew":

> Are you whispering it, and have been all the time, you sea-
> waves?
> Is that it from your liquid rims and wet sands?

It is the sound of the wave dashing the shore's wet sands that the boy translates into the "low and delicious word death."

A SPIRITUAL BIRTH

The "clew," then, is provided not by the sea but rather by the seashore, by the sea and the land jointly. "Liquid rims and wet sands" vividly suggest the land and sea inextricably intermingled or, symbolically, the conjunction of the physical and the spiritual. The sea waves, "delaying not, hurrying not," repeat their single word, "Death, death, death, death, death." The slow and funereal march of the stress ironically recalls the preceding lines of repeated heavy stresses, lines of both joy and sorrow. The sea waves' line not only recalls but also reconciles or merges the joy with the sorrow, for the hypnotic effect ("Creeping thence steadily up to my ears and laving me softly all over") precipitates in the soul of the protagonist not terror but the ecstasy of mystic insight and affirmation. Something of the nature of that insight is suggested parenthetically at the end of the poem. Those sea waves striking unceasingly and rhythmically against the shore, forming the spiritually fertile "liquid rims," are "like some old crone rocking the cradle." The poem ends as it began ("Out of the cradle endlessly rocking"), and the cycle of the experience, like the cycle of life, is begun again. Life and death are not the beginning and end, but rather ceaseless continuations. Death is birth into spiritual life. The sea, as it sends its waves unceasingly to the seashore, is the "cradle endlessly rocking," just as the spiritual world, through the mystic experience of death, provides the "cradle" for man's spiritual birth.

Whitman's Diminished Vision in "As I Ebb'd with the Ocean of Life"

R.W. French

According to R.W. French, Whitman's "As I Ebb'd with the Ocean of Life" is a poem about a diminished world, the world the poet discovers when he puts aside his pride and sees his art within its very minor place in the world. Yet the poet recovers from his dark night of the soul to reassert his vision and to ask the reader's indulgence. He is still a poet, but his scope is scaled down from earlier poems, particularly "Song of Myself." No longer is his focus cosmic. The plight of the individual soul is enough of a battleground for this poem. R.W. French has taught at the University of Massachusetts.

One of the enduring fascinations of *Leaves of Grass* is its constant movement through shifting moods. Continually the book turns on itself, with frequent changes and self-corrections; there is nothing it asserts that it does not at some time deny. It is as full of doubt as it is of faith. Every great Whitman theme is questioned, rejected, reasserted, and questioned again: trust in nature, love of humanity, assertion of the physical, faith in ultimate order, authority of the self, belief in the powers of poetry—these and others are confidently celebrated on some pages and bitterly dismissed on others.

"As I Ebb'd with the Ocean of Life" occupies a crucial place in Whitman's history of doubt and faith, as it moves from a desperate turning against the past to a new awareness, tempered by experience. Starting in anguished rejection, it must find a way to begin again, to go on with life, and in the restrained realism of its perceptions it becomes particularly modern. The poem makes no grand claims, asserts

Reprinted from "From Major to Minor: A Reading of 'As I Ebb'd with the Ocean of Life,'" by R.W. French, *Walt Whitman Quarterly Review*, vol. 7, no. 2, Fall 1989. Reprinted by permission of the *Walt Whitman Quarterly Review*.

no overwhelming universal truths, relies on no supernatural supports; like [English poet William] Wordsworth, Whitman descends to "words / Which speak of nothing more than what we are." The bardic voice has disappeared, and the barbaric yawp is subdued to halting phrases. The poem collapses into fragments, bits and pieces, the insignificant debris of life; but that is not where it ends. Instead of falling into the silence of despair and hopelessness—as well it might—it takes the more difficult and courageous route of building on the harsh reality it perceives. If there is a heroism of ordinariness, this poem exemplifies it; and the challenge that it confronts, finally, is that of [American poet Robert] Frost's Oven Bird: "what to make of a diminished thing." That challenge of course haunts much twentieth-century literature.

A STATE OF DEPRESSION

The poem begins with the poet walking along the beach, "musing," as he says, "late in the autumn day, gazing off southward." The hour and season combine to encourage reflection. . . . While the poet walks, complacent in the pride he feels in his art, he is "seiz'd by the spirit that trails in the lines underfoot. . . ." This spirit leads him into a state of acute depression marked by deep feelings of guilt, inadequacy, and failure. He sees the debris along the shore, the cast-off leavings from the ocean, and in them he sees emblems of his own insignificance. "I too," he discovers, "but signify at the utmost a little wash'd-up drift, / A few sands and dead leaves to gather, / Gather, and merge myself as part of the sands and drift.". . .

The poet had been seeking "types" (metaphors, likenesses, correspondences), and he finds them, although they turn out to be not what he had expected. He looks at the world of nature about him and sees "Chaff, straw, splinters of wood, weeds, and the sea-gluten, / Scum, scales from shining rocks, leaves of salt-lettuce, left by the tide. . . ." The objects are wholly insignificant; there is no glorification here, no sense of infinitude, as there is, for example, in the "mossy scabs of the worm fence, heap'd stones, elder, mullein and poke-weed" of "Song of Myself," line 98. In an earlier apprehension the ordinary could be perceived as "limitless," but that vision will no longer serve. Now we have only debris, the ocean's junk, seen as itself and nothing more. Like Wordsworth in the Intimations Ode, the poet of "As I Ebb'd" must deal with a loss of glory. The world is not what it was; the question now is to find a response to redeem such loss.

A SECTION OF SELF-RIDICULE

The second section begins to resolve that question by asserting similitude. It is a commonplace that Romantic poets see themselves reflected in the images of nature; the outer life mirrors the inner—or, rather, the inner life creates the outer. Falling into depression, the poet easily finds objects to fit—even to exacerbate—his mood. As noted above, he sees himself in the debris washed up along the beach—"I too but signify at the utmost a little wash'd-up drift"—and, in the great passage that follows, he rebukes himself for daring to open his mouth; he dismisses his words as "all that blab" and condemns himself for never having known his true identity:

> O baffled, balk'd, bent to the very earth,
> Oppress'd with myself that I have dared to open my mouth,
> Aware now that amid all that blab whose echoes recoil upon
>   me I have not once had the least idea who or what I am,
> But that before all my arrogant poems that real Me stands yet
>   untouch'd, untold, altogether unreach'd,
> Withdrawn far, mocking me with mock-congratulatory signs
>   and bows,
> With peals of distant ironical laughter at every word I have
>   written,
> Pointing in silence to these songs, and then to the sand
>   beneath.

All, he discovers, has been vanity and self-deception. The tone is bitter; the passage has to be one of the more painful that any poet has ever written, for, undermining from within the poet's confidence in himself and his art, it leaves him exposed and helpless, a mere object of derision. Whitman sees his authentic self—"the real Me"—standing off in the distance, mocking the poet who wrote all those "arrogant" poems—"arrogant" because the poems came out of an ignorance assumed to be knowledge. They are seen now as deceitful and dishonest, the work of a fake, a pretender, an imposter; they have no substance and no truth to them. The poet now realizes that he did not know himself, and he did not know nature; how could he presume to write? The collapse is total and devastating; we see the poet consumed by self-ridicule and the anguished knowledge of failure.

At the end of the second section the poet is despondent; what is surprising is that the poem continues, as there is good reason for it to end at this point. Why go on? The poet finds no meaning or value in life; the extremity of his language—as when he says "I have not once had the least idea who or what I am" and "I have not really understood any thing, not a single object"—indicates clearly the force of his mental depression. His violent self-rebuke has left him incapacitated, bereft of energy and confidence. The poem at this point would seem to have dropped into a pit from which it cannot extricate itself. To make matters worse, this section ends with Nature itself castigating the poet for daring to sing his poems: "Nature here in sight of the sea taking advantage of me to dart upon me and sting me, / Because I have dared to open my mouth to sing at all." Such stern rebuke, from such a source, would seem to leave no answer possible but penitent silence—or at most, barely audible words of contrition and apology, as in the [Biblical] Book of Job, where the Voice from the Whirlwind, comparable to Nature in Whitman's poem, overwhelms Job into submission and self-rebuke. Like Whitman, Job condemns himself even for speaking: "I will lay mine hand upon my mouth. Once have I spoken, but I will not answer: yea, twice; but I will proceed no further."

GAINING HUMILITY

As Job is forced into apology ("I abhor myself, and repent in dust and ashes"), so is Whitman. The poet had called his poems "arrogant"; now, in the third section of the poem, he turns away from the arrogant past and becomes submissive, humble, pleading. No longer pretending to self-sufficiency, he seeks union and reconciliation. Of the opening ten lines of this section, seven, it should be noted, have to do with identity: lines 35-37 (the opening verse of the section) assert an identity with "You oceans both," and lines 40-44 connect the poet to Paumanok, the land, the "father" as opposed to the "fierce old mother," the ocean. Significantly, in this section the poet repeats, with slight variations, what he had said in the previous section ("I too but signify at the utmost a little wash'd up drift" is followed by "I too am but a trail of drift and debris"); but the meanings are different, for the tone has changed. The voice of section 2 is shocked, overwhelmed, stricken with pained discovery, while the voice of section 3, as it comes to accept the identification, is muted and re-strained. The anguish has gone, to be replaced by chastened recognition; the outburst has become a murmur.

The initial perception of identity is not rejected; it is, rather, seen in an altered light. The "little shreds" of debris do indeed stand for the poet and the two oceans, the ocean of life as well as the "fierce old mother." To see these connections is to gain in self-knowledge, and in so doing to move from arrogance to humility; as [American poet] T.S. Eliot wrote in "East Coker," "In order to arrive at what you do not know / You must go by a way which is the way of ignorance." The poet can now with equanimity see himself as drift and debris; that is what it means to be human. To wish to be more than that is to wish to be more than human, to live in an illusion of grandeur, to be willfully blind. The lesson is that of Job, who found his true being in learning his insignificance; it was a gain that could come only through loss. To quote Eliot again: "In order to possess what you do not possess / You must go by the way of dispossession."

In the third section of "As I Ebb'd," the poet achieves humility by recognizing his place in the scheme of things. He is now able to plead submissively, yet passionately, with the father: "Kiss me my father, / Touch me with your lips as I touch those I love, / Breathe to me while I hold you close the secret of the murmuring I envy." As is often pointed out, Whitman generally shows little sympathy for father-figures; the best-known such figure in his poetry, for example, is the distant and fearsome father of "There Was a Child Went Forth," a representation of power, injustice, and oppression. It is a sign of the new-found humility in this poem that the poet can plead as he does with the "father," the land. This is not to say, of course, that Paumanok [Native American word for Long Island] is Walter Whitman, Sr., in any obvious way, but, rather, that the poet can now approach the "father" in a spirit of submission. He speaks out of incompleteness, knowing his intense needs for recognition, for comfort, for love, and for the reassurance of the "secret" that he assumes the father must know. The sense of personal insufficiency behind these needs might be compared with the jauntily confident position taken in lines 989–990 of "Song of Myself" where it is the earth, not the poet, that appears needy: "Earth! you seem to look for something at my hands, / Say, old top-knot, what do you want?"

A MYSTERIOUS WORLD

Strangely, the poet gets no answer from the land, the "father"—a potentially disconcerting turn of events for the poet who once found answers everywhere, who could "hear and behold God in every object." Still, the answer does not come; what the poet hears is murmuring, and moaning, and crying, but this time there is no voice to give him superior knowledge, no word from the sea, no mystic carol of death. The lack of response might be seen as cause for despair, but what we have at this point is not despair, but resignation. The silence is itself a lesson that the poet must learn: for there is no "secret" that he can understand. Like Job, he must come to recognize that the universe is ultimately mysterious, beyond human knowledge. Its grandeur dwarfs human enterprise and human thought; it has nothing of comfort or consolation to whisper to him. He must learn—and it is a difficult lesson for the poet who proclaimed his divinity in "Song of Myself"—that he is not a god, that man is not the measure of things, and that the universe does not exist for anyone's particular good. Nature in this poem is clearly not the beneficent creation of "Song of Myself"; its music is a "sobbing dirge," and, as represented by the sea, it is threatening and potentially destructive. In "Song of Myself," by contrast, the sea was a lover:

> You sea! I resign myself to you also—I guess what you mean,
> I behold from the beach your crooked inviting fingers,
> I believe you refuse to go back without feeling of me,
> We must have a turn together, I undress, hurry me out of
>   sight of the land,
> Cushion me soft, rock me in billowy drowse,
> Dash me with amorous wet, I can repay you. (448–453)

In "As I Ebb'd" the sea is not lover but mother (as of course it is also in "Out of the Cradle Endlessly Rocking"). What's more, it is a "fierce old mother" that moans, "Endlessly crying" for its "castaways"; it rustles up "hoarse and angry" against the poet's feet. The representation is ominous and uncomfortable: a figure of sorrow, lamentation, and sullen hostility. With such there can be no full reconciliation; there can be recognition and acceptance, but hardly love. One must keep one's distance. Thus in the final section the poet dismisses the sea by recognizing that she is to continue in her ways ("Cease not your moaning you fierce old mother"); one must live with the world as it is, however one might wish that it could be otherwise. The fact is that the "ocean of life" is harsh: it has "castaways" that must be mourned; and the music of nature, as noted above, is "a sobbing dirge."

THE FACT OF DEATH

The dirge that the poet hears is music of unrelieved sadness, a true song of death. In this poem death is not to be praised or celebrated, as it is, say, in "Out of the Cradle Endlessly Rocking" or "When Lilacs Last in the Dooryard Bloom'd," and it is not to be dismissed, as it is in line 1289 of "Song of Myself" ("And as to you Death, and you bitter hug of mortality, it is idle to try to alarm me)"; it is simply not available as consolation in any form. Death in "As I Ebb'd" offers no special insights, no entrance into eternity, no enduring calm; it is a way of nature, no more: all life dies, and that is a fact. The view of death that the poem presents—significantly confined to parentheses—is appropriately graphic and clinical: "(See, from my dead lips the ooze exuding at last, / See, the prismatic colors glistening and rolling)". There is nothing to celebrate here, and it is useless to protest. Death and life, both must be endured.

THE PHANTOM READER

The fourth section, then, gives us acceptance, if not reconciliation. The poet opens with imperatives ("Ebb," "Cease not," "Endlessly cry," "Rustle not up so hoarse"), just as he did in the final section of "Crossing Brooklyn Ferry," another poem that moves toward acceptance, although in a different tone. Let things be as they are; everything is in its place. Whatever may be the situation out there, in the world of nature, the poet has achieved his peace; he holds no resentment, no anger ("I mean tenderly by you and all"). He can now turn back to himself, this time without bitter self-reproach, and he can go about his business: "I gather for myself and for this phantom looking down where we lead, and following me and mine. . . ."

And who is this "phantom"? Most probably, the phantom who looks down is the same as the unidentified "You up there walking or sitting, / Whoever you are" in the closing lines; that is, the reader, who appears a number of times in Whitman's poems as "whoever you are" or some such phrase. The reference is important, for it marks the conclusion of the poet's restoration to his calling. As much as any poet who ever wrote Whitman insisted on the necessity of the reader to complete the poem; and among the most prominent characteristics of *Leaves of Grass* is the frequency with which Whitman addresses or otherwise refers to his reader: often he seems conscious of someone looking over his shoulder. What is striking about "As I Ebb'd" is that the poet, having at the start of the poem given up all claims to authority by recognizing that he had never known himself or understood anything, at the end of the poem is prepared to re-assert his claims on a reader. This is a poem that abandons its audience, only to gain it again, on an altered basis; for the poet has to move through the blindness of pride, and then through the blindness of collapse, before he can achieve regeneration and discover that he still deserves an audience. By passing through the darkness, he has gained illumination; though chastened and subdued, he is ready to begin again. Having called out to the land, and to the sea, without an answer, he now calls out to his reader, knowing that there will be no response except, perhaps, at some uncertain date, to the poem itself.

STILL A POET

Reconciled to his calling, he remains a poet, a gatherer along the shore, collecting his fragments. In a brilliant fusion at the close, Whitman brings together the debris of the beach—"loose windrows, little corpses, / Froth, snowy white, and bubbles"—and his poems, those cast-off and disconnected utterances "Buoy'd hither from many moods, one contradicting another, / From the storm, the long calm, the darkness, the swell." Poems are recognized for what they are, fragments tossed up from the sea, from the mysterious depths of creation, perhaps no more than "A limp blossom or two"; for the poet must learn to accept insignificance, his own as well as that of his creations. Not without pain, he is coming to terms with his own humanity, which means the relinquishing of claims to grandeur; now he ceases to be the bard, since he has lost all bardic authority.

"As I Ebb'd" thus shows a poet pulling back, reducing his claims, re-establishing the basis of his work. By the end of the poem he has abandoned his illusion of self-sufficiency, for he knows that life is not a matter of conscious control, no more than the debris scattered along the beach; he and all that pertains to him, he realizes, are "capricious, brought hither we know not whence. . . ." As Ecclesiastes long ago noted, the two operative forces in this world are time and chance. "Song of Myself," rejecting chance, had insisted that time was purposeful: "Immense have been the preparations for me. . . . All forces have been steadily employ'd to complete and delight me. . . ." In "As I Ebb'd," however, that sense of order is abandoned. One must surrender to the randomness of things; that is the only way to establish a proper relationship to the universe as it actually is. The poet is clearly ready by the end of his poem to trust to the workings of chance. Let the poems, the fragments, as "capricious" as the human life that formed them, be "drifted at random"; in time they will find their way to the presence of some audience yet unknown: "We, capricious, brought hither we know not whence, spread out before you, / You up there walking or sitting, / Whoever you are, we too lie in drifts at your feet."

"As I Ebb'd," then, works toward a new realism; it marks a farewell to illusion and self-deception, and it sets out to begin life again as it re-establishes a relationship to the world—or, perhaps, as it establishes for the first time a relationship to the bleak world it has discovered. . . .

Like the Book of Job, it appears to be something of a test case. Suppose that all the illusions of a benevolent and just order were removed: what then? What then would give meaning and purpose to life? "As I Ebb'd" leaves us with fragments—Whitman even uses the word in line 61—to shore against our ruins [an allusion to T.S. Eliot's *The Waste Land*]. Along with the fragments, however, we have human consciousness and a voice to articulate perceptions; for even Job, after all, retained these, and with them he transformed his sufferings into language of the highest art and power. It would be too simple to say that "As I Ebb'd" is "about" poetry, as it is about much else beside; but certainly the theme of poetry is central, for "As I Ebb'd" begins with the poet in his pride and ends with the poet in his humility, and the last lines constitute an offering to a distant reader. The poem takes us into spiritual collapse; but it is poetry that provides the way out of despair by suggesting the redemptive powers of art. It is, the poem implies, the poet's obligation to write of perceived reality, however poor it may appear; surely art may find in that imperative sufficient purpose and justification. As Whitman noted in the 1855 Preface—although perhaps not realizing at the time the directions in which his explorations would lead—"folks expect of the poet to indicate more than the beauty and dignity which always attach to dumb real objects . . . they expect him to indicate the path between reality and their souls." It is not beauty, then, that is the poet's primary concern; throughout his life Whitman had little patience with conventional ideas of artistic beauty, feeling that they interfered with the simple clarity of statement that he valued above all.

SINGING OF THE ORDINARY

There is no beauty in "As I Ebb'd," at least not in any generally accepted sense; what there is in its place is a devotion to the ordinary, the plain, the un-beautiful, for these things, at least, can be trusted not to deceive. The universe may be beyond human comprehension, but the tufts of straw and limp blossoms washed up along the beach exist on a human scale and are accessible to human perception. Indeed, as the poem suggests, they are much like humans, insignificant and accidental. The problem for the poet, the artist, is to give significance to the insignificant and purpose to the accidental; and "As I Ebb'd" succeeds in doing precisely that, for as the ocean's debris provides an emblem of the human condition, it takes on importance. The point is to find the meanings of things within a human context; in that sense the poet can truly indicate a path between reality and the souls of his readers. In "Song of Myself" insignificant objects become significant insofar as they mirror the infinite cosmos; in "As I Ebb'd" they become significant insofar as they mirror the individual human soul. The dramatic shift in scale tells much about the magnitude of change taking place in the mind of the poet.

Form and Structure: A Reader's Guide to Walt Whitman

Gay Wilson Allen

In this excerpt from *A Reader's Guide to Walt Whitman*, noted Whitman scholar Gay Wilson Allen leads the reader through the poem he considers the crowning achievement of Whitman's career, "A Passage to India." Spurred on by technological breakthroughs that brought the world closer together during the late 1800s, Whitman writes of God's cosmic plan to bring the natural world and the world of man into harmony. In the later sections of the poem, which, Allen asserts, neatly break into two parts, the aging poet's concern is his own journey toward death and his desire to become more spirit than body. Gay Wilson Allen taught at New York University and was the author of many books on Whitman, including the biography, *The Solitary Singer.* *[Editors Note: Publisher permits no additions, deletions, or changes to reprinted text. For clarification, please see original source cited below.]*

"Passage to India" is the capstone of Whitman's poetic mythology—not his finest poem (he never really surpassed "Song of Myself"), but the one in which all his theories of the function of poetry and his own ambition to be a "poet-prophet" received final and most nearly coherent expression. One might even say that here he comes nearest to being the "epic" poet some critics[32] have tried to find in his *Leaves of Grass*, but he is a democratized Milton rather than an American Homer.

The seventeenth-century Puritan wrote his Christian epic "to justify the ways of God to man," by which he meant to exonerate God from *injustice* in expelling Adam and Eve from the Garden of Eden, and to reconcile mankind to its inherited curse of

"original sin." Whitman's purpose is not so specifically theological—though it is theological, too, in a broader, more prophetic
sense than Milton's, for he also believes that God created the
earth (the "vast Rondure, swimming in space") for a specific
purpose, and that His will has secretly propelled the human
race through its tumultuous history. By understanding and accepting this plan, mankind can now, Whitman intimates, co-op-
erate in its culminating glory. The poet, the "true son of God," is
the one who can comprehend the plan and "justify" it to
mankind—Whitman uses the word three times, as if to emphasize his Miltonic program.

This is, indeed, a vast program, but Whitman had announced
in his 1855 Preface: "The poets of the kosmos advance through
all interpositions and coverings and turmoils and stratagems to
first principles." More concisely: the "poet of the kosmos" should
indicate the path between reality and the soul.[33] Emerson taught
that man had somehow become separated from nature,[34] and
that salvation lay in healing the breach, which he, like Whitman, strove to accomplish. Whitman's Adam, as we observed of
his "Children of Adam" poems,[35] was prelapsarian; yet Whitman
believed no less firmly than Emerson in the need for restoring a
lost harmony between man and nature, the latter animated by
the breath of Deity.

However, in spite of Whitman's ambition to compete with
Milton, his "Passage to India" can hardly be called an epic
poem except for its range of subject, and he himself intended
it only for an introduction to a collection which would have
(if ever completed) something like the body of an epic. In a
preface to *As a Strong Bird on Pinions Free* (1872), Whitman
revealed his intention to let *Leaves of Grass* stand (in the
1871 edition) as a completed book, "an epic of Democracy,"[36]
and to start a new volume of poems with a more pronounced
"religious purpose." In the same year he published a small
volume entitled *Passage to India,* which he added to *Leaves
of Grass* in 1876, and retained thereafter as a thin cluster. In
his 1876 preface he explained that "*Passage to India,* and its
cluster, are but freer vent and fuller expression to what,
from the first, and so on throughout, more or less lurks in all
my writings, underneath every page, every line, every
where."[37] This poem, then, might be said to epitomize *Leaves
of Grass,* not only the body of poems published by 1871, but
also those that Whitman planned in future years to add to it
for "fuller expression" of its basic intent.

"Passage to India" begins as a topical poem, celebrating three recent epoch-making events: the opening of the Suez Canal, the spanning of the North American continent by railroad, and the completion of the Atlantic cable.[38] Whitman was not alone in looking upon these great engineering feats— "Our modern wonders, (the antique ponderous Seven outvied,)"—as at long last making possible an age of universal peace and brotherhood among the peoples of the world. He begins his poem by "Singing of the great achievements of the present," but they remind him that "the present [is] after all but a growth out of the past"; and in section 2 he turns to the past, takes passage in fantasy to India, the cradle of mankind (as historians then assumed), origin of the oldest myths and fables, of "deep diving bibles" and "the elder religions":

> O you temples fairer than lilies pour'd over by the rising sun!
> O you fables spurning the known, eluding the hold of the
>   known, mounting to heaven!
> You lofty and dazzling towers, pinnacl'd, red as roses,
>   burnish'd with gold!
> Towers of fables immortal fashion'd from mortal dreams!
> You too I welcome and fully the same as the rest!
> You too with joy I sing.

Looking back, he sees "God's purpose from the first":

> The earth to be spann'd, connected by network,
>   races, neighbors, to marry and be given in marriage,
> The oceans to be cross'd, the distance brought near,
> The lands to be welded together.

Therefore, "A worship new I sing," joining to his celebration of explorers, architects, and machinists, the worship of "God's purpose" revealed in their achievements. Once more using musical structure, Whitman envisions the material accomplishments in images of the contemporary newspaper accounts. In section 3 he sees and hears "the locomotives rushing and roaring, and the shrill steamwhistle" reverberating on the plains, over the rivers, through the mountains clear across the continent to the Pacific Ocean. In section 4 he salutes the explorers who in seeking a passage to India discovered America and hastened the end of "man's long probation." Section 5, a paean to the "vast Rondure swimming in space, / Cover'd all over with visible power and beauty," was actually written before the other sections of "Passage to India," and it contains the central idea of the whole poem. In his fantasy of looking down upon the earth from a point high in space (anticipating the astronauts of the twentieth century), he feels that he begins to comprehend the Divine "inscrutable purpose, some hidden prophetic intention . . .":

Down from the garden of Asia descending radiating,
Adam and Eve appear, then their myriad progeny after them,
Wandering, yearning, curious, with restless explorations,
With questionings, baffled, formless, feverish, with never
    happy hearts.
With that sad incessant refrain, *Wherefore unsatisfied soul?*
and *Whither 0 mocking life?*

Ah who shall soothe these feverish children?
Who justify these restless explorations?
Who speak the secret of impassive earth?
Who bind it to us? what is this separate Nature so unnatural?
What is this earth to our affections? (unloving earth,
    without a throb to answer ours,
Cold earth, the place of graves.)

Yet soul be sure the first intent remains, and shall be carried
    out,
Perhaps even now the time has arrived.

Whitman had always striven to be the Orphic poet, but he had never before had a subject which enabled him to make so clear an application of this role, and the application is one which educators and philosophers of the twentieth century were to seek desperately: how to humanize the discoveries and inventions of the explorers, scientists, and engineers. Whitman believes this to be the function of the poet, whom he calls the "true son of God" not because he is in competition with the Christian Son of God but because, like Christ, his life is to be devoted to explaining God's plan of redemption for the human race:

Then not your deeds only O voyagers, O scientists and
    inventors, shall be justified,
All these hearts as of fretted children shall be sooth'd,
All affection shall be responded to, the secret shall be told,
All these separations and gaps shall be taken up and hook'd
    and link'd together,
The whole earth, this cold, impassive, voiceless earth, shall
    be completely justified,
Trinitas divine shall be gloriously accomplish'd and
    compacted by the true son of God, the poet,
(He shall indeed pass the straits and conquer the mountains,
He shall double the cape of Good Hope to some purpose,)
Nature and Man shall be disjoin'd and diffused no more,
The true son of God shall absolutely fuse them.

Christ preached his Gospel, performed miracles with His Father's help, and tried to prepare men and women for God's

Kingdom. This modern poet-son of God has a similar mission to persuade his readers to *see* and comprehend the Utopia in which "All affection shall be responded to," and the breach between man and nature shall be completely healed, "hook'd and link'd together." The poet (artist) works by creating empathy: his readers must see and feel so intensely that they will accept the poet's vision and act upon it. Accordingly, section 6 is a vision of ancient times and people, a montage of human history. In this vision, "the Admiral," Christopher Columbus, appears on the stage at the right time and performs his epical deeds. Though in his personal life he was rewarded by "slander, poverty, and death," he is like the seed planted in the ground (or Frazer's buried god).[39]

> Lies the seed unreck'd for centuries in the ground?
>> lo, to God's due occasion,
> Uprising in the night, it sprouts, blooms,
> And fills the earth with use and beauty.

Of course, one reason for Whitman's strong identification with Columbus was his feeling that he, also a discoverer in the realm of literature and likewise slandered and neglected, would some day be recognized like Columbus and that his *Leaves of Grass* would sprout and bloom and fill "the earth with use and beauty."

Beginning in section 2, Whitman invokes his "soul" to take passage with him back to India and the beginning of history, though until section 7 the invocations are little more than a literary device. But in section 7 this backward journey becomes more personal and psychologically motivated. The poet is still in fantasy circumnavigating the world, back to "primal thought," the "realms of budding bibles," back to "innocent [prelapsarian] intuitions," but this journey becomes in section 8 a quest for more than an imaginative understanding of man's intellectual and religious origins. The poet's spiritual self begins more and more to resemble the Christian concept of "soul." Whitman is now thinking more of his own approaching physical death than of the return to the India of "budding bibles," and his poem becomes a religious lyric—meditative, prayerful, a searching for personal consolation.

> O we can wait no longer,
> We too take ship O soul,
> Joyous we too launch out on trackless seas,
> Fearless for unknown shores on waves of ecstasy to sail,
> Amid the wafting winds, (thou pressing me to thee, I thee to
>> me, O soul,)

Caroling free, singing our song of God,
Chanting our chant of pleasant exploration.

With laugh and many a kiss,
(Let others deprecate, let others weep for sin, remorse,
    humiliation,)
O soul thou pleasest me, I thee.

Ah more than any priest O soul we too believe in God,
But with the mystery of God we dare not dally.

O soul thou pleasest me, I thee,
Sailing these seas or on the hills, or waking in the night,
Thoughts, silent thoughts, of Time and Space and Death,
    like waters flowing.
Bear me indeed as through the regions infinite,
Whose air I breathe, whose ripples hear, lave me all over,
Bathe me O god in thee, mounting to thee,
I and my soul to range in range of thee.

The God to whom the poet prays is of course the same
creator of the "vast Rondure" of section 5:

O Thou transcendent,
Nameless, the fibre and the breath,
Light of the light, shedding forth universes, thou centre of
    them,
Thou mightier centre of the true, the good, the loving,
Thou moral, spiritual fountain—affection's source—thou
    reservoir,
(O pensive soul of me—O thirst unsatisfied—waitest not
    there?
Waitest not haply for us somewhere there the Comrade
    perfect?)
Thou pulse—thou motive of stars, suns, systems,
That, circling, move in order, safe, harmonious,
Athwart the shapeless vastnesses of space,
How should I think, how breathe a single breath, how speak,
    if, out of myself,
I could not launch, to those, superior universes?

This "spiritual fountain" concept of God has traces of
Buddhism (God is an unknowable mystery), of Deism (God
the maker and mover), of Pantheism (God as breath and
pulse), but it is no less anthropomorphic: God is "the Comrade perfect" (a "Calamus" motif) and the "Elder Brother,"
into whose arms the Younger Brother (the poet) melts, almost as in a Christian heaven. However, this final journey
with the soul also resembles the Vedantic return to Brahman, because the poet's soul, his "actual Me," masters the
orbs (stars and planets), mates with Time, smiles at Death,
and fills "the vastness of Space"—see Chari's thesis (page
14).

In section 9 the poet asks rhetorically whether his soul is prepared for such flights to "more than India," to sound "below the Sanskrit and the Vedas." That is, to plunge to the ultimate origin of the intuitions of these sacred writings. Convinced that it is, the poet then bids it to unleash its "bent" (power held in reserve for this purpose), to cut the hawsers, unfurl the sails, and steer for "deep waters only"—into "the seas of God."

The imagery and rhythms of *flowing* are always prominent in Whitman's poetry when he treats the subject of death (as in "The Sleepers," "Out of the Cradle Endlessly Rocking," the latter part of "When Lilacs Last . . ."), and the flowing motif is very effective in some lines (". . . lave me all over, / Bathe me O God . . ."), but at times they become almost a psychological reflex. Section 9 is extremely rhetorical, impassioned, and urgent, but the sailing motif barely escapes (if it does) the triteness of Whitman's ship-of-state cliché in "O Captain! My Captain!" And the poet's identification with Columbus echoes the words of Washington Irving's biography of Columbus (a passage once recited by thousands of school children), "O farther, farther, farther sail!"

"Passage to India" is virtually two poems, the Miltonic "justification" of God's cosmic plan in the first six sections, and in the last three the poet's weariness with the life of "eating and drinking" and his intense longing to become all-spirit.

NOTES

32. See Chapter IV, note 1. [1. Ferner Nuhn, "Leaves of Grass Viewed as an Epic," *Arizona Quarterly*, VII, 324–338 (Winter 1951); James E. Miller, "America's Epic," in *A Critical Guide to Leaves of Grass* (Chicago, 1957), 256–261; Roy Harvey Pearce, *The Continuity of American Poetry* (Princeton, 1961), 69–83.]

33. Preface, 1855 edition, *Leaves of Grass: Comprehensive Reader's Edition*, 714.

34. Cf. especially "Nature."

35. See p. 69 [of original source].

36. *Leaves of Grass: Comprehensive Reader's Edition*, 739.

37. *Ibid.*, 745.

38. *Walt Whitman's Poems*, ed. G.W. Allen and C.T. Davis (New York, 1955), 243–248.

39. Fraser, "The Ritual of Death and Resurrection," *Golden Bough*, 692 ff.

Catalogues and Meaning in "Crossing Brooklyn Ferry"

Stanley K. Coffman Jr.

One of Walt Whitman's most prevalent techniques is his use of catalogues, or strings of objects and impressions. Stanley K. Coffman Jr. here shows how Whitman took Ralph Waldo Emerson's suggestion about the poetry in "bare lists of words," then manipulated his lists into catalogues that suggest the very meaning of his poem. "Crossing Brooklyn Ferry" incorporates both the spiritual and the physical worlds, and through his lists Whitman suggests that we must accept not just the higher spiritual values, but the physical world as well, in all of its wonderful variety. Stanley K. Coffman has taught at the University of Oklahoma. He is the author of *Imagism: A Chapter for the History of Modern Poetry.*

The justification for the "bare lists of words" which mark the Whitman poem is usually found in Emerson's essay on "The Poet": "Bare lists of words are found suggestive to an imaginative and excited mind." According to Emerson, the universe is the externalization of the soul, and its objects symbols, manifestations of the one reality behind them. Words which name objects also carry with them the whole sense of nature and are themselves to be understood as symbols. Thus a list of words (objects) will be effective in giving to the mind, under certain conditions, a heightened sense not only of reality but of the variety and abundance of its manifestations.

It is perfectly possible that a transcendentalist, who sees reality in a special way, might find the catalogue suggestive, though it is worth noting that Emerson qualifies this—an "excited mind." If one is a transcendentalist, he can accept the

Reprinted from "'Crossing Brooklyn Ferry': A Note on the Catalogue Technique in Whitman's Poetry," by Stanley K. Coffman Jr., *Modern Philology,* vol. 51, no. 4, May 1954. Reprinted by permission of The University of Chicago Press.

words in these lists as metonyms [symbols of Larger Ideas]; not exclusively or even primarily interested in the form of the poem, he can substitute the sign for the thing signified, or, for purposes of poetry, he can reverse the process and be satisfied with their effectiveness. But not many readers will be content with this; if the catalogues are to be successful, they must function in such a way that their meaning comes from within the poem and not from reference to something outside it. . . .

PATTERNS IN WHITMAN'S LISTS

Whitman turned Emerson's passing comment into a major technique of his verse, but there may also have been some question in his mind about the adequacy of the purely philosophical argument for the catalogue. Occasionally, and on important occasions, he manipulated his lists so carefully that they are not fairly to be described as "catalogues," ordered them so that they became aesthetically expressive, conveyed meaning by their form. The catalogues in "Crossing Brooklyn Ferry" are excellent examples of what he could do with the device.

Two sections of this poem, 3 and 9, consist almost wholly of lists, but they are by no means "bare lists." In section 3 the catalogue begins with the sea gulls:

> Watched the Twelfth-month sea-gulls, saw them high in the air
>   floating with motionless wings, oscillating their bodies,
> Saw how the glistening yellow lit up parts of their bodies and
>   left the rest in strong shadow.

There is an abundance of concrete detail here, mainly appealing to the sense of sight and the sense of motion. This first image in the long series begins by directing the imaginative vision upward, where it is immediately held by the floating, oscillating motion of the birds, and then is concentrated upon their colors, sharply contrasting light and darkness. Out of these details the whole passage grows. The motion of the gulls continues in their "slow-wheeling circles" and "gradual edging toward the south"; then is repeated in the flying vapor, the "swinging motion of the hulls," perhaps in the "serpentine" pennants, the white "wake," the "whirl" of the wheels, the "scallop-edged waves," "the ladled cups," the frolicsome "crests." The light imagery, beginning with the "glistening yellow" of the gulls, extends through the "reflection of the summer sky in the water," the "beams," the "spokes of light" in the "sunlit water," the haze and the vapor flying in "fleeces," the "white" sails, the "pennants," the "white" wake, the "glistening" crests. "Crests," in fact, contains overtones of *both* light and motion, as do "shimmering," the "white" wake, and the figure of the "centrifugal spokes of light."

However, the pattern established by recurring images of a particular motion and a particular color undergoes a change as the catalogue proceeds, a change effected naturally and realistically within the scene at hand, a sunset scene. The exhilaration and buoyancy achieved by the clusters of light and motion images are altered with "The flags of all nations, the falling of them at sunset." The waves are now seen in "twilight," and the imaginative vision is no longer so markedly directed upward and toward the horizon; instead, it is necessarily fixed by the failing light upon what is immediately before it, the docks, the ships in the river, a "shadowy group." An image pattern carefully prepared for in the contrast of light *and* dark on the gulls' bodies, in the motion of birds away toward the south and out of the scene, and in the "violet" tinge on the fleecelike vapor, has now become dominant. As the sense of motion becomes a falling one, losing its vigor and soaring quality, so the light, glistening, shimmering, changes to shadows and darkness and then to the "wild red and yellow" of the foundry fires burning into the "night"; the flags fall at sunset, and the firelight, though it burns spasmodically in the night ("flicker" echoes the original, majestic, oscillating light of the gulls), ultimately is cast "down," into the "clefts of streets."

We observe, then, that the images of this catalogue are presented as lists but that the list is not of separate objects, each of which, according to transcendentalist theory, becomes symbolic of the whole. At least, the catalogue does not depend for its expressive value upon any philosophical assumptions about the nature of the word. Instead, the words become effective as they function in the context of other words, which is to say, they become effective aesthetically: they work through a pattern of motion and light, which is first established and then altered. Their status as individual symbols disappears in the sense of a single pattern of motion and light, first evoking exhilaration, which gradually gives way to a feeling of the forbidden and threatening in the fire and darkness. There is no question but that certain of the images are symbolic; the figure of the head, with its halo of divinity, reflected in the water certainly has this meaning; but even this is subordinated to the total effect, which becomes the aim and result of this catalogue.

COMPARING CATALOGUES

The changes which take place are more sharply defined when the reader compares this catalogue with the one that concludes the poem. He is struck by the reappearance in section 8 of, first, the "sunset," then the "scallop-edg'd waves," and, finally, the "sea-gulls oscillating their bodies," the "hay-boat" and the "belated lighter." In section 8 these details are only a part of a passage of rhetorical questions, but they (and the rhetorical nature of the questions) prepare for section 9, which is again a listing of details. These, as might now be expected, are basically the same as in section 3. There are the "crested" and frolicsome waves; and once again the "scallop-edg'd" epithet is applied to them, as once again the sea gulls are seen wheeling "in large circles high in the air." There are the summer sky reflected in the water, the spokes of light about the poet's reflection, the ships, the white sails, the flags; and the foundries once again cast their red and yellow light into the darkness.

A CHANGE IN TONE

But there is also a number of differences. The first is a difference in tone, which derives in part from the imperative mode of the verb that is used throughout to begin the lines, giving them conviction and assurance that they did not have before. Though the objects named are the same, though the sunset occurs and with it the falling motion and the disappearance of natural light, the awareness of this is overcome by the force of the imperative—"Flaunt away, flags . . . be duly lower'd at sunset." Though the light changes to the glare of foundry chimneys, Whitman defies this wildness—"Burn high . . . cast black shadows . . . cast red and yellow light . . . !" And the final motion is not a falling one; the fires are commanded to cast their light "over the tops" of the houses, but not then down into the streets. Other details are reintroduced in such a way as to reinforce the difference; "Stand up, tall masts of Mannahatta! stand up, beautiful hills of Brooklyn," for example, transforms the masts and hills, previously only mentioned, into images that intensify the quality of soaring and exhilaration in a new and final way.

STRUCTURE OF THE POEM

The two catalogues are, however, so basically similar in imagery that a parallelism between them is inescapable, and they are further related by the fact that in tone they are the poem's passages of greatest intensity, even though the quality of elation is lost in one (it does not lose its intensity) and maintained in the other. Occurring as they do at the middle and end of the poem, they provide an over-all framework, a structural basis upon which the poem rests. It rises in intensity to section 3, breaks, and rises again to the climax in section 9, an organization emphasized by the flat, prosaic statement of the brief section 4, which serves as a kind of punctuation. And this structure forces the reader to question its meaning. Why is the feeling altered in section 3 and sus-

WHITMAN'S CATALOGUES

John Ciardi, one of America's premier poets and translators, and Miller Williams, who served as the inaugural poet for Bill Clinton in 1997, suggest that we can tell much about the workings of Whitman's mind by noting what the poet includes and what he leaves out in his catalogues.

Simple statements of fact, and even the simple names of things, convey sensory suggestion. One very definite sort of effect can be achieved in poetry by the device called the catalogue, which consists simply of a list of names of things, or of sensory impressions, though in practice the catalogue tends to become a mixture of both names and metaphors. Walt Whitman has used the catalogue more extensively than any poet writing in English. The following passage from "Song of Myself" will illustrate both the basic quality of the catalogue as a simple listing of things, and the tendency for some metaphoric comparison to become involved in the list. As a first exercise, one might do well to underline every element in the catalogue that is simply the name of a thing, and to circle every element that involves some sort of metaphoric comparison.

Song of Myself (26)

Now I will do nothing but listen,
To accrue what I hear into this song, to let sounds contribute
    toward it.

I hear the bravuras of birds, bustle of growing wheat, gossip of
    flames, clack of sticks cooking my meals.
I hear the sound I love, the sound of the human voice,
I hear all sounds running together, combined, fused or following,
Sounds of the city and sounds out of the city, sounds of the day
    and night,
Talkative young ones to those that like them, the loud laugh of
    work-people at their meals,

tained and intensified in section 9? What has happened between sections 3 and 9 that finally enables the poet to keep his assurance in the naming of the catalogue's objects? What significance is there to the inclusion of new images in the final catalogue?

It can be shown that the catalogues not only function as patterns of imagery which have different effects upon the reader as patterns but, by their differing effects, provide the key to the meaning of the poem. In other words, they are expressive aesthetically not only in themselves but within the larger over-all structure of the poem. In section 1 Whitman

> The angry bass of disjointed friendship, the faint tones of the sick,
> The judge with hands tight to the desk, his pallid lips pronouncing a death-sentence,
> The heave'e'yo of stevedores unlading ships by the wharves, the refrain of the anchor-lifters,
> The ring of alarm-bells, the cry of fire, the whirr of swift-streaking engines and hose-carts with premonitory tinkles and color'd lights,
> The steam-whistle, the solid roll of the train of approaching cars,
> The slow march play'd at the head of the association marching two and two,
> (They go to guard some corpse, the flag-tops are draped with black muslin.)
>
> I hear the violincello, ('tis the young man's heart's complaint,)
> I hear the key'd cornet, it slides quickly through my ears,
> It shakes mad-sweet pangs through my belly and breast.
>
> I hear the chorus, it is a grand opera,
> Ah this indeed is music—this suits me.
>
> A tenor large and fresh as the creation fills me,
> The orbic flex of his mouth is pouring and filling me full.
>
> I hear the train'd soprano (what work with hers is this?)
> The orchestra whirls me wider than Uranus flies,
> It wrenches such ardors from me I did not know I possessed them,
> It sails me, I dab with bare feet, they are licked by the indolent waves,
> I am cut by bitter and angry hail, I lose my breath,
> Steep'd amid honey'd morphine, my windpipe throttled in fakes of death,
> At length let up again to feel the puzzle of puzzles,
> And that we call Being.

John Ciardi and Miller Williams, *How Does a Poem Mean?* Second Edition. Boston: Houghton Mifflin, 1975.

had introduced the materials of his poem: the flood-tide and the clouds, objects of nature; the crowds of people, which, like the natural world, are seen as external to him, to his self. There is no comment other than this; but he has established the basis for a question that is of recurring importance in his verse: What is the relationship of the "I" of the individual identity to that which is external to it? More specifically in the terms of this poem: What is the status of the physical and objective and what attitude shall we assume toward it?

Then in section 2 he dwells at more length upon both external "things" and the "others," considering the human being in this poem, as is clear from his introductory section, from this point of view. Now, however, he *uses* the external, both human and nonhuman, to heighten his sense of the oneness of all experience, that is, tending to ignore the status of individualization in his concentration upon the unity of the spiritual reality behind it. Uppermost in his mind is the "simple, compact, well-join'd scheme" into which every object, as individual, is disintegrated; in place of things, he sees the "sustenance" derived from them; in place of past and future, the "similitudes" between them; in place of single images, the "glories strung like beads"; in place of the "others," the "ties between me and them." Specifically, he dwells upon the feeling of oneness with the men and women of the future, who will encounter the same externals, the same images; and, since these will be his readers, he is hoping to reach them through the objects as bridges. As usual in his major poems, he is making some comment on the problems of the poet or his poetry.

The direction in which he is moving becomes clear with the opening lines of section 3, which presents the first catalogue, or extensive listing of objects: "It avails not, time nor place—distance avails not." Dissolving the categories of time and space in his contemplation of that outside him, he loses his awareness of its individuality and of his own and approaches the mystic experience of mergence with a transcendent reality. From a short incantatory stanza, continuing the incantatory style of section 2, with its suggestion of a magical invoking of a spiritual reality in which all identity disappears, he moves into the first climax of the poem, the catalogue where the objects flow in upon him, where he becomes them, where a rapport with life is felt through the inescapably positive tone of the passage.

As we have seen, however, the mood passes, is altered; the exhilaration of the opening lines is transformed, with the sense of the original motion falling and failing, in the presence of the foundries, the darkness of the city's streets, as if these were the objects which did not suit the visionary unity and therefore broke the sense of it. There is no question but that the last objects in the list are presented as alien and forbidding, and it would appear that Whitman is now further complicating his subject. In addition to considering the human as well as the natural object, he is to cope with the manmade, the object that is typical of his own modern industrial civilization. After the short series of comments in section 4, whose past tense and matter-of-fact tone admit the change of mood, come the questions that open section 5 and indicate further that his first approach to an understanding of the physical and objective has not been wholly successful:

What is it then between us?
What is the count of the scores or hundreds of years between us?

The questions are only partially rhetorical. To a certain extent they may be seen as such, suggesting that in the mysticism of the catalogue passage he has transcended time and space (and reached the modern reader). But the organization of the poem, and especially the nature of what follows in its second major division, call for further consideration of their meaning. In section 5 he begins again with the assertion that the categories of time and space do not really matter, but he develops his poem now from a totally different point of view, which in one sense denies what he has just said about them. If in the first division of the poem (secs. 1–3) he has been concerned with an attitude of what in the 1855 "Preface" he calls *sympathy,* he now becomes concerned with its opposite, *pride;* the emphasis now is upon the "I," the self (note, in this connection, his revisions of the poem which cut the "I" from four of the first five lines of the first catalogue).

In section 6, then, he is attending to the self and, with particular reference to the ugly side of identity, the "wolf, the snake, the hog." That this emphasis is productive is clear from the opening line of section 7: "Closer yet I approach you." He is closer to the "others" of the future (as they are to him) for his recognition of the ugly, the sensual, the elements in his own nature normally thought of as separating him from others. And, as these elements are of the senses, of the physical, they create a basis for sympathy for all objects, all "things," as he says: "I too had been struck from the float forever held in solution." This is, of course, a different kind of sympathy from that of the first division of the poem, where the physical nature of things or of the self was not recognized as having its own separate and unique character. The metaphor of the float held in solution, which contains the answer to the problems studied in the poem, is crude and difficult to handle, but it is central and deserves special comment.

IMPORTANCE OF THE PHYSICAL WORLD

As the problem of the nature of the physical, objective world is stated here, it resembles the problem of evil, as the transcendentalist might define it, but considered more specifically and realistically than was usual for this philosophy. Whitman recognized very clearly the limitations imposed by the senses, by that which gave his physical nature as well as that of the rest of the external world. The identity provided by the physical gives the sense of life, the awareness of life; but, by virtue of its physicality, it presents at the same time the problem of divisiveness and separateness and the potential for the ugly and evil. Thus evil is regarded in somewhat the same way as in the Christian myth of the Fall, though without placing the burden for the Fall upon man. In order to become man, he must assume the physical, with its limitations; and were he not to become man, the existence in which Whitman so positively believed as the end of all Life would not be possible, the spiritual itself being by itself without meaning or significance.

These implications are more fully developed elsewhere, as in "Out of the Cradle." For the present poem, we find Whitman's meaning expressed in the closing lines, as he addresses the "dumb, beautiful ministers":

> You have waited, you always wait, you dumb, beautiful ministers,
> We receive you with free sense at last, and are insatiate henceforward,
> Not you any more shall be able to foil us, or withhold yourselves from us,
> We use you, and do not cast you aside—we plant you permanently within us,
> We fathom you not—we love you—there is perfection in you also,
> You furnish your parts toward eternity,
> Great or small, you furnish your parts toward the soul.

The conclusion which he reaches in "Crossing Brooklyn Ferry" is that the physical is necessary that we may learn the meaning of spiritual reality but that it must for this reason be allowed to maintain its physical and objective reality; and, though this reality may be seen to have its limitations, these are not only shared by all objects but must be accepted as inevitable accompaniments of the way in which the reality of the spirit can be made manifest. We do not gain in understanding them, *or* spiritual reality, if we attempt to ignore or dissolve their real existence. They must remain objects, dumb but beautiful in their ministering to us.

This would be true of all manifestations, not only those in the world of nature, but those that are man-made; thus the fires of the foundries are no longer seen as alien, or their status as real ignored, but are accepted with all their apparent limitations, like all the objective world. Thus, too, other humans are encouraged to maintain their objectivity, their individuality, in a more balanced, less extremely idealistic view of life. Paradoxically, Whitman approaches the reader of later generations more closely by insisting upon the individuality and objective reality of himself and the reader than by "transcending" this in an idealist's unity. The final catalogue, then, includes the young men, the other humans, and the affirmative images of the city objects, with a clearly defined understanding of their status:

> Expand, being than which none else is perhaps more spiritual,
> Keep your places, objects than which none else is more lasting.

SYMPATHY VERSUS PRIDE

The over-all structure of the poem, on the basis of this interpretation, may be seen to reflect the motion of the ferry, which gives the poem its present title and a background symbol that insures its specific meaning. The poem moves between two extremes, or from one extreme to another, each tested in the presence of the objects of the catalogues. Using Whitman's terminology, the first extreme may be designated as *sympathy*, i.e., loss of the sense of self, transcendence of it, so that the individual soul may become one with the world-soul and experience the conviction of unity in variety. When, however, the objective world is approached in this way alone, it becomes, at the close of the first catalogue, alien; it excludes the poet, who is now, for the moment, separate from it. In spite of Whitman's description of this as the approach through sympathy, it is, for the theme of

this poem, clearly not adequate in itself; if it is not supple-
mented by its opposite, it provides no key to the significance of
the external world.

The other extreme is that of *pride*, in Whitman's vocabulary
a designation for intense, concentrated awareness of self, even
though in this case the awareness is primarily of the unpleasant
aspects of individuality. In preparation for his second approach
to the external, he assumes an attitude directly opposed to the
first one; and, as it emphasizes the physical in him, it leads him
to regard the physical in other "objects" and thus to respect their
identities as he respects his own (though it is also true that he
respects his own more after seeing it as a link between the self
and the external world). The result is, as has been indicated, the
ability to sustain his ecstasy in their presence and, accepting variety in unity, to identify himself more securely with them, to
achieve another sympathy now, which has its source in respect
for objectivity and individuality.

THE ACCEPTANCE OF VARIETY

As the motion of the boat is from one shore to the other, so the
movement of consciousness is, characteristically for Whitman,
from an extreme of awareness of soul, which is single and universal, to the other extreme of awareness of the physical, which
forms the soul into self and which thus constitutes the basis for
the identities of the world. Each of these provides a way of
knowing the external and thus leads to a catalogue of objects
seen in an ecstasy of understanding. This movement is perhaps
to be felt also in the rise and fall of the tide and certainly in the
oscillating motion of the imagery in the two catalogues; but it is
equally important not to ignore the tone of the closing stanza.
Like many of his final passages, this reflects a modification of
tone, in that it suggests a more subdued level of calm resolution
and assurance, which have been achieved out of the play of opposites or extremes. The poet speaks from a point of view that
has achieved a proper balance between these opposites, and
thus the poem moves from a sense of unity in variety to the opposed (and for the transcendentalist just as valid) sense of variety in unity, and finally to a steady acceptance of the variety
on its own terms.

"The Sleepers": Whitman's Dream of World Harmony

Anne Waldman

Anne Waldman uses a line from the French poet Arthur Rimbaud, "I Is Another," as a way to suggest the empathy and restorative power Whitman holds for poetry in "The Sleepers." Waldman traces the poem's movement from a descent into a dream world of death to a vision of the entire world restored and joined together in harmony. This poem upholds Whitman's reputation as the poet of democracy. In Whitman's final vision, love restores, heals, and brings together all of mankind. Anne Waldman is a performance poet who has published numerous books of poetry including "Baby Breakdown" (1970), "Fast Speaking Woman" (1975), "Makeup on Empty Space" (1983), "Iovis: All is Full of Jove" (1993), and "Troubairitz" (1993). She has taught at the Jack Kerouac School of Disembodied Poetics at Naropa Institute.

Walt Whitman's poem "The Sleepers" opens with the line "I wander all night in my vision" and proceeds to describe the poet's travels in his nocturnal imagination. With unflagging enthusiasm, he pictures a host of colorful sleepers, meeting them "face to face," "bending with open eyes" over their "shut eyes": children in cradles, drunkards, married couples, corpses, "sacred idiots," and the blind. Moving from bedside to bedside, he lists a great variety of slumberers. Then, as if exemplifying [French poet] Arthur Rimbaud's "I is another," he expands further, empathizing with all of them: actor, actress, voter, politician, emigrant, exile, stammerer, male and female, beloved and lover, requited and unrequited. There is a wonderful and unexpected moment

Reprinted from "The 'I' Is Another," by Anne Waldman, in *The Teachers and Writers Guide to Walt Whitman*, edited by Ron Padgett (New York: Teachers and Writers Collaborative, 1991). Copyright © 1991 by Teachers and Writers Collaborative. Reprinted by permission of the Teachers and Writers Collaborative.

when his excitement drives him further into his poem:

> O hotcheeked and blushing! O foolish hectic!
> O for pity's sake, no one must see me now! . . . my clothes
>   were stolen while I was abed,
> Now I am thrust forward, where shall I run?

Many of us have had similar dreams of finding ourselves seriously underdressed.

A DESCENT INTO DEATH

The next section of the poem is different. In it, none of the figures are sleeping, and the poet descends not into sleep but into death. Whitman suddenly ages and identifies with an old woman darning her grandson's socks, next with a "sleepless widow looking out on the winter midnight," then with the light of the stars glittering on the snow. The cold and pallor of the snow lead him to seeing a shroud, and, with typical Whitmanic magic, he becomes the shroud, on a corpse underground. Like the tribal shaman (or anyone who has just gotten a good report after a scary visit to the doctor), the one who returns from the underworld tells the living to value what they have: "It seems to me that everything in the light and air ought to be happy; / Whoever is not in his coffin and the dark grave, let him know he has enough."

The third section describes a "beautiful gigantic swimmer" who struggles against sea waves that bash him around until he drowns. This peculiar and haunting section sounds as though it might have come from one of Whitman's own dreams.

Section 4 is something of a continuation of section 3: "I turn but do not extricate myself." Standing on a beach, the poet witnesses a shipwreck at night: "I hear the burst as she strikes. . . . I hear the howls of dismay. . . ." He searches the beach "with the crowd," and in the morning helps "pick up the dead and lay them in rows in a barn."

The fifth section begins with more death imagery (a description of George Washington weeping over the slaughter of his young soldiers) but it veers off into what sounds like a tableau vivant of the General bidding good-bye to his army. Whitman doesn't tell us whether these are dream scenes or historical scenes that, in the memory, take on the aura of dreams.

He is more explicit in section 6: "Now I tell what my mother told me today as we sat at dinner together." One morning, when his mother was still living at home with her parents, an astonishingly beautiful Indian woman wandered in and stayed until the middle of the afternoon, and then she left, never to be seen again. His mother had wanted her to stay, and missed her terribly, and remembered her all those years. The section concludes with a curse against Lucifer, who separates people, who interferes and permeates all experience with death.

Restoring the World

As if the poet has had enough of death, section 7 builds into a quiet ode to the beauty of all the dreaming persons the poet has observed in his peripatetic vision. The poem is infused with "love and summer," and everything is made right: the immigrants and exiles return to their homelands, where they are welcomed warmly. Everyone is made equal and restored, made beautiful in the "dim night," individuals united in a cosmic peace.

But Whitman goes even further; in section 8 he joins whole continents together:

> The Asiatic and African are hand in hand .. the European and American are hand in hand,
> Learned and unlearned are hand in hand .. and male and female are hand in hand.

These repetitions have a lulling, soothing effect, as this section rises into an ecstatic hymn of "matings." The sexes embrace, parents embrace children, teachers students, masters slaves. The ill are restored to health: the insane become sane, the paralyzed supple. Whitman's vision performs miracles! His voice is vatic—exorcizing evil, embracing the cosmos, healing those in strife and pain—but, at the same time, surprisingly down-to-earth.

The closing lines of "The Sleepers" invoke and salute the night that is the archetypal Mother, the poet's muse, the *sine qua non* [essential element] for what has happened in the poem. The poet himself was "yielded" (born) from night. Night has allowed his illumination of a unified and perfected humanity, and so he acknowledges his muse's power.

A Straightforward Poem

"The Sleepers" is a fairly straightforward poem. Its language is accessible. In his open letter to Emerson, included in the second edition of *Leaves of Grass*, Whitman proclaimed that he would "meet people and The States face to face"—the way he meets the sleepers in the poem—"to confront them with an American rude tongue," by which he meant ordinary, vernacular language. The poem is also straightforward in that it comes directly from the poet's heart. Without the intermediary of symbols or "literary" maneuvering, the reader experiences both the trajectory of a powerful revelation and his or her own place in it. Whitman's vision is of a true democracy, in which our strength is a "unity in diversity." There is room for everyone in this attractive, healing vision, in which everyone in the entire world is in love with everyone else.

We can't be sure how the poem was composed, but because "The Sleepers" is a rather long poem, it would have been difficult to write in one sitting. Notice the shifts in mood between the different sections, and how the poem picks up the same theme again and again, but introduces and colors it in different ways. Although it has an undeniable flow and continuity, it starts and stops. It reiterates constantly. Notice, too, how within stanzas Whitman uses dots, dashes, semicolons, and colons to keep the poem moving along, and how he uses periods (or other stop punctuation) at the end of each stanza. For example, the first stanza of section 8 (which includes fourteen very long lines) opens with "The sleepers are very beautiful as they lie unclothed" and proceeds to describe those sleepers in a list that is enhanced by punctuation that keeps the flow alive and fluid, as in:

> The felon steps forth from the prison . . . . the insane becomes
>   sane . . . . the suffering of sick persons is relieved,
> The sweatings and fevers stop . . . the throat that was unsound
>   is sound . . . the lungs of the consumptive are resumed . . .
>   the poor distressed head is free . . .

eventually moving to a last line that calls the whole stanza together in a final end-stop: "They pass the invigoration of the night and the chemistry of the night and awake." After a breath, the next stanza's opening line shifts the focus abruptly to the personal "I": "I too pass from the night." Whitman also varies the pace of his poem by questioning and exclaiming, as in "The murderer that is to be hung next day . . . . how does he sleep? / And the murdered person . . . . how does he sleep?" or "What are you doing you ruffianly red-trickled waves?" and "I am a dance . . . . Play up there! the fit is whirling me fast" or "O love and summer! you are in the dreams and in me." He also skillfully exercises the present tense throughout, giving the poem its immediacy, timelessness, and "averaging" aspect. We are thrust into a permanent state of inspiring—and ironically active—slumber.

READING "THE SLEEPERS"

Read "The Sleepers" the way it was written: with feelings and senses open. Feel the pulse of the language, the heave of Whitman's lines. (You could read it aloud solo or with others reading individual lines.) As you read, visualize the sleepers, as Whitman does; let your mind and imagination expand. Try not to hold back. You might make a list of the active verbs he uses—almost all his verbs, as noted, are in the present tense. Notice how he uses the pronoun "I" and how that contrasts with his descriptions of others. Notice also how we move back and forth from his imagined and projected vision to his more experiential "personal" vision. The former is all-inclusive; the latter seems linked particularly to the poet's own psychological need to reshape the world through the act of writing. Do we share the same need, or is it enough to be included in his fantasy of a united humanity? It is intriguing to think about where we are situated, as audience. Between the two? Somewhere between sleeping and waking?

Whitman's *Calamus* Poems: Desire and Fears

Bettina L. Knapp

Whitman's *Calamus* poems were for years interpreted as celebratory of male bonding, but it was no
secret that the poems were also suggestive of homosexual love. Bettina L. Knapp here explains the dual
meaning of the word "calamus" and interprets a
number of the more well-known poems in the collection. The poems are often thinly veiled accounts
of sexual love, and Whitman's desires and fears
come across strongly throughout the volume. Bettina
L. Knapp has taught at Hunter College. She is the author of numerous books on literary figures including
Emily Dickinson, Edgar Allan Poe, and others.

Calamus may be considered a meditation on the mysticality
of friendship, love, and the sexual act. While Whitman calls
for the creation of a secret camaraderie, by inference, among
homosexuals, bonding is also to be effected on a larger scale,
universally and politically—thus helping to democratize society the world over. Songs of loneliness, urgings for long-
lasting and solid relationships between men, the *Calamus*
poems leave the reader with a yearning for connectedness,
not only between couples, but between the poet and the society of which he is a part.

CALAMUS DEFINED

The "calamus" (Greek, *kalamos*) is a plant, stalk, or grass
with long, narrow leaves and a phallic-looking root resem-
bling the penis and testes. Because it grows near ponds and
marshes, that is, in secluded areas—"in paths untrodden"—it
is identified with the poet in general and Whitman in particu-

lar: a man who felt alienated from society because of his outspokenness on sexual matters. On the other hand, because of the calamus's shape, it becomes a metaphor for Eros, love and relatedness, a way of life the poet felt was crucial to his vision of democratic America.

In that *calamus* (Arabic, *qalam*) also means the quill of a feather, used as a pen in the West until the fifteenth century, such an image may also suggest the metier of the writer. In Islamic tradition, it is believed that Allah created the qalam out of light a thousand years before he brought anything else into being. When he ordered the qalam to write, it shuddered and asked: "What must I write?" Allah answered: "Destiny." As a symbol of universal intelligence, light then flowed from its point as ink from a pen and it began inscribing onto sacred tablets all that was to happen until the Resurrection. Thus was a new world order ushered in via the word—for Islam and for Whitman.

Since *calamus*, symbolized by the pen, conflated spirituality and mentation [mental activity], as well as physicality, in that it also represented the phallus, Whitman's title indicated a generative force within the universe. It linked essentials— the sexual with the sacred—thus substituting earthly multiplicity (and frequently discord), for spiritual and physical oneness during the period of gestation: prior to the birth of the poem.

DREAMS OF A UTOPIAN SOCIETY

Idealistic, even simplistic, Whitman, a true utopian, failed in his grand scheme of things to take human nature into account. Since time immemorial, prophets, philosophers, man-gods, and saviors have planted their credo into the hearts and minds of humanity with little or no resulting amelioration of earthly tragedies. Still, no diminution of attempts to find an answer to life's dilemmas was forthcoming in Whitman's day. Economists and political scientists had been busy creating societies that would, they hoped, bring financial and spiritual stability into being, basing their ideas on the fundamental principle of love and camaraderie. . . .

Whitman's ideal society existed in his mind alone—as a dream, an illusion enshrouded in maya's [the appearance of the world] veil. Not a philosopher per se, although he loved to philosophize, Whitman was above all a poet. And, in *Calamus*, he was a deeply poignant poet of homosexual love. The *Cala-*

mus cluster reveals not only a restless and anguished psyche, but a condition of ambivalence concerning his "secret." Despite his courageous proclamation to Emerson that he would speak the truth about his sexual proclivities, he did so only in veiled, ambiguous, and illusive terms. Understandably, perhaps. Had he not felt the stigma of being marginalized in a heterosexual society?

Love between men in *Calamus*, and elsewhere in *Leaves of Grass*, is most frequently presented under a disguise: via symbols, allusions, conceits, role-playing (substituting a female for a male lover), equivocal metaphors, coded language. Other strategies are also used by Whitman as a means of obfuscation: by alternating highly lyrical and/or cacophonous sonorities, he sweeps the reader into his *feeling* realm, thereby submerging any kind of objective understanding of the true nature of his sexual inclinations. . . .

A NEED TO LOVE AND BE LOVED

Emotionally spent at times, hence frequently subject to periods of despondency, Whitman . . . frequently underwent a numinous [supernatural] experience: moments of religious ecstasy. Bursting with excitement, filled with a sense of liberation, he yielded during these privileged instances to his impulses, which blossomed into what seemed like endless verbal permutations and constructs.

Although the *Calamus* poems have no dramatic continuity and Whitman was forever changing and reordering them for new editions, a prevailing need is evident in all of them: the desire to bind himself to another—*to love* and *be loved*. Confessional to a certain extent, although this tone was probably a poetic strategy to deceive his readers further by masking his real intent, some of his *Calamus* poems remind one of conversations with a dear friend—or even of seductions. Similar dialogues in prose are inscribed in his Notebooks: they were his means of explaining himself to his audiences, of revealing his sorrows, as well as his spiritual and physical needs.

"IN PATHS UNTRODDEN"

Whitman invites his readers "In Paths Untrodden" to follow him on a journey defined as a search for adhesiveness—a higher form of male love. As leader and guiding power of a new society and religious approach to life, the poet takes his disciples on mysterious walks into unknown areas. Although the verb *to tread* means to walk, dance, step, beat, crush, trample, or subdue, it also refers to copulation with regard to male birds. Since Cro-Magnon times, birds have been identified with the soul, as attested to in the Lascaux cave paintings and in later religious and literary texts, including [the ancient Greek philosopher] Plato's *Dialogues.* Whitman's linkage between soul, walking, and population suggests a need for that potent connecting cosmic principle—love.

> In paths untrodden,
> In the growth by margins of pond-waters,
> Escaped from the life that exhibits itself,
> From all the standards hitherto publish'd, from the pleasures, profits, conformities.

As the prophet of a new society and father figure for male youth, the poet will lead/lure and tread with them—and the reader as well—into unknown dimensions: those marshy lands where the phallic calamus plants grow. There they will be awakened, enlightened, spiritualized—initiated into a new world. In isolation, like the initiates of old—the word *initiate* is derived from the Latin *initium,* "going within," meaning "to enter"—the poet's followers will penetrate into fresh territories: open the door onto a different way of viewing life. Only by experiencing deeper insights into the life process may initiates pass from a so-called inferior or superficial state of understanding to a superior one. Only then may they begin to realize their potential.

In the all-male environment into which the poet lures the reader, the initiate finds himself in a position to receive secrets that would have otherwise been denied him, thus paving the way for him to be reborn into another domain. Perils, nevertheless, are implicit in the renunciation of the world. So are inexpressible joys.

> That the soul of the man I speak for rejoices in comrades,
> Here by myself away from the clank of the world,
> Tallying and talk'd to here by tongues aromatic,
> No longer abash'd (for in this secluded spot I can respond as I would not dare elsewhere.)

That he feels free to convey his feelings in a *temenos,* or sacred space, far from society, yields the poet ineffable pleasure. Yet, the experience of polarities is crucial in the learning and love experience. Were he to remain far from the madding crowd and live out an ideal relationship with a partner for a protracted period of time without the application of judgmental faculties, stasis, aridity, or a mechanical quality in the love experience could ensue. The same is true of the individuals who refuse to follow the poet into "paths untrodden": their daily activities become rote. To fracture and fragment the known, to venture into untapped areas, paves the way for deepening relationships, while also opening the door onto greater riches.

What Whitman offers his reader in dazzling arrays of images, powerful rhythms, and visceral tonalities are revelations of a whole secreted shadowy realm. The new insights gleaned, he hopes, will serve to overthrow society's restrictive "standards," which he considers deleterious to the individual and thus to society as a whole. To his readers, he offers pleasure and not sorrow, freedom and not constriction. Yet, in Whitman's use of harsh, unpleasant guttural and palatal sounds, as in the word *clank* ("Here by myself away from the clank of the world") and *abash* ("No longer abash'd"), he is also warning those who seek to follow him that strength, perseverance, even heroism, are needed to "dare" cut free from the crowd and live out one's existence in a "secluded" world—perhaps as a pariah.

Among the calamus, and far from social reproach and oppression, the poet sings out his song—born from his needs and cast from his desire for "manly attachment." Far from the world of deceptions and difficulties, his *temenos* has yielded him nutritive and gestating powers, which he now realizes have extended and completed himself in "this delicious Ninth-month in my forty-first year." Ready for rebirth, he sings the purity of each new love episode.

> To tell the secret of my night and days,
> To celebrate the need of comrades.

Is the poet really free, as he claims to be? Or does he seek a protective male environment into which to withdraw—there to live out his isolated love experience, as well as to compose his new poetics based on the verbalization of sexual episodes?

"SCENTED HERBAGE OF MY BREAST"

Focusing on the death motif in "Scented Herbage of My Breast," the poet makes us privy to a *Liebestod* [a song from Richard Wagner's opera, *Tristan and Isolde*] experience. Having been initiated into the male sexual order, he dies to the heterosexual one, to be reborn into a sphere where "perennial roots, tall leaves" will always be available to him. Such phallic images, as well as mystical soliloquies, threnodies, and apostrophes, reoccur throughout the poem: coded references to a world beyond.

> O slender leaves! O blossoms of my blood! I permit you to tell
>   in your own way of the heart that is under you,
> O I do not know what you mean there underneath yourselves,
>   you are not happiness.

The genital analogies in the above and other passages have spiritual as well as creative applications. Identifiable with the [Egyptian god of the underworld] Osiris and Christ myths, they tell of the ordeals of those who seek to bring forth a new way or world order, including dismemberment and crucifixion. Only after Osiris and Christ descended into an underworld were both made privy to larger knowledge, followed by rebirth and deification.

Whitman experiences a similar ascesis [self-discipline] when writing. After his ascension/descent (for the mystic these are the same), or period of withdrawal into himself, the timeless/spaceless regions he has spanned open him up to revelation: "Yet you are beautiful to me you faint tinged roots, you make me think of death." Emerging into light again, he is reborn into the "calm" beatitude that comes with fulfillment.

The imagery of leaves, running through the poem, draws upon a primitive vegetal world, signifying both sexual and spiritual fertility. In keeping with Whitman's coded language, leaves as well as other vegetative images include both phallic and vaginal elements. The passage from vegetal to animal to human may be associated with the evolution of a latent idea dwelling inchoate [newly born] in the poet's collective unconscious: its passage into consciousness; its leap into the poem—its life eternal as a biocosmic symbol.

In that vegetation symbolizes the development of a world of possibilities—as seed, sperm, or word—that will become actualized into differentiated matter, the root plunged deep into the earth or the idea embedded in the mind may be said to be endowed with infrahuman nature. In Genesis we read: "God made you be born from the earth as a plant." Leaves, whether growing from the calamus plant or understood as *qalam*, identified with the quill or pen, or as leaves of paper, are to be used by the poet to engrave his sacred experience.

> Grow up taller sweet leaves that I may see! grow up out of my
>   breast! . . .
> Do not fold yourself so in your pink-tinged roots timid leaves!

Do not remain down there so ashamed, herbage of my breast!
Come I am determin'd to unbare this broad breast of mine, I
    have long enough stifled and choked;
Emblematic and capricious blades I leave you, now you serve
    me not.

The mere mention of genital metaphors floods the narrator
with desire, once again conflating sexuality with poetics. The
poet will set the example and become guide to the uninitiated
disciple and reader, leading those who have patiently waited for
someone to "take control of all." Not only will their yearning for
man-to-man love be fulfilled, thereby liberating them from society and its "entire show of appearance," but the experience will
enable them to reconnect with their own depths—their own
roots—by living out the death and resurrection ritual. . . .

"WHOEVER YOU ARE HOLDING ME NOW IN HAND"

More dramatic and perhaps more aggressive than the previous poems, "Whoever You Are Holding Me Now in Hand," addresses the reader overtly, enticing him to become a follower,
to interpenetrate with the author, and become "a candidate
for my affections." On the other hand, one may ask, Is the poet
really addressing the reader or is he talking to his lover? The
poem's title, which is also its opening line—"Whoever you are
holding me now in hand"—may reveal the author's need to
give himself to the reader as is, without his mask.

The poet warns the reader that he is not what he purports
to be and that there may be grounds for suspicion and fear on
the part of those hearing his song.

I give you fair warning before you attempt me further,
I am not what you supposed, but far different.

That the reader may seek to immerse himself in the poet's
world might prove to be "destructive": lead to doubt and un-
certainty; to rejection of previous moral standards that had
once meant security and calm. Furthermore, the initiation period into this new way would be demanding: "Your novitiate
would even then be long and exhausting." Yet, without making any promises, the poet entices the stranger to follow his
way. The use of indirection and misdirection serves to confuse
the reader, to tease him into participation, offering him a
glimpse into his garden of sensual delights.

Here to put your lips upon mine I permit you,
With the comrade's long-dwelling kiss or the new husband's
    kiss,
For I am the new husband and I am the comrade.

The reader or stranger, now the object of the poet's seduction, is induced to leave the world of conformity, to abandon the material domain, to separate himself from society, and to experience a rite of passage that would prepare him for the trials of the *real* world: endow him with faith in himself, with strength to pursue his vision, and with the ability to carve out his own independent path.

The road, the poet warns again, is not easy. The reader is again told that if he is not prepared to sacrifice everything he has in life, as so many other creative spirits have done before, "Put me down and depart on your way."

Then the poet makes a fascinating about-face, changing his tactics most subtly to more provocative, yet more passive, attitudes. The androgynous [having both male and female characteristics] poet entices the stranger to his fold: the paradisaic soul/body complex.

> Or if you will, thrusting me beneath your clothing,
> Where I may feel the throbs of your heart or rest upon your hip,
> Carry me when you go forth overland or sea;
> For thus merely touching you is enough, is best,
> And thus touching you would I silently sleep and be carried
> eternally.

Sensitive and loving, the androgynous poet, responding as male and female to the joys of tactile encounters, fondles, touches, palpates, and rubs parts of the body. In so doing, he is flooded with, paradoxically, sensations of serenity and of tantalizing excitement. In either case, the ambiguity of the feelings experienced may be likened to the orgasmic experience: as pleasure principle or as the intense sense of fulfillment and liberation following the creative poetic act.

Intellectual and abstract theories are arid fabrications of the mind, Whitman declares. Even his own "leaves" (he is referring to the calamus, but also to the leaves in a book) are empty without life's succulent energy.

> But these leaves conning you con at peril,
> For these leaves and me you will not understand,
> They will elude you at first and still more afterward, I will certainly elude you,
> Even while you should think you had unquestionably caught me, behold!
> Already you see I have escaped from you.

Reading teaches nothing. Only the experience *itself* has the capacity to titillate and activate emotion—thereby bringing the poem to birth. Nor can the experience be possessed or contained in a word or line. It may only be sensed or intuited.

The poem, like lovemaking, becomes a verbal replica of the privileged moments known to the participants. As an artistic construct, the poem remains an artifice: a concretization of ecstasy, a mirror image of higher truths that exist in a metasphere. And if the illusion the poet seeks to realize for the reader cannot provoke him into participation, he has failed in his intent. If such is the case, he asks him directly and in no uncertain terms, to "release me and depart on your way."

"For You O Democracy"

In "For You O Democracy," Whitman sings of companionship in a landscape "thick as trees," of good fun "along the rivers of America," of watching and joining his friends as they swim, row, race, and wander about from the great lakes to the prairies and mountains, "With the love of comrades, / With the life-long love of comrades."

Objectivity but also symbolism mark Whitman's verbal canvas, studded as it is with phallic images of trees reaching up to the heavens and metaphors of the womb, in the waters flowing along the byways of the New World. Just as the poet requires insemination, then periods of gestation, to foster his work, so, too, does America in order to fulfill its potential.

Come, I will make the continent indissoluble,
I will make the most splendid race the sun ever shone upon,
I will make divine magnetic lands. . . .

The plethora of Whitman's water images introduces a whole subliminal sphere of prenatal and preconscious existence: the undifferentiated realm of nonknowing, of unconcern, shorn of all problems. Since water dissolves hard matter, it may be looked upon, psychologically, as a liquefying agent, making solid and problematic conditions—be they sexual or intellectual—more malleable.

Why, one may ask, does the author entitle his poem "For You O Democracy"? Because democracy not only represents the ideal form of government for the poet, but because he conceives of it as a mother figure. By conflating the ideal and the real, he is also paying homage to his own mother. Although he occasionally smarted from her subtly dictatorial ways and sought to evade the burdens she had placed upon him, Whitman adored her. Understandably, compassionate and loving mother figures prevail in many of Whitman's poems, including "These I Sing in Spring" from *Calamus*. In the latter poem, Mother Earth and the Water Mother figure prominently in a fertile atmosphere of wild flowers, trees, and grasses of all sorts. Democracy is identified with the mother; camaraderie with males, who are children of sorts, bounding about gleefully in natural surroundings.

"OF THE TERRIBLE DOUBT OF APPEARANCES"

Love, a disastrous experience, no doubt, has brought the poet to the brink of despair. Fear is intense and traumatic. Questions, nevertheless, arise in the reader's mind. Were the love experiences undergone and then depicted in the poem *real?* Or were they fantasy? illusion? dream? masturbatory sequences? Or, perhaps, in keeping with Platonic tradition, emanations from a cosmic metamind, from the realm of Idea?

> Of the terrible doubt of appearances,
> Of the uncertainty after all, that we may be deluded,
> That may-be reliance and hope are but speculations after all,
> That may-be identity beyond the grave is a beautiful fable only. . . .

Whitman is haunted by the thought that what he has taken to be truth, be it in the love experience or in the creation of a poem, might merely have been a stratagem. For the Hindu, illusion and/or deception is symbolized as maya's veil, a power that serves to halt humankind's vision, allowing them to perceive only the world of multiplicity and not that of primordial unity. . . .

For Whitman . . . emotional in his encounters and in his relationships with people, as well as in his work, "doubt" left him in a state of turmoil. . . . If, as he fears in the poem, "reliance and hope are but speculations," then everything comes into question: his own identity as well as cosmic powers.

> The skies of day and night, colors, densities, forms, may-be these are (as doubtless they are) only apparitions, and the real something has yet to be known. . . .

Most painful are his doubts concerning his talent, his needs, and his sexual proclivities. The intensity of his anguish, the fearsomeness of the mockery leveled at him by others, fill him with a sense of failure—and dread. Should he have followed in the well-worn tracks of a [American poet Henry Wadsworth] Longfellow or a [British poet Alfred, Lord] Tennyson? Or is his anguish merely a mirage or fantasy?

And what of his love experiences? Has he really read the hearts and thoughts of his love objects clearly? Or has he been deceived by his feelings toward them? Whitman, who has always *felt* into relationships rather than reason them out or question the motivations of himself or others, decides to probe no longer. To enjoy the love of the moment will be sufficient. "When he whom I love travels with me or sits a long while holding me by the hand."

Whether his loves are just a memory or even an illusion, they have brought him momentary satisfaction. He, therefore, has no need of engaging in philosophical discourse or speculations, or probing into the world of Ideas, Forms, or Intellect.

> I cannot answer the question of appearances or that of identity beyond the grave,
> But I walk or sit indifferent, I am satisfied,
> He ahold of my hand has completely satisfied me.

Doubt remains, nevertheless, as to whether Whitman was or was not satisfied with his chance encounters or momentary relationships. That he had to define his attitude in "Of the Terrible Doubt of Appearances" leads one to believe that although he longed to function as a detached and objective creature, he never really succeeded in accomplishing this feat. . . .

"RECORDERS AGES HENCE"

Because the fear of being unloved as man and poet again corrodes the author's sense of well-being, he admonishes his followers to "Publish my name and hang up my picture as the tenderest lover." Anguish mounts within him when aloneness prevails, and the poet probes the depths and reality of his love experiences. Encountering an abyss within himself, and within others, he dwells in the dread of torment. "Who knew too well the sick, sick dread lest the one he lov'd might secretly be indifferent to him. . . ."

The gutturals and sibilants in the above line, in addition to the repetition of such words as *sick, sick,* serve once again to point up Whitman's powerful sense of inadequacy, his fear of loneliness—and his contradictory nature, since he needed to live away from others so as to better indwell. The particularly acute sense of distress inhabiting "Recorders Ages Hence" stems to a great extent from the cruel criticisms meted out to him by his detractors. . . .

"CITY OF ORGIES"

In "City of Orgies," Whitman discloses his passion for the anonymity large cities afford him. There, amid the multitude, he is free to indulge in orgies, to cruise, to court young bus drivers, soldiers, sailors, thieves, priests, and any others that strike his fancy.

On the other hand, like Paris for [French poet Charles] Baudelaire, Whitman's Manhattan makes him more keenly aware of his isolation. Observer and voyeur, he accepts the fact that he will never quite succeed in losing himself in the multitude, in divesting himself of that deeply rooted sadness that permeates the world of one who lives on the fringes of society.

Moods, however, alternate swiftly in "City of Orgies," in rhythm with the urban landscape as viewed by the observing poet. All seems mobile, floating—houses, windows, streets, the shifting crowd of lads he meets during his days and/or evenings devoted to gay cruising and to playing male games.

> Offering response to my own—these repay me,
> Lovers, continual lovers, only repay me.

"THAT SHADOW MY LIKENESS"

Reminiscent of Plato's allegory of the cave (described in his *Republic*), the poet sees himself as double. One part of him, like the uninstructed beings enchained in a cave in the bowels of the earth, lives the life of a pariah [outcast], in bleakness and blackness. The other side of him, yearns to move up from the world of shadows into a sun-drenched world—where Idea and Reality dwell.

> That shadow my likeness that goes to and fro seeking a liveli-
>   hood, chattering, chaffering.
> How often I question and doubt whether that is really me.

The shadow, understood psychologically, is a group of personal characteristics that the individual in question considers inferior or weak and that his ego's self-esteem will not allow him to recognize. Because he can neither assimilate nor accept these qualities in himself, his conscious considers them negative. Should Whitman reject his shadow, the darker and more problematic side of his personality, he would not only be joining the status quo in repudiating what he considered his "baser" side, but more importantly, he would be repudiating a part of himself—his own chaotic elements. To do so would be to destroy any possibility of facing his contradictions and thus dealing with what he and society considered destructive.

Whitman needed courage to overcome the vilifications *Leaves of Grass* elicited, as is made clear by the following example from Rufus Griswold, one of his most outspoken detractors, wrote:

In our allusions to this book [*Leaves of Grass*] we have found it impossible to convey any, even the most faint idea of its style and contents, and of our disgust and detestation of them, without employing language that cannot be pleasing to ears polite; but it does seem that some one should, under circumstances like these, undertake a most disagreeable, yet stern duty. The records of crime show that many monsters have gone on in impunity, because the exposure of their vileness was attended with too great indelicacy. *Peccatum illud horribile, inter christianos non nominandum* [that horrible sin not to be mentioned among Christians].

Bitter rejection is not an uncommon fate for revolutionaries, especially in their lifetime, and *Calamus* [is] indeed revolutionary: thematically, for its brazen approach to sex; visually, for the poet's painterly prose, colorful panoramas, and explicit visions; rhythmically, for the bodily vibrations and undulations the subtext triggers in its attempt to replicate copulation; sonorously, for the flow of the poem-songs, which, when voiced, are as lyrical as [an] operatic sequence.

The Spiritual World of "Eidólons"

Harry R. Warfel

"Eidólons" differs from much of Walt Whitman's poetry in that it has a regular pattern of stanzas. But in subject matter, the poem is consistent with Whitman's philosophy. "Eidólons" are spirits or souls that exist all around us. Whitman suggests that, ultimately, the world is more spiritual than material. The poet's job, like the prophets of old, is to sing to the people of this spiritual world and teach that we are all part of one larger soul, called the "oversoul" by transcendental thinkers such as Ralph Waldo Emerson. Harry R. Warfel has taught at the University of Florida.

It has been a matter of frequent remark that the somewhat regular four-line stanzas of 'Eidólons' stand in sharp contrast to the free-verse poems at the beginning of *Leaves of Grass*. No one seems to have noticed that a further regularity may be discerned in the way the thought of the twenty-one stanzas is structured into five separate units. The fourth unit, stanzas 13 to 17, contains twenty lines; each of the others contains sixteen lines. In each unit the initial stanza announces a proposition and the final stanza rises to a climactic statement in the progressively demonstrated thesis. The concluding stanza of the poem ties together the thought of the whole poem. In its overall rhetorical arrangement and in its inner dynamics of maneuvered syntax and metaphor to achieve a rich baroque music, 'Eidólons' is a masterpiece of Emersonian 'metre-making argument' [Emerson's definition of poetry].

The central idea of 'Eidólons' is that the phenomenal universe exists for the purpose of creating eidólons or souls, all of which merge ultimately into the Over-Soul, and that the prophet-bard's responsibility is the eclaircizement [making

Reprinted from Harry R. Warfel, "The Structure of 'Eidólons,'" *Walt Whitman Newsletter*, December 1958.

clear] of this major doctrine of the Perennial Philosophy. This theme had been worked out in 'Passage to India' in a larger, programmatic way; in this poem, recent engineering feats, when set against deeds accomplished in earlier time cycles, prove the existence of God's purpose to reveal through selected men the law of the soul's operation and the need for the prophet-bard to demonstrate the possibility of union by the human soul with the Over-Soul. In 'Song of Myself' the final section represents Walt as disembodied and becoming one with Nature, a symbolic action reflecting his view that the universe is composed of Soul and that man's last journey is to the Over-Soul. By 1876, when 'Eidólons' was published, Walt's convictions were solidified by the doctrines explicit in the evolutionary theory, and he used facets of this theory as the central image upon which to base his 'argument.'

NATURE CREATES EIDÓLONS

The first unit, stanzas 1 to 5, begins much as Emerson's *Nature* (1836) concludes: the thought in the poem comes from a seer (Emerson has a poet) who, himself a transcender of time and space, explains that the phenomenal universe has as its reason for existence the creation of eidólons. In stanza 2 the seer tells Walt not to write about incidents in time and space but to put eidólons first 'as light for all and entrance-song of all.' The image 'light' may stand on its literal level, but more likely the suggestion of 'heavenly light' is intended to accompany the image of 'entrance' to 'all.' 'All' lifts the thought to metaphysical totality, so that the poem promises to give a key to the all-encompassing extent of the answer finally to be given. Stanza 3 presents an evolutionary sequence which reaches completion ('the summit' and 'the merge at last' of the rounded circle), meanwhile creating its eidólon, and then starts again on a new cycle. . . . Stanza 4 reinforces the thought of the preceding stanza and brings a climax to the unit by stating that all matter, which is in a constant state of flux, and that the changes occurring through natural action ('the ateliers, the factories divine') give shape to eidólons.

MEN CREATE EIDÓLONS

The second unit, stanzas 5 to 8, carries forward the theme by showing that individuals, who seem to be building 'solid wealth, strength, beauty,' 'really build eidólons.' In stanza 6 man's inventions and deeds—each of which becomes an 'ostent evanescent,' that is, a momentary phenomenon or manifestation which may be seen physically—occur wholly to create eidólons. Stanza 7 reinforces this statement by saying that the eidólon of each person sums up the entirety of his physical, mental, and emotional experience. Stanza 8, which by 'pinnacles' recalls the evolutionary image of 'summit' in stanza 3, climaxes the second unit by asserting that the ascension process is based upon an 'old, old urge' or *élan vital* [life force] which dynamically thrusts upward beyond 'science and the modern.' This 'urge' is in the eidólon or soul. Here Walt has taken a most important step in his argument, for he repeats the concept of the 'repressless' soul ('Passage to India,' line 169) which pushes onward steadily in making known God's increasing purpose. A dual action exists, that of nature and man in creating eidólons and that of the soul in impelling this creation. Emerson put the same idea this way in 'Circles': 'These things proceed from the eternal generation of the soul. Cause and effect are two sides of one fact.'

'THE MIGHTY EARTH-EIDÓLON'

The third unit, stanzas 9 to 12, moves forward to the larger eidólons which are created by nations and to those which are formed by separate aspects of nature. The climax comes in stanza 12, where 'orbic tendencies' shape 'the mighty earth-eidólon.' The concept of the Over-Soul's dynamism mentioned in 'the old, old urge' in stanza 8 is now enriched by mystical language: 'Exalté, rapt, ecstatic.' An image of birth is used, as in 'Song of Myself,' to indicate that the visible form of nature has in it the creative source of its own making. Thus Walt has progressed into the cosmos by successively enlarging the eidólon or soul until it is coextensive with the universe.

THE UNIVERSE IS COMPOSED OF SPIRIT

Walt now asserts in the fourth unit, stanzas 13 to 17, that the universe is not material but spiritual. In *Nature* (1836) Emerson stated the idea thus: 'The noblest ministry of nature is to stand as the apparition of God. It is the organ through which the universal spirit speaks to the individual, and strives to lead the individual back to it.' In stanza 13 Walt says that 'All space, all time' are 'Fill'd with eidólons only.' In stanza 14 all phenomena, small and large, are 'The true realities, eidólons.' In stanza 15 the 'purport and end' of the universes is God, 'the permanent life of life, Eidólons.' In stanza 16 the thought is undergirded by a contrast: beyond the materialistic facts gleaned by scholars lies 'The entities of entities, eidólons.' Stanza 17 concludes the fourth unit with a Brahman utterance asserting the overriding quality and permanence of the Over-Soul, the eidólons.

THE PROPHET-BARD'S RESPONSIBILITY

At the beginning of the poem the seer laid upon the poet a charge to understand the spiritual nature of the universe. In the fifth unit the poet states the responsibility now accruing to him as a result of his knowledge. In stanza 18 the prophet-bard, who will rise to ever-higher summits and pinnacles, will be a mediator between the infinite, permanent Over-Soul and the people of today, and he will also interpret to them these ideas of God and of eidólons or souls. In stanza 19 his own yearning soul will, through 'Joys, ceaseless exercises, exaltations,' be prepared to meet other eidólons or souls. The nature of the soul is explained in stanza 20: it is permanent but it is housed in an impermanent body, and this body is the only hint which is available concerning the form of the soul. The soul is 'the real I myself' (cf. 'O soul, thou actual Me.' 'Passage to India,' line 208); it is 'An image,' that is, an intangible yet real manifestation; it is an eidólon. The concluding stanza echoes Emerson's statement in 'The Poet': 'The condition of true naming, on the poet's part, is his resigning himself to the divine *aura* which breathes through forms. . . . He is capable of a new energy . . . by an abandonment to the nature of things, . . . suffering the ethereal tides to roll and circulate through him.' That is, the poet does not really speak from himself or choose his topics; rather, by yielding himself fully to the Over-Soul, he will become the spokesman of God. Or as Emerson put it in 'The Problem':

> The passive master lent his hand
> To the vast soul that o'er him plann'd; . . .
> Himself from God he could not free;
> He builded better than he knew.

CHAPTER 4

Influence: Other Poets Evaluate Whitman

READINGS ON
WALT WHITMAN

Whitman Celebrates All Americans

Langston Hughes

Langston Hughes, a prominent member of the Harlem Renaissance, admired Whitman for his politics as well as his poetry. Whitman wrote without frills in a simple style that differs from most poetry of his era. He was a writer for all of the people and a true poet of democracy. Langston Hughes is the author of numerous poems, stories, and other works. One of his famous poems is "I, Too, Sing America," alluding to the poetry of Whitman.

[Whitman] had been an editor of the Brooklyn *Eagle*, but was fired there in 1848 because he refused to support Governor Cass of Michigan who advocated the continuation of slavery. Whitman called people like Cass "Dough Faces," because of their condonance of Southern slavery. Whitman abhorred slave catchers and those who gave them aid or supported their political beliefs. In the New York *Evening Post*, Whitman wrote:

> We are all docile dough-faces,
> They knead us with the fist,
> They, the dashing Southern Lords,
> We labor as they list.
> For them we speak—or hold our tongue,
> For them we turn and twist.

There had been a half-dozen or so slaves on the ancestral Whitman farm, and young Walt had played with them as a child. Perhaps that is where he acquired his sympathy for the Negro people and his early belief that all men should be free—a belief that grew to embrace the peoples of the whole world, expressed over and over throughout his poems, encompassing not only America but the colonial peoples, the serfs of tsarist Russia, the suppressed classes everywhere.

Reprinted from the Introduction, "The Ceaseless Rings of Walt Whitman," by Langston Hughes, to *I Hear the People Singing: Selected Poems of Walt Whitman* (New York: International, 1946). Reprinted by permission of Harold Ober Associates Incorporated.

In our own land, Walt Whitman lived intensely within the currents of his time, absorbed in the democratic strivings growing in America and taking root like wind-blown seeds in varied soils around the world. His physical self wandered from the Long Island countryside to the Brooklyn ferries and Broadway trolley cars, from urban foundries and shops to Mississippi river boats and the fields of battle during the Civil War. His spiritual self roamed the earth wherever the winds of freedom blow however faintly, keeping company with the foiled revolutionaries of Europe or the suppressed coolies of Asia.

Because the vast sweep of democracy is still incomplete even in America today, because revolutionaries seeking to break old fetters are still foiled in Europe and Asia, because the physical life of the Brooklyn ferries and the Broadway street cars and the Mississippi river banks and the still fresh battlefields of World War II continue to pulse with the same heartbeats of humanity as in Whitman's time, his poetry strikes us now with the same immediacy it must have awakened in its earliest readers in the 1850's.

The good gray poet of democracy is one of literature's great faith-holders in human freedom. Speaking simply for people everywhere and most of all for the believers in our basic American dream, he is constantly growing in stature as the twentieth century advances and edition after edition of his poems appears.

WHITMAN'S SIMPLE LANGUAGE

Walt Whitman wrote without the frills, furbelows, and decorations of conventional poetry, usually without rhyme or measured prettiness. Perhaps because of his simplicity, timid poetry lovers over the years have been frightened away from his *Leaves of Grass*, poems as firmly rooted and as brightly growing as the grass itself. Perhaps, too, because his all-embracing words lock arms with workers and farmers, Negroes and whites, Asiatics and Europeans, serfs, and free men, beaming democracy to all, many academic-minded intellectual isolationists in America have had little use for Whitman, and so have impeded his handclasp with today by keeping him imprisoned in silence on library shelves. Still his words leap from their pages and their spirit grows steadily stronger everywhere:

. . . I give the sign of democracy.
By God! I will accept nothing which all cannot have their
    counterpart of on the same terms. . .

So there is no keeping Whitman imprisoned in silence. He
proclaims:

I ordain myself loosed of limits. . . .
Going where I list. . . .
Gently, but with undeniable will, divesting myself of the
    holds that would hold me.

WHITMAN'S POEMS CONTAIN US ALL

One of the greatest "I" poets of all time, Whitman's "I" is not
the "I" of the introspective versifiers who write always and
only about themselves. Rather it is the cosmic "I" of all peoples who seek freedom, decency, and dignity, friendship and
equality between individuals and races all over the world.

The best indication of the scope of Whitman's poems
might be found in his own *Song of the Answerer* where he
writes about poetry:

The words of true poems give you more than poems,
They give you to form for yourself poems, religions, politics,
    war, peace, behavior, histories, essays, daily life and every-
    thing else,
They balance ranks, colors, races, creeds, and the sexes. . . .
They bring none to his or her terminus or to be content and
    full,
Whom they take they take into space to behold the birth of
    stars, to learn one of the meanings,
To launch off with absolute faith, to sweep through the cease-
    less rings and never be quiet again.

In this atomic age of ours, when the ceaseless rings are
multiplied a millionfold, the Whitman spiral is upward and
outward toward a freer, better life for all, not narrowing
downward toward death and destruction. Singing the greatness of the individual, Whitman also sings the greatness of
unity, cooperation, and understanding.

. . . all the men ever born are also my brothers, and the
    women my sisters. . . .

As an after-thought he adds:

(I am large, I contain multitudes).

Certainly, his poems contain us all. The reader cannot help
but see his own better self therein.

Honoring Walt Whitman

Louis Simpson

Louis Simpson acknowledges the influence of Walt Whitman on his own poetry while pointing out the flaws in Whitman's work. Simpson chiefly admires Whitman for his imagery, his "pictures," while asserting, contrary to popular belief, that Whitman was not a mystical poet. Whitman knew much about the mass of men, but little of individuals and actual circumstances, argues Simpson. Simpson "honors" Whitman by learning from the elder poet's mistakes and attempting to surpass him. In addition to his numerous books of poetry, Louis Simpson has published studies of such twentieth-century poets as Dylan Thomas, William Carlos Williams, T.S. Eliot, and Ezra Pound.

> He most honors my style who learns under it how to destroy the teacher.
>
> "Song of Myself"

I began reading Whitman seriously around 1959. I had read him before that out of curiosity, but in 1959 I was changing from writing in regular meters and forms to writing in irregular meters and forms, and Whitman was one of the poets I read to see how they did it.

I liked the pictures in Whitman's poems: cavalry crossing a ford, a tree standing by itself. I liked his idea of a "Muse install'd amid the kitchenware," i.e., making poetry out of common things. This seemed useful in view of the part played by machinery in our lives a hundred years later.

On the other hand, his whooping it up over the chest-expansion of the United States didn't do a thing for me. His wish for young men to throw their arms about his neck struck me as incomprehensible. I was put off by his use of big-sounding words or French words. He was capable of

"Honoring Whitman" by Louis Simpson from *Walt Whitman: The Measure of His Song*, edited by Jim Perlman, Ed Folsom, and Dan Campion (Holy Cow! Press, 1981; 2nd revised ed., 1998). Reprinted by permission of the publisher.

writing long passages naming countries he'd read about or heard about, the names of mountains and rivers, the races of men, et cetera.

> I see the Brazilian vaquero,
> I see the Bolivian ascending mount Sorata. . . .

I don't see how anyone could ever have read these passages in Whitman with pleasure.

At times, however, he was capable of a surprising compression of thought and style—he was almost epigrammatic: "The nearest gnat is an explanation," "Trippers and askers surround me."

WHITMAN'S IDEAS

On the whole I found Whitman exhilarating. His freedom of line and style, and his interest in pots and pans, bringing them over into poetry, were what I needed at the time.

So far I haven't mentioned Whitman's "philosophy." It consists of two or three ideas. One, it is possible to merge in your feelings with others, and it is possible for others to merge in their feelings with you. Two, if this occurs over a distance, or over a span of time, it seems to annihilate space and time. This is a kind of immortality. Three, in order to convey your feelings to others you must, by a process of empathic observation, using all your senses, take things into yourself and express them again. The senses are "dumb ministers" of feeling . . . through them we know one another. The poet is the manager of this process—he puts what we feel and see into words. . . .

WHITMAN WAS NOT A MYSTIC

It may appear that I've overlooked Whitman's mystical, visionary side. I haven't overlooked it, but Whitman doesn't strike me as mystical or visionary—he is a naturalist first and last. He wills to see things—even "The Sleeper" is laid out and proceeds according to plan. His most ecstatic passages are descriptions of sexual intercourse or frottation.

> I mind how once we lay such a transparent summer
>   morning,
> How you settled your head athwart my hips and gently
>   turn'd over upon me . . . .

These lines are addressed to his soul, but can there be any doubt as to what is actually happening? Sex may be the link with a mystery, but at least let us see that it is sex and not

POUND MAKES HIS PEACE WITH WHITMAN

The famous (and notorious) American poet Ezra Pound acknowledges that he has much in common with the poet he once disdained.

A Pact

I make a pact with you, Walt Whitman—
I have detested you long enough.
I come to you as a grown child
Who has had a pig-headed father;
I am old enough now to make friends.
It was you that broke the new wood,
Now is a time for carving.
We have one sap and one root—
Let there be commerce between us.

rush to find an alternative explanation. There is the kind of reader who, having no knowledge of religion, is always looking in books for the secret of the universe. . . .

I don't want to suggest that Whitman is only a picture-artist. "When Lilacs Last in the Dooryard Bloom'd" and "Out of the Cradle Endlessly Rocking" hold our attention through rhythm and sound as well as imagery. But as rhythm and sound are operating just as audibly in his empty, monotonous, forgettable poems, I do not think that Whitman's impressiveness depends on rhythm and sound. It is what he describes that makes him a poet. Rhythm and sound are only an aid to this.

Critics who wish to pore over a phrase in Whitman, or the structure of a line, and show how perfectly suited it is to his purpose, should choose a banality and show why the meter and phrasing are perfect. This is the trouble with criticism that concentrates on technique—it is an *arrière-pensée* [backward thinking]. We know that the poetry is fine, and set about finding reasons why the meter and the syntax had to be just so. But these things in themselves do not make fine poetry. If nothing worthwhile is being said, meter, syntax, and the rest of the prosodist's and the grammarian's bag of tricks are so much useless baggage.

There are ranges of poetry that lie beyond Whitman. Of situations such as occur in people's lives he appears to have known very little, and these are our main concern. He is good at describing shipwrecks, which are infrequent, but does not show affections, attachments, anxieties, shades of feeling, passions . . . the life we actually have. The human appears in his poems as a crowd or as a solitary figure . . . himself, looking at others.

In recent years [the late 1970s] there has been talk by American poets of developing new kinds of consciousness which would, presumably, enable us to advance beyond the merely human. But it is self-evident that if we are to continue to exist it will be as human beings, not some other species. Our poets are trying to be like stones . . . another way of saying that they would rather be dead. Paul Breslin made the point clearly in an article ("How to Read the New Contemporary Poem," *The American Scholar*, Summer, 1978) but the thought had occurred to me independently. According to Breslin, our poets of darkness and stones are trying to escape the consequences of being human. They are trying to cast out the ego and live in a Jungian universe of archetypes.

Readers of this kind will find Whitman reassuring—he never becomes involved. "I am the man," he states, "I suffer'd, I was there." The passage may be so well known because it is so refreshing, in the wasteland of his usual detachment. He is a stroller, an onlooker, a gazer, and has nothing to say about what goes on in the houses he is passing, or behind office or factory windows, or in the life of the man turning a plough. He does not seem to know what people say to each other—especially what men say to women, or women to men. Reading Whitman's poetry one would think that the human race is dumb—and indeed, as he tells us, he would rather turn and live with animals.

His poetry is about a spectacle . . . a crowd on the ferry, "the fine centrifugal spokes of light round the shape of my head in the sunlit water." But the actualities of human society are a closed book to him. It isn't the "proud libraries" that are closed to him—indeed, at times we could wish they were. What is closed is the life of the individual, and the lives of two, and three.

WHITMAN'S MASSES OF MEN

Whitman has plenty to say about man *"En-Masse."* His optimism about the common man reflects the optimism of the bankers and railroad-builders in the Gilded Age. Man *"En-Masse"* provided them with labor and then with a mass-market. But optimism about the masses seems out of place in our century. The masses elect mass-murderers—if we survive it will not be due to the good nature of the common man. Whitman's view of mankind is of no use at all—it doesn't help when it comes to understanding one another and building a community.

As he has so little to say about actual circumstances, Whitman is not among the very great, realized poets. There is hardly any drama or narration in his poetry—ideas aren't realized in action. We rise from reading Whitman with the feeling that he has talked about life rather than created it.

Building on his achievement we may hope to do much better, as he himself, in one of his generous moods, said that we would.

Whitman Is Overrated

Lewis Putnam Turco

Lewis Turco dissents from the common opinion that Whitman is America's greatest, most innovative and influential poet. Turco asserts that in matters of style, point of view, and experimentation, Whitman did nothing new. Whitman's chief prominence lies in his poetic expression of transcendentalist Ralph Waldo Emerson's philosophy and his presentation of the poetic "I" as a metaphor for America. But these traits are of more interest to literary historians than to those interested in the beauty of poetry. Lewis Turco has taught at the State University of New York at Oswego. He has published numerous books of poetry and is also the author of *The Book of Forms: A Handbook of Poetics.*

It was Whitman who put Emerson's theories into practice, and that is why he is considered to be a Great Poet, not because he wrote great poems and maintained a high level of competence in the body of his work. It will be objected that Whitman can be considered great on other grounds: he broke with tradition and wrote in a whole new mode which freed American poetry from the constraints of English prosody. Even if this were true, which it is not, such a defense is historical and not literary. It is a scholar's defense, not that of a writer or a reader.

That Whitman was thoroughly familiar with Emerson's work is well documented, but he need not have been. As [critic Hyatt] Waggoner points out in *American Poets*, everything he required was contained in the essay "The Poet." "This is true not simply because the essay states nearly all the ideas Whitman was later to express in his poetry, or even because the essay recommends that the ideal poet should write in the *manner* of the author of *Leaves of Grass*. It is true because Emerson's idea of what a poet is and does was

Reprinted from *Visions and Revisions of American Poetry*, by Lewis Putnam Turco. Copyright © 1986 by Lewis Putnam Turco. Reprinted by permission of The University of Arkansas Press.

precisely the idea Whitman needed if he was to move beyond journalism and mediocre versifying."

WHITMAN'S EARLY POETRY

Waggoner is being kind. Whitman was not, in his earlier pieces, a mediocre versifier—he was simply execrable. There was no way in the world he was ever going to be able to handle the language metrically—he had a tin ear and a ham hand. Here is an entirely typical product of Whitman's early pen—not juvenilia, but an adult piece from his days as a journalist:

> Old Grimes
>
> He lived at peace with all mankind,
>   In friendship he was true;
> His coat had pocket-holes behind,
>   His pantaloons were blue.
>
> Unharmed, the sin which earth pollutes
>   He passed securely o'er,—
> And never wore a pair of boots
>   For thirty years or more.

It is all but impossible to find these early verses in any popular edition of Whitman's work, even in volumes with such titles as *The Collected Poems* and *The Complete Poems*, edited by such people as Malcolm Cowley. One must go to one of the rare multivolume scholarly editions if one wants to read Whitman as a benighted non-American, in those days when he went to social events in a top hat and cape, carrying a nob-head cane, in order to write a story for a newspaper. Later, realizing that he was a poor traditional craftsman, Whitman became the first American to discover what many others, including Emerson, were struggling to discover—namely, that poetry may be written in prose. Everyone else thought it had to be written in verse, which explains why a person such as [American novelist Herman] Melville, who was also a failed versifier, was much more the successful poet in his later novels, for a succinct definition of *poem* might be this—that something said well is something well said, but something said superbly is a poem.

American and British poets were so locked into the *verse = poetry, prose = something else* syndrome that it would cause a huge ruckus in the early twentieth century, and people would go around calling prose *vers libre* or "free verse" till minds were so confused it would take half a century even to begin to sort things out. Only [American poet] Amy Lowell would

WHITMAN'S SYMBOLIC SPIDER

Whitman's "A Noiseless Patient Spider" combines close observation of nature with larger symbolic implications.

A Noiseless Patient Spider

A noiseless patient spider,
I marked where on a little promontory it stood isolated,
Marked how to explore the vacant vast surrounding,
It launched forth filament, filament, filament, out of itself,
Ever unreeling them, every tirelessly speeding them.

And you, O my soul where you stand,
Surrounded, detached, in measureless oceans of space,
Ceaselessly musing, venturing, throwing, seeking the spheres
  to connect them,
Till the bridge you will need be formed, till the ductile anchor
  hold,
Till the gossamer thread you fling catch somewhere, O my
  soul.

In the first stanza the speaker describes a spider's apparently tireless effort to attach its thread to some substantial support so that it can begin constructing a web. The speaker reveals his attentive interest by the hinted personification of the spider, and his sympathy with it is expressed in the overstatement of size and distance—he is trying to perceive the world as a spider sees it from a "promontory" surrounded by vast space. He even attributes a human motive to the spider: exploration, rather than instinctive web-building. Nevertheless, the first stanza is essentially literal—the close observation of an actual spider at its task. In the second stanza the speaker explicitly interprets the symbolic meaning of what he has observed: his soul (personified by apostrophe [direct address] and by the capabilities assigned to it) is like the spider in its constant striving. But the soul's purpose is to find spiritual or intellectual certainties in the vast universe it inhabits. The symbolic meaning is richer than a mere comparison; while a spider's actual purpose is limited to its instinctive drives, the human soul strives for much more, in a much more complex "surrounding." And of course, the result of the soul's symbolized striving is much more open-ended than is the attempt of a spider to spin a web, as the paradoxical language ("surrounded, detached," "ductile anchor") implies. *Can* the human soul connect the celestial spheres?

Laurence Perrine and Thomas R. Arp, *Sound and Sense*. 8th edition. Fort Worth: Harcourt Brace, 1992, pp. 81–82.

have sense enough in those early days to introduce the term "polyphonic prose." Meanwhile, the scholars and teachers went around trying to justify Whitman's lines as some kind of hybrid metric and, of course, it couldn't be done.

WHITMAN DID NOTHING NEW

If Whitman was the first American to write straightforward prose poetry, he was hardly inventing something new. Grammatic parallelism is in all likelihood the oldest prosody in the world—the Chaldeans were using it in the *Gilgamesh* epic at the beginning of history. For that matter, the Bible—even the King James version—is written in the grammatic prose parallel systems of Hebrew prosody. . . . [G]rammatically parallel structures tend to exhibit parallel rhythms; they thus give a sense of verse, but they are much easier to write.

The fact is that Whitman was no less derivative, in his own way, than his un-American Anglophile compatriot poets. Though he could not have been aware of Christopher Smart's experiments with prose poetry because they were not published until the twentieth century, Whitman could hardly have missed the work of another Englishman, Martin Farquhar Tupper, whose *Proverbial Philosophy* appeared when Whitman was nineteen. One can still, if one digs a little, find a reference here and there to Whitman's connection with Tupper. The following passage is from *Everyman's Dictionary of Literary Biography*, edited by D. C. Browning and published in 1962:

> [Tupper] wrote many works in prose and verse, only one of which, *Proverbial Philosophy* (1838), had much success. But the vogue which it had was enormous especially in America, where a million copies were sold. It is a singular collection of commonplace observations set forth in a form which bears the appearance of verse, but has neither rhyme nor metre, though its rhythms, inspired by biblical passages, are said to have influenced Walt Whitman. Tupper's name has become a byword for the trite and platitudinous.

Meanwhile, Whitman's name—because Whitman was an American—has become a byword for the innovative and oracular, not for the derivative and banal.

A million-copy best-seller in the fledgling United States! Whitman would have had to be deaf and blind to miss Tupper. It is a pity that our own great American bard of the people was comparatively ignored, according to Kreymborg, who says that *Leaves of Grass* "was intended for the divine average and the average ignored it, as to this day they ignore it. In the literature of the world, there is no greater irony, no greater tragedy, than the neglect paid by the people to a man of genius embracing the gamut of the Common American man and lifting it to a continuous chant resounding round the earth."

If it is true that the man in the street ignored Whitman, it needs to be pointed out that the man in the street, particularly in America, ignores all poetry, all poets. It is a segment of the educated middle class that sometimes patronizes American poetry, even if its members do not read it—teachers, students, other writers, for the most part. When it comes to this element of society, Whitman did as well in his own time as anyone else, including the Schoolroom Poets. *Leaves of Grass* went through twelve editions between 1855 and 1892, and it is still going through edition after edition. Furthermore, even Whitman's early verses had wide circulation in the pages of some of the newspapers of the day, and a *Selected Poems*, edited by Arthur Stedman, was published in 1892, the year of the poet's death.

In many anthologies of poetry published in the nineteenth century, even obscure ones with titles like *The Royal Gallery of Poetry* (1888), *Cyclopedia of British and American Poetry* (1881), and *Representative Poems of Living Poets* (1886), Whitman is well represented. He is included in nearly all the standard anthologies of the period, and he has been represented in anthologies and textbooks ever since. *Leaves of Grass* was reviewed in the leading periodicals and journals of the day, and to cap everything Emerson, the foremost critic of the period, praised his work fulsomely. What does this prove? That although Whitman was unable to persuade the common laborer to read poetry, the Good Gray Poet was, almost from the start, a member in good standing of the American literary establishment. That he was controversial merely emphasizes the point.

WHITMAN'S STRENGTH WAS SELF-PROMOTION

If Whitman was no technical innovator, and if he was no literary pariah, he was perhaps the first American poet who recognized the value of public relations as a means of building a reputation. No doubt his years as a journalist provided him with the training he needed in order to harness the medium (no one could yet use the plural *media*) and make it pull the Whitman bandwagon. In the same edition of

Everyman's Dictionary of Literary Biography that makes the connection between Tupper and Whitman, the article on the latter says that "Whitman is the most unconventional of writers. Revolt against all convention was in fact his self-proclaimed mission. In his verse he established a new tradition of freedom of form and expression, while in his treatment of certain passions and appetites, and of unadulterated human nature, he was at war with what he considered the conventions of an effeminate society; but after all reservations, there is real poetic insight and an intense and singularly fresh sense of nature in his best writings.". . .

WHITMAN BECAME AMERICA

Whitman was, however, an innovator in one important sense, and perhaps this is what makes the difference: he fused the populist credo and the egopoetic narrator so that the "I" of his poems became symbolic of America. In other words, Whitman *became* America, or so he would have his readers believe. By whatever means this brilliant—and brilliantly simple—fusion was brought into being and focused upon the American audience, it became almost impossible to talk about Whitman the poet, to criticize his work, without seeming to criticize America itself.

When his work is stripped of all extraneous considerations, perhaps his only intrinsically "great" poem is "A Noiseless, Patient Spider," as memorable a piece of writing as any in the language. It is also atypical of Whitman's work. The level of his competence was not very high—he retained his poor ear throughout his life; his poems are too long, too disorganized, too pompous, too repetitious, too boring; he is too determinedly, one-sidedly, unrelievedly optimistic—nobody can be that affirmative all the time. Whitman is not interested in humanity except possibly as an abstraction—there are no living people in his poems, though there are many lists of people; there are no characters except himself, and even his Self comes off as symbolic, not palpable, a two-dimensional persona.

If, however, we must look at Whitman as the embodiment of a Transcendentalist theory of literature, as a literary-historical watershed leading to all those democratic prose poems of the twentieth century, as an image of all those just and liberal and worthy things we would like to think we hold in our heart-of-hearts as a nation, then perhaps he was a Great Poet. That still doesn't make him worth reading as literature.

Chronology

1819

Walt Whitman born May 31 in West Hills, Long Island.

1823

The Whitman family moves to Brooklyn, New York.

1825–1830

Attends public school in Brooklyn.

1830

Begins work as an apprentice printer.

1835–1836

Works as printer in New York City.

1836–1838

Works as a teacher at East Norwich, Long Island; subsequently teaches at Hempstead, Babylon, Long Swamp, and Smithtown.

1838

Becomes editor and publisher of the *Long Islander* in Huntington.

1841

Begins work as a printer in *New World* office.

1842

Edits first the *Aurora*, then the *Evening Tattler;* novel *Franklin Evans* published.

1845

Returns to Brooklyn; writes for the *Long Island Evening Star.*

1846

Becomes editor of the *Brooklyn Daily Eagle.*

1848

Travels to New Orleans to work on the *New Orleans Crescent;* returns to New York to edit the *Brooklyn Freeman.*

1849

Returns to live with his family; begins running printing office and working in family housing business.

1855

Leaves of Grass published on or about July 4; Walter Whitman Sr. dies July 11; begins long, intermittent correspondence with Ralph Waldo Emerson.

1856

Second edition of *Leaves of Grass* published.

1857–1859

Edits the *Brooklyn Daily Times.*

1860

Third edition of *Leaves of Grass* published by Thayer and Eldridge of Boston.

1861

Civil War begins as Fort Sumter is attacked by Confederates; brother George Whitman enlists.

1862

Upon hearing of George's injury, travels to Fredericksburg, Virginia, to search for him; works part-time as a clerk in Washington, D.C.; begins to make hospital visits.

1864

Returns to Brooklyn due to illness.

1865

Given an appointment as clerk in Department of the Interior; meets friend and companion Peter Doyle; Abraham Lincoln assassinated April 14; Whitman fired from job and reinstated in the attorney general's office; *Drum-Taps* published.

1866

Whitman's friend and supporter William O'Connor publishes *The Good Gray Poet.*

1867

John Burroughs writes the first biography of Whitman; fourth edition of *Leaves of Grass* published.

1868

William Michael Rossetti publishes *Poems by Walt Whitman* in London.

1871

Democratic Vistas and fifth edition of *Leaves of Grass* published.

1873

Suffers first paralytic stroke on January 23; Louisa Whitman, the poet's mother, dies on May 23; lives with brother George in Camden, New Jersey.

1876

Relationship with Harry Stafford begins; Whitman lives on Stafford Farm; British press accuses America of neglecting Whitman; sixth edition of *Leaves of Grass* published.

1879

Lectures in Philadelphia; travels to Colorado; visits brother Jeff in St. Louis.

1880

Travels to Canada.

1881

Makes a last visit to Long Island.

1881–1882

Seventh edition of *Leaves of Grass* published.

1882

The notorious Irish playwright Oscar Wilde pays Whitman a visit in Camden.

1883

Richard Bucke's biography of Whitman published.

1884

Buys house on Mickle Street in Camden.

1885

Friends and supporters buy Whitman a horse and buggy.

1888

Suffers severe paralytic stroke; *November Boughs* and eighth edition of *Leaves of Grass* published.

1890

Plans and pays for tomb in Harleigh Cemetery, Camden.

1891

Goodbye My Fancy published.

1892

Ninth edition of *Leaves of Grass* published; dies March 26, buried in Camden, New Jersey.

FOR FURTHER RESEARCH

Gay Wilson Allen, *The New Walt Whitman Handbook.* New York: New York University Press, 1975.

——, *A Reader's Guide to Walt Whitman.* New York: Farrar, Straus, and Giroux, 1970.

Roger Asselineau, *The Evolution of Walt Whitman.* Cambridge, MA: Harvard University Press, 1960.

Harold Bloom, ed., *Walt Whitman.* New York: Chelsea House, 1985.

Philip Callow, *From Noon to Starry Night: A Life of Walt Whitman.* Chicago: Ivan R. Dee, 1992.

David Cavitch, *"My Soul and I": The Inner Life of Walt Whitman.* New York: Beacon Press, 1985.

Richard Chase, *Walt Whitman Reconsidered.* New York: Sloane, 1955.

Ezra Greenspan, ed., *The Cambridge Companion to Walt Whitman.* Cambridge: Cambridge University Press, 1995.

Milton Hindus, ed., Leaves of Grass *One Hundred Years After.* Palo Alto, CA: Stanford University Press, 1955.

Justin Kaplan, *Walt Whitman, A Life.* New York: Simon & Schuster, 1980.

Bettina L. Knapp, *Walt Whitman.* New York: Continuum, 1993.

Robert K. Martin, ed., *The Continuing Presence of Walt Whitman: The Life After the Life.* Iowa City: University of Iowa Press, 1992.

Edwin H. Miller, *Walt Whitman's Poetry: A Psychological Journey.* New York: New York University Press, 1969.

James E. Miller, *A Critical Guide to* Leaves of Grass. Chicago: University of Chicago Press, 1957.

——, *Walt Whitman.* New York: Twayne, 1962.

Ron Padgett, ed., *The Teachers & Writers Guide to Walt Whitman.* New York: Teachers & Writers, 1991.

Roy Harvey Pearce, *The Continuity of American Poetry.* Princeton, NJ: Princeton University Press, 1961.

——, *Whitman, a Collection of Critical Essays.* Englewood Cliffs, NJ: Prentice-Hall, 1962.

Catherine Reef, *Walt Whitman.* New York: Clarion Press, 1995.

David S. Reynolds, *Walt Whitman's America: A Cultural Biography.* New York: Knopf, 1995.

Howard J. Waskow, *Whitman: Explorations in Form.* Chicago: University of Chicago Press, 1966.

William White, ed., *1980: Leaves of Grass at 125: Eight Essays.* Detroit: Wayne State University Press, 1980.

Paul Zweig, *Walt Whitman: The Making of the Poet.* New York: Basic Books, 1984.

INDEX